Professional Ethics
in Criminal Justice

Third Edition

Professional Ethics in Criminal Justice

BEING ETHICAL WHEN NO ONE IS LOOKING

Jay S. Albanese
Virginia Commonwealth University

Prentice Hall

Boston   Columbus   Indianapolis   New York   San Francisco   Upper Saddle River
Amsterdam   Cape Town   Dubai   London   Madrid   Milan   Munich   Paris   Montréal   Toronto
Delhi   Mexico City   São Paulo   Sydney   Hong Kong   Seoul   Singapore   Taipei   Tokyo

Editorial Director: Vernon Anthony
Senior Acquisition Editor: Eric Krassow
Editorial Assistant: Lynda Cramer
Director of Marketing: David Gesell
Senior Marketing Manager: Adam Kloza
Senior Marketing Coordinator: Alicia Wozniak
Senior Marketing Assistant: Les Roberts
Production Manager: Holly Shufeldt
Creative Director: Jayne Conte
Cover Designer: Suzanne Duda
Cover Photo: Fotolia
Full-Service Project Management/Composition: Integra Software Services
Printer/Binder: Courier Companies, Inc.

Library of Congress Cataloging-in-Publication Data

Albanese, Jay S.
Professional ethics in criminal justice: being ethical when no one is looking/Jay S. Albanese.—3rd ed.
    p. cm.
  Includes bibliographical references and index.
  ISBN-13: 978-0-13-137565-9
  ISBN-10: 0-13-137565-2
  1. Criminal justice, Administration of—Moral and ethical aspects. 2. Law and ethics.
3. Critical thinking—Examinations, questions, etc. I. Title.
HV7419.A43 2012
174'.9364—dc22

                                      2010032984

10 9 8 7 6 5 4 3   V013

Prentice Hall
is an imprint of

www.pearsonhighered.com

ISBN-10:   0-13-137565-2
ISBN-13: 978-0-13-137565-9

To
Thomas and Kelsey

A book about the most important subject of all:
Being ethical when no one is looking

BRIEF CONTENTS

CONTENTS

PREFACE

Scandals involving unethical and immoral behavior are reported in the news nearly every day, leaving the impression that ethical conduct is on the decline. The news has become "what went wrong today."[1] For example, thirty-eight students were forced to leave the University of Virginia in the largest plagiarism scandal in the school's 200-year history. A professor used a computer program that found duplicated phrases in students' term papers.[2] A questionnaire administered at thirty-one U.S. universities found that two-thirds of respondents admitted cheating on a test or major assignment at least once while in college.[3] In a study at one institution, 51 percent of criminal justice majors admitted to committing acts of academic dishonesty.[4] In the United Kingdom, the Universities and College Admissions Service reported that it had discovered 1,000 fraudulent statements of qualifications in 2004—more than twice the usual number—involving applicants who had falsified their grades or scores on entrance exams. Oxford University expelled eleven current students for fake qualifications.[5]

However, stories of ethical conduct are also reported, although less often. In New Jersey, for instance, tickets to the baseball play-offs at Yankee Stadium somehow fell out of a delivery truck. The individual tickets were worth as much as $2,600 each. They were found on the sidewalk by seventh graders as they walked home from school. They turned the tickets over to the police, resulting in a great deal of public praise and free tickets to a Yankees game, a New Jersey Nets basketball game, and special recognition from their town.[6]

In the criminal justice system, we see a similar dichotomy between reports of corrupt behavior on the one hand and virtuous behavior on the other. Three officers in Los Angeles were convicted for fabricating evidence and framing gang members to obtain false convictions. In Oakland, police were found to have planted drugs on suspects and beaten them.[7] At the same time, seven police officers in New York were honored for extraordinary bravery in subduing a suspect who opened fire on them with two dozen weapons when they responded to a call at his home. In a similar way, twelve police officers on Long Island were cited for heroism and bravery in making 154 drug arrests as part of an undercover operation targeting drug dealers.[8]

Watchers of television news and readers of newspapers know that bad news and scandals make up most of the news; stories of ethical behavior are not deemed as newsworthy as are unethical actions. Therefore, we hear and read about bad behavior all the time, although most people we know engage in ethical conduct most of the time. It is, therefore, difficult to know how ethical people really are when we are barraged by stories of bad behavior in the media yet experience very little of it ourselves. Nevertheless, instances of unethical conduct are frequent and serious enough to warrant our concern.

Why do people who have wealth and status steal? Why would students lucky enough to be accepted into a prestigious university cheat and jeopardize their status? In the same way, why are many police officers honest and even heroic, whereas others are corrupt? Why do most people go into a supermarket and pay for their food, whereas others put it in their pockets and steal it? Questions of ethics underlie virtually every decision we make, and it's important to understand how to make these decisions correctly and their central importance in our lives. This book is useful in several important ways:

- It helps students recognize ethical decisions and provides the framework for analyzing ethical dilemmas.

- The three major ethical schools of thought are presented in a clear and cogent way, so students can apply them with an understanding of their strengths and limitations.
- Critical thinking exercises reporting on situations from real life are presented in each chapter, helping the students apply ethical principles to actual cases.
- Ethics Checkup exercises are included in each chapter and report on criminal justice cases to assist students in understanding ethical content in criminal justice decisions.
- Ethics in the Movies is featured in each chapter, summarizing a recent film that deals with ethical issues and asking students to make the connections to ethics.
- Ethics in Books is featured in every chapter, summarizing the content of popular books that deal with relevant issues with questions for the student to understand the implications for ethics.
- Ethical decision making and criminal justice decision making are integrated in a systematic way, illustrating the fundamental connection between ethics and criminal justice.
- The connections between law and ethics, and crime prevention via internal mechanisms (ethical training) versus external mechanisms (law enforcement), are presented to highlight the fundamental importance of ethics in personal and social life.
- It shows how ethics do not merely help individuals make decisions, but, with practice, how they work to create an ethical person who can make moral choices in difficult situations.

From elementary school forward, there is an apparent belief that education is little more than the accumulation of facts. As a result, we see many well-educated people making very bad decisions. The most important life skill of all is often never taught: How to make decisions in the face of conflicting demands. That is what this book is all about.

It's been said that in contemporary society everyone is claiming rights, but no one is accepting responsibilities. Unethical behavior is blamed on others, and rationalizations after the fact are used in a vain effort to justify immoral behavior. This book shows the fallacy of this kind of reasoning; it also shows how many people are making morally appropriate choices every day, and why these people are the ones worthy of admiration and, when all is said and done, the people we'd like to become.

Notes

1. Ann Medlock, "The Courage to Stick Your Neck Out," in M. Josephson and W. Hanson, Eds., *The Power of Character* (San Francisco, CA: Jossey-Bass, 1998), p. 337.
2. "Cheating Scandal Rocks University of Virginia," *USA Today* (March 7, 2002), p. 3.
3. D. McCabe, "The Influence of Situational Ethics on Cheating among College Students," *Sociological Inquiry*, vol. 62 (1992), pp. 365–374.
4. Charisse T. M. Coston and David A. Jenks, "Exploring Academic Dishonesty among Undergraduate Criminal Justice Majors: A Research Note," *American Journal of Criminal Justice*, vol. 22 (1998), pp. 235–248.
5. "Student Fraud Hits Record Level," *BBC News* (October 28, 2004).
6. "Talk about Temptation: Box-Seats for New York Yankees Playoff Games Lying on the Street," *Associated Press* (October 1, 2004).
7. Matt Lait and Tina Daunt, "The Rampart Verdicts: L. A. Will Feel Ripple Effect of Corruption for Years," *Los Angles Times* (November 16, 2000), p. 1; Terence Monmaney, "Rampart-Like Scandal Rocks Oakland Justice System," *Los Angeles Times* (December 11, 2000), p. 1.
8. Greg Wilson, "Heroic Cops Are Honored," *New York Daily News* (November 12, 2000), p. 3; Robert Geary, "Gulotta Cites Twelve Officers for Heroism," *New York Daily News* (January 12, 2000), p. 9.

ACKNOWLEDGMENTS

To write a book like this, one incurs a number of intellectual debts. After all, the notions of good and evil, right and wrong, and the ethical and the unethical are among the oldest and most central issues in all human experience, and they have been debated and lived over many lifetimes.

Mortimer J. Adler (1902–2001), the distinguished American philosopher and educator, piqued my interest in ethics in several of his more than fifty books, including *Six Great Ideas, How to Think about God*, and *Desires Right and Wrong*. As the person most responsible for the selection and organization of the Great Books of the Western World and the Herculean effort, The Syntopicon, which organizes all the great books around the 102 great ideas they discuss, Adler's work had a significant influence on my thinking about ethics. I was later able to participate in two of his seminars at the Aspen Institute, and he is one of the few great people who was as good in person as he was in his writings. Making philosophy "everybody's business" was truly his life's work.

Journalists Bill Moyers and William F. Buckley also deserve credit for highlighting the work of Mortimer Adler in their television programs. Their efforts helped illuminate the connection among the great ideas and great thinkers and the everyday life of professionals and students.

I have been an educator for most of my career, and my students at Niagara University and Virginia Commonwealth University have served as a sounding board, as I attempted to place ethics center stage in their lives and developed new courses on ethics at each of those institutions. It is interesting that older students caught on much more quickly in this effort; Aristotle would have predicted this, as we will see later. I thank my students for their thoughtfulness and good questions along the way.

As a criminologist, my field of study centers on the bad. Bad decisions, and sometimes bad people, take up a lot of my time. On the other hand, life experience makes it clear that good decisions and good people far outnumber the bad. And even though good and bad lie at the core of criminology, criminology books never use this terminology or perspective. Perhaps we need more ethically trained criminologists writing the books, because ethics provides the foundation for making sense of all subsequent analyses of crime and criminal justice.

The ideas expressed in this book were reviewed by many, including D. Kall Loper, University of North Texas; G. Larry Mays, New Mexico State University; Kerry L. Muehlenbeck, Mesa Community College; Joseph Keith Price, West Texas A&M university; Raymond L. Sparks, California State University–Bakersfield; and Harry Osborn. I thank them for their efforts and, of course, take responsibility for inaccuracies that remain.

My editor, Eric Krassow, was great to work with, and his encouragement and persistence were both well balanced and effective. Rex Davidson and Lynda Cramer kept the editorial process moving, especially when an author is prone to slow down just when things need to speed up.

My family has become used to my typing away at the computer as I write and rewrite sections of the manuscript, always looking for interesting examples in my reading to make concepts clear, contemporary, and lively. I thank them for their patience. My faithful dog and cat, Coby and Stripey, and their constant need for attention caused me to rethink ideas sometimes two or three times as they coaxed me to pet them, get up for more pet food, and open and close the door to let them out—and then back in—countless times. I suppose I should thank them for that.

As always, I remain interested in feedback from readers, whether it is good or bad, as I endeavor to help you distinguish those same two ideas.

Jay S. Albanese
Herndon, Virginia

ABOUT THE AUTHOR

JAY S. ALBANESE is professor in the Wilder School of Government and Public Affairs at Virginia Commonwealth University. He served as chief of the International Center at the National Institute of Justice (NIJ), the research arm of the U.S. Department of Justice, from 2002 to 2006. Dr. Albanese received his Ph.D. and M.A. degrees from Rutgers University and his B.A. from Niagara University. He was the first Ph.D. recipient from the Rutgers School of Criminal Justice. Dr. Albanese is author or editor of fifteen books that include *Organized Crime in Our Times* (6th ed., Elsevier, 2011), *Criminal Justice* (4th ed., Allyn & Bacon, 2008), *Transnational Crime and the 21st Century* (Oxford University Press, 2011), *Comparative Criminal Justice Systems* (with H. Dammer, 4th ed., Wadsworth, 2011), and *Combating Piracy: Intellectual Property Theft and Fraud* (Transaction, 2009). Dr. Albanese is recipient of the Elske Smith Distinguished Lecturer Award from Virginia Commonwealth University and the Scholar Award in Criminal Justice from the Virginia Social Science Association. He has served as executive director of the International Association for the Study of Organized Crime and is a past president of the Academy of Criminal Justice Sciences, the White Collar Crime Research Consortium, and the Northeastern Association of Criminal Justice Sciences.

Professional Ethics
in Criminal Justice

CHAPTER 1

Recognizing Ethical Decisions
Ethics and Critical Thinking

Learning Objectives:

- To develop the ability to understand the essence of good character.

- To distinguish between morals, values, and ethics.

- To recognize the concept of moral relativism.

- To understand the importance of critical thinking to ethics.

- To increase awareness of the connection between etiquette and ethics.

Character is destiny.

—Heraclitus (540–480 B.C.)

S uppose you are a parent, and you want your son or daughter to marry a person who has at least one exceptional quality. You can choose from incredible wealth, exceptional good looks, high intelligence, superior athletic skills, creativity, or extraordinary character. Which would you choose?

Virtually everyone would choose character first, which illustrates the fundamental importance people place on good character, despite the attention given to other skills and attributes in daily life. As seen on the news regularly, the other attributes are often wasted on people when good character is lacking.

Good character can be defined as consisting of three qualities:

- good principles (to guide actions),
- conscience (to internalize those principles), and
- moral courage (to act on them).[1]

Ethics are fundamental to character because they specify the guiding principles on which character is built.

Ethics are all around, yet people often fail to realize it. Recognizing ethical decisions when people make them is a fundamental first step in developing ethical awareness. Perhaps the only thing worse than an unethical decision is the failure to be aware of it!

WHAT ARE ETHICS, AND WHAT IS ETHICAL?

It's fun to begin by trying to imagine behavior that's morally neutral. Are there actions you can take that have no moral content and, therefore, lie outside the scope of ethics?

It turns out there are very few behaviors of this type. You can wear wrinkled clothes or clothes with holes in them. You can decide whether to get up early tomorrow morning. You can decide whether to say "hello!" to the toll collector on the highway, and you can decide not to brush your teeth today. These actions usually have no moral content (although long-term neglect of teeth, e.g., can affect your health and insurance costs and make you a bad role model for younger siblings, thereby incurring important personal and social consequences).

It is clear, however, that there are very few examples of actions that lack moral content. The vast majority of behaviors a person engages in have moral content and are included within the purview of ethics.

TO WHAT TYPES OF THINGS OR BEINGS SHOULD WE LIMIT THE DISCUSSION OF ETHICS?

Discussions of ethics are limited to human beings. Lower animals lack the capacity to reason, functioning by instinct rather than by freely willed choices between alternate courses of conduct (e.g., can a migratory goose choose *not* to fly south in winter?). In the classic film *The African Queen*, Humphrey Bogart's character, Charlie, went out on a binge for an evening of drunkenness and told Rosie the missionary (Katherine Hepburn) it was "only human nature." She replied, "We were put on earth to rise above nature." This exchange illustrates the responsibility of human beings for the rational and ethical exercise of their free wills.

Certain categories of human beings are exempt from discussions of ethics. People who are mentally ill and young children are traditional exceptions to criminal responsibility because of their inability to understand the consequences of their actions. For the same reason, they cannot be held to ethical standards, which also require the capacity to contemplate and comprehend the impact of one's actions.

WHAT IS THE DIFFERENCE BETWEEN MORALS AND ETHICS?

Morals are good conduct; they constitute permissible behavior. Morals are the rules that prescribe proper action. **Ethics** is the study of morality, that is, the study and analysis of what constitutes good conduct (i.e., morals).

Laws provide only the baseline or boundaries of civil behavior. Moral behavior requires more than the law requires (i.e., there are many legal actions that are immoral). Take the example of the cashier who mistakenly returns to you $20 in change after you make a purchase, when the actual amount returned should have been only $2. You have no legal obligation to return the money, but there is a clear moral obligation to do so. A person of good character is one who engages consistently in moral conduct, regardless of what the law demands. Sometimes integrity is used to describe someone of good character, but it is more correct to say that a person of good character acts routinely in accord with the moral virtues (which are detailed in Chapter 2).

Ethics is central to criminal justice because morality is what distinguishes right from wrong—in differentiating the government's moral authority to enforce the law from the immorality of the crime itself. In other words, "Only by being moral can criminal justice be distinguished from the very crime it condemns!"[2]

WHAT ARE VALUES?

Values are judgments of worth of attitudes, statements, and behaviors. Factual judgments (i.e., judgments based on facts) can be verified empirically through observations, whereas value judgments can be verified only through reason. Factual judgments *describe* something, whereas value judgments *characterize* it by making evaluative statements about it.

Sometimes it can be said that people claim one set of beliefs, whereas they actually endorse the opposite. For example, some preach love, nonviolence, hard work, family values, and self-discipline. However, others may glorify and act with hate and violence and praise luck and celebrity—things not worthy of glory or praise. The failure to recognize such misguided conduct makes people little more than billiard balls on the pool table of life. Each person controls his or her actions; each person must think about these actions and be responsible for them and their consequences.

WHY IS CRITICAL THINKING FUNDAMENTAL TO ETHICS?

Many things that are praised or rewarded in contemporary life are unworthy. Things that are portrayed as important (e.g., money, power, advantage) often promote unethical conduct by encouraging rash, selfish, or unlawful behavior. **Critical thinking** is the ability to evaluate viewpoints, facts, and behaviors objectively in order to assess the presentation of information or methods of argumentation to establish the true worth or merit of an act or a course of conduct.

Consider the case of the person who plans to host a Super Bowl football party at his house and decides he wants a large-screen plasma television for the party. Unfortunately, he cannot afford one, so he comes up with the idea of "buying" one using his credit card the week before the Super Bowl and then returning it to the store the week after the Super Bowl, claiming he "doesn't like it" or it "takes up too much space." Apparently, people have been doing this, and major electronic retailers are now charging restocking fees on returned products. Similarly, Best Buy stores have said that students bought laptop computers to write term papers and then returned the laptops. A camcorder was returned as defective, but the videotape left inside showed the camera had been dropped into a swimming pool.[3] This behavior is not clearly illegal, but it is clearly unethical. An understanding of ethical principles applied critically to different scenarios helps individuals to discern clever ideas from immoral ones.

Education in school has largely become the accumulation of facts. How to make decisions is not routinely taught (i.e., how to *use* facts in a principled way). Critical thinking involves the development of abilities to sort through facts intelligently, as well as half-truths, lies, and deceptive arguments, to determine the actual value of a statement, position, or behavior. Ethics takes critical thinking one step further by explicitly teaching methods of principled reasoning and responsibility for actions. Continued examination of one's beliefs and actions is the only way to know all aspects and implications of a belief or action and whether that belief or action is still worth holding or doing. If people don't challenge their own moral beliefs, others who do not agree with them will challenge them. Therefore, both critical thinking and ethical thought are crucial for proper behavior.

CAN MORALITY BE TAUGHT?

Morals and ethics are not acquired naturally; they must be taught. As has been said, "Character may determine our fate, but character is not determined by fate."[5] In fact, it's hard to see another way to teach children. It is very inefficient and painful to teach only through experience. A lot of unnecessary pain results from having to learn through bad decisions. Learning proper methods to make ethical decisions is necessary in order to avoid the pain of unethical conduct. It can be argued that moral values were more effectively transmitted 50 to 100 years ago than they are today. Religious beliefs (containing many ethical principles) have been marginalized by many; objections to "values" being taught in schools continue; and there is a decline of intact families and extended families, who often serve as effective role models for acceptable personal and social behavior.

Manners and etiquette are precursors to morals. **Etiquette** tells how people should interact with others in all social relations, whereas morals express ethical obligations toward others in behavior. Therefore, people who are ill mannered (e.g., rude, inconsiderate, self-centered) are also likely to engage in unethical conduct because of their selfish view of the world and failure to value the views or claims of others. America's first president, George Washington, compiled a short book titled *Rules of Civility and Decent Behavior in Company and Conversation* (1744), which included a list of 110 maxims designed to polish manners and emphasize the important virtues. These maxims included "speak not evil of the absent, for it is unjust," "undertake not what you cannot perform, but be careful to keep your promise," and "labour to keep alive in your breast that little celestial fire called conscience."[6] Many of these rules of etiquette refer to a state of mind and motivation, which underlie the principles for expectations of ethical conduct.

Ervin Staub conducted a study of altruism to answer the question, "Why did ordinary people risk their lives to protect Jews hiding from the Nazis during World War II?" He found that "heroes evolve, they aren't born." As such, he found people took early steps toward altruistic behavior and then began to see themselves differently. He concluded, "Goodness, like evil, often evolves in small steps."[7] His work suggests that ethical conduct probably proceeds in the same way, from smaller acts to more consistent courses of conduct. In an analogous way, a study of students and counterfeit sunglasses discovered that students who knew they were wearing counterfeit glasses were more than twice as likely to cheat on a simple test, leading the researchers to conclude that a seemingly innocuous activity (like wearing fake clothing or sunglasses) has an impact on moral behavior.[8] Therefore, small steps may be the path toward either ethical or unethical conduct.

So does studying ethics guarantee ethical conduct? As ethicist Elizabeth Kiss writes, "Character education is no panacea. By itself, it will not repair disintegrating schools, neighborhoods, or families, dry up the drug trade, or create jobs. But it can be an important part of efforts to invest in our children's development and well-being."[9] Teaching and learning ethics certainly does not guarantee moral conduct in the future, but people who take classes in English or math may or may not become avid readers and use their mathematical knowledge, but that doesn't make taking those courses any less worthwhile. Ethics provides the way to see that there is a greater purpose to life than self-interest. Familiarity with the principles of ethical conduct can "leave students with the understanding that they are moral agents, that they have moral responsibilities, that there are methods for evaluating and defending their own positions" on moral questions.[10]

WHAT IS MORAL RELATIVISM?

Moral relativism is the belief that morals can be different, but none are better than another. **Moral relativism** is synonymous with situational ethics, which holds that there are no universal moral standards. For example, infanticide was accepted in ancient Greece and in parts of today's China, but it is immoral elsewhere. Are various social rules, traditions, and morality simply different, or can they be wrong?

Yes, they can be wrong; it is important not to confuse local habits and customs with human nature that is common to all humankind. Guiding human potential and action in a moral direction is the subject matter of ethics. The potential of human beings is specific to the species.[11]

Every society agrees that arbitrary killing is wrong and that property theft, assault, and other behaviors hurt the continuing existence of society. In fact, there is more general agreement about basic human values, human rights, and the universality of modern codes of conduct than we are sometimes led to believe. Those who say it is wrong to be judgmental about difficult questions of conduct are saying that all viewpoints have equal moral validity. This is not true, of course, and in many ways it is a cop-out, making no demands on you nor expecting anything from the conduct of others. Ethical relativism attempts to *justify* the way people behave, rather than focusing on how people *ought* to behave, which is the real subject matter of ethics.

Sometimes relativism is confused with tolerance. Tolerance accepts that there are moral principles, but people should not have the views of others imposed on them. Relativism sees nothing wrong with imposing views on others because there are no general principles (so nothing can be wrong). Clearly, true relativism is rare because nearly everyone believes that some things are morally wrong. Ethics provides principles for distinguishing acts that are morally right from those that are morally wrong.

In a similar way, ethics rejects the notion of "moral intuition," where a person merely seeks out a "commonsense" position on ethical issues without referring to ethical theory or perspective. Without guiding principles, moral intuition can be misleading or provide no guidance at all (e.g., it is difficult to find a commonsense position on in vitro fertilization). Developing and following moral principles give human decision making both meaning and a dispassionate rationale. Objective moral rules help a person to recognize ethical decisions and to act on them with consistency and purpose.

HOW CAN WE CHOOSE WHAT TO BELIEVE AND HOW TO ACT ETHICALLY?

A framework for making ethical decisions is needed. Such a framework begins with a search for universal principles. Many of these principles are based in religious traditions (e.g., Jewish, Christian, and Islam), where it is shown that persons of high moral character not only do what is right but they also do it for the right reasons. People value and respect those who do more than what is morally required (e.g., Mother Theresa, who created homes for the poor, dying, and unwanted around the world for more than 45 years).

Moral rules can also be derived independently of religious beliefs because desirable human conduct can be prescribed and achieved through application of rational principles. Certain actions can be seen as objectively right or wrong (a natural law), and people can choose between them as human beings. For example, societies agree that murder, theft, lying, and similar actions are immoral. Basic values are also necessary for society to work effectively (e.g., honoring contracts, respecting others). Therefore, moral rules are often associated with religious beliefs, but they can be derived through the application of independent rational principles as well.

Sometimes the following questions are asked: "Why be moral?" and "Why not simply pursue self-interest and grab whatever advantage you can?"

Actually, ethical behavior is often in our self-interest. There is happiness to be found in acts that benefit others, respect is accorded those who have high moral standards, freedom is found from succumbing to our basest desires, and living openly and cooperatively with others rather than secretively and fraudulently are among the many benefits of acting ethically. The benefits achieved by those who act unethically (e.g., taking unfair advantage, committing theft) are usually short-term gains that are either quickly exhausted, must remain secret, or are not easily shared, and they result in pain or penalty when the conduct becomes known.

The remainder of this book provides the basics of ethical thinking to guide individual decision making. Critical thinking exercises are provided throughout the book, so students can practice applying ethical principles to actual situations.

ETHICS IN BOOKS

Ethics is everywhere, even in the books we read, which sometimes are written without ethics specifically in mind. Here is a summary of such a book, followed by questions that ask you to reflect on the ethical connections.

THE WORLD ACCORDING TO MISTER ROGERS

Fred Rogers
(Hyperion, 2003)

Fred Rogers was host of the public television program *Mister Rogers' Neighborhood* for more than 30 years. It was a children's program that appealed to adults as well, because Mr. Rogers spoke directly to the viewer in a calm, conversational tone about significant personal and social issues of concern to children and young people.

The book is comprised of short quotes from Mr. Rogers on the subjects of courage, love, discipline, and relationships with others ("we are all neighbors"). In one excerpt, he recounts a story from his childhood:

"When I was a boy and I would see scary things in the news, my mother would say to me, 'Look for the helpers. You will always find people who are helping.'

To this day, especially in times of 'disaster,' I remember my mother's words, and I am always comforted by realizing that there are still so many helpers—so many caring people in this world."

In another quote, at the very end of the book, he observes, "So in all that you do in all of your life, I wish you the strength and the grace to make those choices which will allow you and your neighbor to become the best of whoever you are."

Fred Rogers received honorary degrees from more than forty colleges and universities and was inducted into the Television Hall of Fame in 1999. He was also the recipient of the Presidential Medal of Freedom in 2002, the nation's highest civilian award for exceptional public service. Fred Rogers died in 2003.

QUESTIONS

1. Can you offer an explanation based on ethics of why there always seems to be so many "helpers," offering to assist and ease those suffering from disasters, whether they are man-made or natural disasters?

2. In the book's final quote, why do you believe he says it takes "strength and grace" to make choices in life, rather than simply making ethical decisions?

ETHICS IN THE MOVIES

Movies seek to entertain and inform the audience about a story, incident, or person. Many good movies also hit upon important ethical themes in making significant decisions that affect the lives of others. Read the movie summary here (and watch the movie if you haven't already), and answer the questions to make the ethical connections.

THE EMPEROR'S CLUB

Michael Hoffman,
Director (2002)

The Emperor's Club tells the story of a classics teacher William Hundert (Kevin Kline) at a private school for boys, who fixes the result of an academic competition, allowing a well-connected student to get away with cheating, and how subsequent events change him, but not the student.

The teacher is clearly very talented and works to build character in his students: "a man's character is his fate," "how will history remember you?" The problem student, Sedgewick Bell (Emile Hirsch), is a disrespectful rule violator, but the other boys think he is very cool. He is the son of a powerful U.S. senator, who seems to care little about his son but threatens him to do well in school.

The problem student does indeed improve greatly in school, and the teacher allows him to participate in the annual best final three competition conducted in a quiz show format—even though he actually finished fourth. During the competition, the teacher sees the student cheating, but the headmaster tells him to ignore it, and the teacher finds a way to make him lose the competition anyway.

The movie then jumps forward 25 years, and the problem student is now a rich man running for senator, who wishes to give a large endowment to the private school on the condition there is a re-run of the competition in which he cheated and lost years earlier. The class is reassembled, the competition is replayed, and his former teacher finds he has cheated again—and does not let him win.

The film ends in unpredictable fashion, but the teacher learns that he will not succeed in reaching every student and is gratified by the response he received from his other former students. The film succeeds in portraying an excellent teacher who makes a mistake, and how that mistake plays out years later, as the former problem student appears to make the same mistake with his own son as his father did with him.

QUESTIONS

1. Was it ethical for the teacher to allow the student into the competition to reward his improvement even though he did not actually finish in the top three?
2. Was it morally permissible for the headmaster to ignore the cheating student (probably because his father was a powerful senator)?

Discussion Question

If the study of ethics does not guarantee ethical conduct, why do it?

Critical Thinking Exercises

All ethical decisions affect others (by definition), and ethical decision making is achieved consistently only through practice. Even though the discussion of the principles of ethical decision making begins in Chapter 2, please respond to the following scenarios based solely on your ability to think critically. It will be interesting to see if your reasoning or answers change if you examine these first five critical thinking exercises after finishing this book!

Important note on method: *Critical thinking requires the ability to evaluate viewpoints, facts, and behaviors objectively to assess information or methods of argumentation to establish the true worth or merit of an act or course of conduct. Please evaluate these scenarios, starting with analyzing pros and cons of alternate views,* before *you come to a conclusion. Do not* draw a conclusion first, *and then try to find facts to support it—this frequently leads to narrow (and incorrect) thinking.*

To properly evaluate the moral permissibility of a course of action using critical thinking skills

1. *Begin with an open mind (no preconceptions!),*
2. *Isolate and evaluate the relevant facts on both sides,*
3. *Identify the precise moral question to be answered, and*
4. *Apply ethical principles to the moral question based on an objective evaluation of the facts, only then drawing a conclusion.*

1.1 Teenagers and Drug-Sniffing Dogs

Drug use by teenagers is a fundamental fear of most parents. Coupled with images on the news, reports of government statistics about rampant drug use, and periodic tragedies at schools around the country, most parents have been shown a clear link between drug use and tragedies of all kinds.

You are the parent of a teenager, who is showing all the signs of being a teenager. Your child is not very talkative to you, but is very talkative with friends; doesn't want to be seen with you or the family at stores or on vacation; does not seem interested in being an "A" student anymore; has lousy taste in music; wears unattractive clothing and hairstyles; and wants to get even more body parts pierced. These behaviors have not gone unnoticed by you, and you fear that drug use might be at the root of it.

You contact Detector Dogs against Drugs, one of a growing number of private security firms in the United States that trains dogs and is licensed by the Drug Enforcement Administration to contract with schools, corporations, or parents to conduct dog-led searches of teenager's rooms and lockers for drugs.[12] The fee is $250 to $750 for the search, but you don't know what some of today's drugs look like or the places where your teenager might hide drugs in the house.

You wait for your teenager to leave for school one day to have the search conducted without his or her knowledge or presence. You don't believe that confronting your teenager with your suspicions will be fruitful, and if the search turns up nothing, then you will know your fears are unfounded.

- Evaluate the moral permissibility of your Detector Dogs against Drugs search of your child's room.

    (*Hint*: You will find that in ethical scenarios, there are usually the interests of two competing parties to consider. You should evaluate them separately [i.e., the strengths and weaknesses of each side's arguments] before drawing a conclusion.)

1.2   Sentenced to the Newspaper

Judges in several states are now permitted to sentence men who solicit prostitutes to buy ads in local newspapers to run their photos and the charges against them as a form of humiliation and shame. In some places, the names of the men can be placed on Web sites or even on a billboard.[13]

- Is such a sentence for soliciting prostitutes morally permissible?

    (*Hint*: Here again it is necessary to comparatively assess the competing interests of the community [i.e., judge in sentencing] versus the interests of the offender.)

1.3   Brewing Up a Storm

An undercover police officer was on duty inside a bar conducting surveillance activities on crime suspects. The officer bought a beer to maintain her cover.

Unbeknownst to the officer, buying the beer automatically qualified her for a contest sponsored by a beer company. The grand prize winner would win a new car worth $20,000. It was later announced that the undercover officer was the grand prize winner.

Her employer, the New York City Police Department (NYPD), believes the car should be turned over to the department because she bought the beer with department money and was on duty at the time.

The officer argues that the car should be hers because her employer did not require her to buy beer at the bar. She

merely had some good luck, and the department wishes to capitalize unfairly on her good fortune. The case was sent to the city's Board of Ethics to settle the dispute.

- As a member of the Board of Ethics, how would you evaluate the competing claims of the officer and the NYPD?
- Would your answer be different if the undercover officer walked into the bar and was awarded the new car for being the 10,000th customer inside the bar?

1.4   Internet Predator Sting

A number of local law enforcement agencies are working with Perverted-Justice.com, a private organization that received nationwide attention after assisting a television news program, *Dateline*, to run sting operations to catch men using Internet chat rooms to meet children for sex. Founded in 2003, the private organization claims to have done work with police resulting in more than 200 convictions of online predators thus far.

Perverted Justice's volunteers pose as children online in Internet chat rooms. Very quickly, they receive private messages from men of a sexual nature. If a man solicits sex, the volunteer works to obtain his phone number and address. In a phone call, a volunteer with a young-sounding voice sets up a meeting for a rendezvous. Law enforcement officials are brought in to make an arrest at the meeting location.

NBC television's *Dateline* series is titled "To Catch a Predator," which videotapes the men lured to locations around the country where they believe they are meeting a minor for sex. Perverted Justice sometimes telephones the men's wives, girlfriends, employers, and neighbors, labeling them as pedophiles. Only after the men apologize and enter counseling does Perverted Justice consider removing their information from their Web site.[14]

Supporters say the volunteer organization is a grassroots movement that is protecting children from online predators in a preventive way. Critics call it a vigilante effort that harasses suspects prior to their conviction and invades their privacy rights and also of those who know them or are related to them.

- Do you believe that police agencies should work with Perverted Justice?
- Can you identify the potential ethical issues in dealing with Internet predators in this way?

1.5   An Honest Golfer

On his twelfth hole of the first round of Qualifying School at Deerwood Country Club (a tryout required if one wishes to play on the PGA tour), professional golfer J.P. Hayes' caddie reached into his golf bag, pulled out a ball, and flipped it to Hayes, who missed the green with his tee shot. He then chipped on and marked his ball. It was then that Hayes realized the ball was not the same model *Titleist* with which he had started his round. That was in violation of the one-ball rule, which stipulates that a player must play the same model ball throughout a round.

The result is a two-stroke penalty on your final score. Hayes recovered well enough to put himself in position to finish in the top twenty and advance to the third and final round of Qualifying School. The top twenty-five finishers in that round earn exempt status for the entire 2009 PGA season and can play in all the tournaments.

Hayes then realized something else—not only did he play the wrong ball, he might have played a ball that wasn't even approved for play at all. "It was a *Titleist* prototype, and somehow it had gotten into my bag," he said. "It had

been four weeks since *Titleist* gave me some prototype balls and I tested them. I have no idea how or why it was still in there . . . I called an official in Houston that night and said, 'I think I may have a problem.' He said they'd call *Titleist* the next day. I pretty much knew at that point I was going to be disqualified."[15]

It would have been easy to either do nothing or blame the caddy, but Hayes rose above both those temptations, putting all the blame on himself and asserting that every other professional golfer would have done exactly the same thing. Hayes already has more than $7 million in career earnings, but his action takes him off the PGA tour for a year until he can try to requalify next year, costing him some career stability and significant potential earnings.

• Evaluate the moral permissibility of Hayes' decision to report on his own actions.

Key Concepts

Good character *2*
Morals *2*
Ethics *2*

Values *3*
Critical thinking *3*

Etiquette *4*
Moral relativism *5*

Notes

1. Michael S. Josephson and Wes Hanson, Eds., *The Power of Character* (San Francisco: Jossey-Bass, 1998), p. 4.
2. Jeffrey Reiman, "Criminal Justice Ethics," in P. Leighton and J. Reiman, Eds., *Criminal Justice Ethics* (Upper Saddle River, NJ: Prentice Hall, 2001), p. 2.
3. Chris Woodward, "Circuit City Tacks 15 Percent Fee on Some Returns," *USA Today* (December 26, 1997), p. B3.
4. "Nintendo No-No," *USA Today* (August 21, 1991), p. 3.
5. Michael S. Josephson, *The Power of Character* (San Francisco: Jossey-Bass, 1998), p. 2.
6. George Washington, *Rules of Civility and Decent Behavior in Company and Conversation (1744)* (Bedford, MA: Applewood Books, 1994), p. 20.
7. Ervin Staub, *The Psychology of Good and Evil: Why Children, Adults, and Groups Help and Harm Others* (London: Cambridge University Press, 2003), p. 55.
8. Francesca Gino, Michael I. Norton, and Dan Ariely, "The Counterfeit Self: The Deceptive Costs of

Faking It," *Psychological Science*, vol. 21 (2010), pp. 712–720.
9. Elizabeth Kiss, "In Praise of Eccentricity," in M. Josephson and W. Hanson, Eds., *The Power of Character* (San Francisco: Jossey-Bass, 1998), p. 335.
10. Vartan Gregorian, "Our Moral DNA," in M. Josephson and W. Hanson, Eds., *The Power of Character* (San Francisco: Jossey-Bass, 1998), p. 115.
11. Mortimer Adler, *Ten Philosophical Mistakes* (New York: Scribners, 1985), p. 161.
12. Brendan I. Koerner, "Mom, A Dog Is Here Sniffing, Um, Oregano," *U.S. News & World Report* (October 5, 1998), p. 62.
13. "Shame Works, So Use It," *USA Today* (September 1, 2004), p. 8.
14. Jason Trahan and Chris Colgin, "Campaign against Child Sex Predators Draws Critics," *The Dallas Morning News* (September 10, 2006).
15. Jay Busbee, "J.P. Hayes Is As Honest As We Like to Think We Are," *Devil Ball Golf* (November 19, 2008).

CHAPTER 2

Virtue Ethics
Seeking the Good

*It is possible to fail in many ways . . . while to
succeed is possible only in one way.*

—Aristotle (384–322 B.C.)

Learning Objectives:

- To understand the centrality of moral virtue to understanding the ethics of Aristotle.

- To appreciate the hierarchy of goods and the difference between real and apparent goods.

- To recognize the distinctions among virtue ethics, stoicism, and hedonism.

- To increase understanding of the linkage between the moral virtues in pursuing real goods.

- To develop skills in applying moral virtues and real goods in evaluating ethical dilemmas.

Virtue is one of the most revered words in all language. It is associated with character, good judgment, and ethical decision making. **Moral virtue** can be defined as "the habit of right desire" or the disposition to make right choices.[1] The right path to follow in seeking virtue has been the source of much debate over the centuries, and the leading proponents of virtue ethics and their ideas are presented in this chapter.

THE ROLES OF SOCRATES AND PLATO

The beginnings of virtue ethics can be traced to Aristotle's distinguished predecessors, Socrates and Plato. Socrates (470–399 B.C.) lived in Athens and essentially wandered the streets, engaging people in conversations about the meaning of life, knowledge, and virtue. He intellectually challenged those who followed him by constantly asking questions in a way that forced them to come to conclusions on their own. Socrates is the source of the saying, "The unexamined life is not worth living." Socrates' method of teaching, often questioning widely held but incorrect beliefs in an exchange with his students, was known as the dialectic method. This use of questions and answers to arrive at truth was later termed the **Socratic method**, in honor of Socrates' skill as a teacher. Socrates saw knowledge (wisdom) and virtue as synonymous. He believed that a person who knows what is right will act rightly. Aristotle modified this view, as is explained later in this chapter, claiming that intellectual virtue and moral virtue are distinct attributes. Socrates' impact on both thinking about ethics and his method of teaching was enormous. It is difficult to find a later thinker who was not influenced by Socrates in some way. He remains one of the most significant of all historical figures.

Socrates did not write his thoughts on paper, but his most famous student, Plato, did. Plato (428–348 B.C.) became a student of Socrates at age 20 and was disillusioned with the corruption in Greek politics, highlighted when his mentor Socrates was put to death in 399 B.C. by the government.[2] Plato founded the Academy in Athens, where he taught and wrote on many subjects, organizing and adding to the ideas of Socrates. His work was influential and remains so, and his book *The Republic* sets forth his views on ethics, describing a plan for an ideal city where few laws are needed because of the highly developed moral character of its inhabitants. Plato's statement, "If you want justice, you must be moral," identified what he saw as the connection between individual moral conduct and the ideal society.[3]

Aristotle (384–322 B.C.) enrolled in Plato's Academy at age 17 and was a lifelong student of Plato, later forming his own school, the Lyceum, after Plato's death. Aristotle wrote more than 400 works while at the Lyceum on a broad array of subjects, including astronomy, biology, logic, politics, physics, and ethics. The breadth of his knowledge was remarkable. Considered by some to be the most intelligent person who ever lived, Aristotle studied, taught, and wrote about every subject that was known during his time.[4] In the *Nicomachean Ethics*, he provided the first systematic study of ethics in the history of the Western world.

When Alexander the Great died in 322 B.C., his empire was challenged, and anyone who had been friendly with him was threatened. Aristotle, a close friend, was indicted for treason for his teachings. Faced with a choice between trial (and certain execution) or exile, Aristotle chose to flee. He left Athens, recalling the death of Socrates 76 years earlier, saying he was not going to give Athens a chance to "sin twice against philosophy." Aristotle died shortly thereafter in 322 B.C. at the age of 62. The worldwide influence of his work continues today.

NICOMACHEAN ETHICS OF ARISTOTLE

Virtue ethics are most closely associated with Aristotle whose approach to ethics asks, "How ought people live their lives?" His book is titled the *Nicomachean Ethics*, and it can be difficult reading.

The book gets its name from **Nicomachus**, Aristotle's son. It is unlikely that Aristotle intended the book to appear in its present form. Most of Aristotle's works had been lost since his time. The book was probably put together from the notes of his students, and Nicomachus probably didn't want to leave anything out. (One can imagine what a modern textbook would read like if it was composed from the notes taken by the students in the class!)

Aristotle believed that discussion of ethics is wasted on the young. The young lack experience in actions, and they tend to follow their passions and follow action rather than knowledge in making decisions. Therefore, life experiences in taking actions and making decisions are important to learn ethics effectively. Reflections about one's past and future actions, and the motivations for them, are central to understanding and incorporating ethics in a person's life.

A HIERARCHY OF GOODS

Aristotle sees all human activities aimed at some good, but some goods are subordinate to others. For example, work is good, but work toward helping the sick or destitute, versus work toward making yourself rich, seems to have more value. Therefore, there is a **hierarchy of goods**. In attempting to define true goods, Aristotle finds that good and pleasure are often confused.

> To judge from the lives that men lead, most men, and men of the most vulgar type, seem (not without some ground) to identify the good, or happiness, with pleasure; which is the reason why they love the life of enjoyment.[5]

According to Aristotle, those living the political life seek happiness through honor, which he believes is superficial, depending more on those bestowing the happiness than the person who is receiving it. Others seek happiness through money making, but money is merely useful for the sake of something else. And money cannot buy anything that guarantees happiness. Pleasure is often selfish because it involves only you, whereas things that bring true happiness usually involve others as well.

This leads Aristotle to ask whether there are things that are good in themselves (as opposed to things that are simply useful). He finds that those things that are pursued for their own sake (rather than for something else) are good in themselves. These "real goods" include food, shelter, and health (all bodily goods); wealth (enough to live decently), pleasure, and knowledge (all goods needed for livelihood); and liberty, friends/loved ones, and civil peace (all social goods). **Real goods** are things we *ought* to desire regardless of whether we really do. According to Aristotle, real goods should be the focus of all ethical action. They are presented in Table 2.1.

There also exist **apparent goods**, which are pursued by many people; some are innocuous and some are noxious. Innocuous apparent goods might be love of sweets, good music, and fine wine. These remain innocuous only if they are pursued in moderation and do not interfere in the pursuit of real goods. Noxious apparent goods are those that involve treating real or apparent goods as ends in themselves and usually involve pleasure, wealth, fame, or power. Wealth is

TABLE 2.1 The Real Goods		
Bodily Goods	**Goods Needed for Livelihood**	**Social Goods**
Food	Wealth (above subsistence level)	Liberty
Shelter	Pleasure	Friends/loved ones
Health	Knowledge (understanding/wisdom)	Civil peace

needed only to exist decently above the subsistence level, and fame and power are not needed at all; in fact, fame and power often lead to self-indulgence and other behaviors that violate the moral virtues discussed later.

THE ULTIMATE GOOD

The ultimate good is happiness, according to Aristotle. All the other real goods we pursue are for the sake of happiness (or eudaimonia), which is the life that is most desirable (i.e., much more than contentment or joy commonly associated with the term *happiness*). We choose happiness not for anything other than itself. Aristotle believed further that happiness is the *final* good, the ultimate end of all desire achieved at the end of a complete life. Therefore, happiness cannot be experienced at a given moment; it can be achieved only through virtuous action (not thought alone).

Although virtuous action is required to achieve ethical happiness, some degree of good fortune is also required. External goods are required to achieve happiness. Being born into slavery or another oppressive condition can limit the opportunities to achieve happiness, as would friends lost by death. So both moral virtue and good fortune are operative means to happiness.

A complete life is needed to achieve happiness because many changes occur in life; there are ups and downs; "one swallow does not make a summer, nor does one day; and so too one day, or a short time, does not make a man blessed and happy."[6] Aristotle recognized that all people face misfortune during their lives, but a happy person can never become miserable. "For the man who is truly good and wise bears all the chances of life becomingly and always makes the best of circumstances, as a good general makes the best military use of the army at his command, and a good shoemaker makes the best shoes out of the hides that are given him."[7] So misfortune is a hindrance but not a permanent obstacle to real goods and ethical happiness.

STOICISM AND HEDONISM

There were two other approaches to virtue that emerged around this same historical period: stoicism and hedonism. Neither of these has endured in the same way that Aristotle's ethics have, but they are important to understand.

Stoicism was a philosophy of serenity, tranquility, and impassiveness to suffering. Epictetus (ca. 50–138) was the leading stoic. Similar to Socrates, he lectured rather than wrote, maintaining that inner peace is the ultimate virtue in the face of the difficulties faced in life. In his words, "Externals are not in my power, choice is."[8] Epictetus spoke of virtue and of courage, but in a different way than Socrates and Aristotle, emphasizing that life's events are to be accepted through self-control, abstinence, and submission to the will of God. Christianity was born during this period, and stoicism was incorporated into Christian religious thought. Calm acceptance of events beyond one's control had great appeal because this was seen as a way to submit to the will of God.

Hedonism views pleasure as the ultimate virtue. A leading hedonist, Epicurus (341–270 B.C.), believed prudence and tranquility were the most important pleasures because these virtues helped people avoid pleasures that might hurt them. Epicurus also stressed measured pleasures, such as friendship, peace, and contentment, rather than fleeting sensual pleasures.[9] **Egoistic hedonism**, however, sees pleasure as physical gratification of the senses. This is the common image the term suggests today. According to egoistic hedonism, immediate pleasure is good in itself; acts that do not bring pleasure are immoral.[10] This view ultimately contradicts experience,

> ## ETHICS CHECKUP
> ### ATM Trouble
>
> In a survey, people were asked what they would do if the automatic teller machine (ATM) gave them $200 too much during a transaction. Fifty percent of those responding would keep the money. Occasional news reports of faulty ATMs suggest that many more people than that take advantage of overpayments.[11]
> *On what principle(s) would you make your decision, if you received such an overpayment?*

however, because things we desire may not be healthful or may hurt others, such as rich foods or seeking wanton sexual pleasure. Like the stoics and the hedonists, Aristotle's theory of moral virtue recognizes the importance of pleasure, courage, and temperament, but he places them in the context of all other goods and virtues and how they must be balanced for ethical conduct to result. Aristotle's more evenhanded approach is one of the reasons why it became the most prominent theory of moral virtue.

MORAL VIRTUE

Moral virtue is excellence of character. It suggests more than the specific moral connotation the term has today. It refers to a quality in a person who seeks real goods in a morally correct manner. Aristotle identified two types of virtue: intellectual and moral. Intellectual virtue consists of learning or all the creative activities of the intellect that help us achieve our potential. Moral virtue develops as a result of habit (by exercising them); it does not occur naturally. Aristotle uses the example of the lyre (harp) player who becomes proficient only through continuous playing and practice: "So too we become just by doing just acts, temperate by doing temperate acts, brave by doing brave acts."[12] Of course, if moral virtue was innate, the discussion of ethics would be irrelevant because people would be born either good or bad, and that would be the end of it. There would be nothing gained from activity, study, practice, or habit. Because moral virtue must be learned through practice, teaching, exposure, support, and good habits are very important to ethical conduct.

Virtue ethics are sometimes seen as frustrating because Aristotle does not provide a precise formula for how to act in specific situations. Instead, he prescribes real goods to be sought and moral virtues to guide the quest, but individuals must find their own way in applying them in particular circumstances. As Aristotle observed, good conduct cannot be prescribed any more than the conduct required for good health. Avoiding defect or excess is an important guide, as are general principles, but there is no formula to track every possible ethical dilemma (or good or bad food) that might arise in the course of a lifetime.

Judging moral virtue can be difficult. Some people can be "two faced"; they may appear to engage in virtuous conduct but they are not really virtuous people. For example, a man might engage in an overt act of generosity (perhaps by giving a large charitable donation) to appear virtuous, but he really does it to impress a woman or to gain some kind of advantage. How is one to distinguish a virtuous act from a truly virtuous person? Isolated acts can be misleading unless they proceed from excellence in character, and excellence in character must be developed over time by doing virtuous acts. In the words of Aristotle, "It is by doing just acts that the just man is produced, and by doing temperate acts the temperate man; without doing these no one would have even a prospect of becoming good."[13]

ACHIEVING MORAL VIRTUE

Aristotle provides specific ideas regarding the methods to achieve moral virtue. Virtue is a kind of mean, or average, that aims at the intermediate. For example, it is good to be truthful, but a person might revel in telling everyone he or she sees about each occasion in which he or she told the truth or perhaps refuse to tell a small child about the Easter Bunny because he or she believes it to be a lie. It is clear that truthfulness can be taken to an extreme. Likewise, a person might be congratulated on winning the Nobel Prize and say, "Oh, it was nothing." Clearly, this is a gross understatement. Therefore, the intermediate, or mean, is a truthful person who is not boastful (excess) and not prone to understatement (deficiency). Moral virtue is a mean between two vices involving excess on the one hand and deficiency on the other.

As noted earlier, there are also "apparent" goods, which are things that appear good to certain people but are not. Celebrity, popularity, and influence are common examples of apparent goods that are often desired but do not constitute real or needed goods. In addition, there are some things that are bad in themselves (such as larceny and murder) that are always wrong. There is no "intermediate" to be sought in these things because these acts are always wrong under all circumstances. Given these constraints, Aristotle recognizes, "It is no easy task to be good . . . to find the middle . . . anyone can get angry—that is easy—or give or spend money; but to do this to the right person, to the right extent, at the right time, with the right motive, and the right way, that is not for everyone, nor is it easy; wherefore goodness is both rare and laudable and noble."[14] So given this broad outline of virtuous conduct, it is clear that, except in cases of acts bad in themselves, virtue seeks the mean, based on the facts of the situation. Seeking the mean is a principle found also in Eastern philosophies, such as Confucianism and Buddhism, which contend that the life of virtue and inner tranquility comes from seeking the middle, or noble, path.[15]

Moral virtue implies that our actions are voluntary and the products of choice. If our actions were not products of free choice, people would contribute nothing; it would be as if the wind simply pushed them in one direction or another. Children and those who are mentally ill also engage in voluntary action, but not in choice, because they cannot be expected to understand the consequences of their actions. The actions of lower animals are guided by instinct rather than conscious choice, so moral virtue is a unique goal to adult humans who have the power to make choices and engage in activities that pursue real goods or apparent goods. In Aristotle's day, for example, the penalties for crimes committed while drunk were doubled because of the underlying principle that individuals have the volition to choose whether to drink. Likewise, people are punished who violate laws because of ignorance when they should have known of the law's existence, so ignorance is not an excuse. As Aristotle says, "We assume that it is in their power not to be ignorant." Nevertheless, some people lead "slack" lives as a result of ignorance or self-indulgence, but that does excuse them from the moral obligation to act virtuously. The moral virtues constitute a short list. They are summarized in Table 2.2.

Aristotle described ten moral virtues: courage, temperance, prudence, justice, pride, ambition, having a good temper, being a good friend, truthfulness, and wittiness. These are the ten traits that people are morally obligated to act on as they seek real goods according to virtue ethics. The moral virtues have in common their emphasis on maintaining an even disposition while adhering to firm principles, showing restraint in one's actions, and placing the common good over individual gain.

The exercise of moral virtue is guided by the four **cardinal virtues** (temperance, courage, prudence, and justice), none of which is able to exist by itself. It is on these four cardinal virtues

TABLE 2.2   The Moral Virtues

Defect	Mean	Excess
Cowardice	Courage	Rashness
Self-indulgence	Temperance	Inhibition/self-denial
Using excessive care leading to inaction	Prudence (practical wisdom—choosing the right means for the right reason and end)	Too carefree/extravagant
Providing less than is due	Justice	Giving more than is due
Undue humility	Pride	Vanity
Laziness	Ambition	Blind ambition (love of honor at the expense of others)
Unmoving/not responsive	Having a good temper	Irascibility
Being exploitive	Being a good friend	Obsequiousness
Understating	Truthfulness	Boastfulness
Boorishness	Wittiness	Vulgar buffoon

that the remaining virtues are anchored. Recognition of the cardinal virtues can be traced to Plato, and, after Aristotle, they were later adopted by St. Thomas Aquinas (ca. 1225–1274) in his work *Summa Theologica*.[16] Plato and Aquinas identified wisdom, courage, temperance, and justice as the four cardinal virtues because they focused on the ideal society. Aristotle identified the same virtues, substituting prudence (practical wisdom) for wisdom because his focus was on ideal personal conduct, and he also saw intellectual virtue as distinct from moral virtue (as noted earlier in this chapter).

Table 2.2 also shows the excess and deficiency or defect in seeking moral virtues. It is virtuous to be ambitious but not to be lazy or have blind ambition. It is virtuous to have courage but not to be rash or cowardly. Therefore, moral virtues lie at the mean between excess and defect. As Michael Josephson has summarized, a person of character must work especially hard to overcome "self-righteousness, self-delusion, and selfishness," which are variations of some of Aristotle's excesses and defects from the moral virtues.[17] Self-righteousness is the character trait that leads people to overestimate how ethical they really are. It blinds people to their true moral shortcomings. Self-delusion refers to the capacity to rationalize conduct and make excuses in a vain effort to justify conduct that is morally impermissible. These rationalizations include comparisons to others (who behave worse); relying on the law to guide all moral conduct; or blaming a corrupt system to justify conduct, rather than relying on objective ethical standards. Selfishness places an individual's personal interest above the interests of others in all circumstances, causing myopia in determining ethical behavior.

THE HABIT OF MORAL VIRTUE

To summarize, virtue ethics require a person to seek real goods according to the moral virtues. People who do this habitually are morally virtuous. Moral virtue, sometimes called the habit of right desire is, according to American philosopher Mortimer Adler, the "process of conquering one's childish tendencies toward indulgence in immediate gratification."[18] Although the exact course of conduct in certain situations is not specified, Aristotle's ethics provide guidance for being a virtuous person, knowing that a virtuous person will likely choose the ethically correct path because of his or her reliance on the moral virtues to seek real goods. Morality is more than following rules according to virtue ethics. Adler summarized it in this way: "Living as he ought by habit, the man of good character has no need of rules of conduct; moral virtue as good habit dispenses with rules."[19] As Aristotle concluded, "We are the masters of our actions from the beginning to the end."[20]

Virtue ethics is based on the idea that if a person seeks the right things (the real goods) in the proper ways (via the moral virtues), the result will be a morally virtuous person engaging in ethical conduct. Individuals should seek the good for its own sake; so a good person is one who lives well, meeting his or her potential as a human being.

There is some empirical support for the value we place on the virtues. A study of college students in the United States and Korea found consistent results in their ranking of "what is satisfying about satisfying events?" They were asked to identify what occurrences (their content and characteristics) during the previous month had made them the happiest ("most personally satisfying"). The answers given were those events that involved autonomy/independence, competence/effectiveness, relatedness/belongingness, and self-esteem/self-respect. Security/control in times of privation also was important. However, the study participants deemed pleasure/stimulation, self-actualization/meaning, popularity/influence, and physical/bodily health less important. The least important kind of event involved money or luxury.[21] Many of these kinds of events correspond to the moral virtues (Table 2.2). According to the study's author, past research has also shown that although Americans have been getting richer in recent decades, wealthier people are generally no happier than the less well off. This study provides evidence that the things that bring true happiness involve virtues and personal development rather than acquisition of goods.

Some psychologists have referred to character as "emotional intelligence," although ethics has nothing to do with emotions and little to do with intelligence. *Character*, as used by psychologists, is the ability to motivate yourself in the face of frustration, control your impulses, delay gratification, regulate your moods, and so on.[22] As sociologist Amitai Etzioni writes, character is "the psychological muscle that moral conduct requires" to overcome emotional barriers that prevent ethical decision making.[23]

Aristotle's moral virtues have been summarized in many different ways over the years and appear in codes of ethics of all kinds. The *Character Counts!* education programs summarize the six pillars of character as trustworthiness, respect, responsibility, fairness, caring, and citizenship.[24] The Boy Scouts' oath pledges, "On my honor I will do my best to do my duty to God and my country and to obey the Scout Law; to help other people at all times; to keep myself physically strong, mentally awake, and morally straight."[25] And, of course, there is the Golden Rule: "Do unto others as you would have them do unto you," another motto that highlights several of the moral virtues.

Rushworth Kidder, president of the Institute for Global Ethics, interviewed twenty-four distinguished individuals from sixteen countries who were known for their conscientiousness and character. These people came from different religious, political, social, and cultural backgrounds, and he asked them, "If you could construct a global code of ethics for the twenty-first century, what would be in it?" Their answers centered on eight widely shared values: love, truth, freedom, fairness, unity, tolerance, responsibility, and respect for life.[26] Aristotle would likely support all these expressions of virtue, but he would note that none of them incorporate *all* the moral virtues; hence, his effort to identify a comprehensive list.

Aristotle emphasizes that ethical conduct requires practice so that it becomes a habit. Therefore, ethics both causes our actions and is the result of our actions. In Aristotle's words, "We are what we repeatedly do." The Critical Thinking Exercises at the end of the chapter are designed to help students develop the habit of moral thinking.

TABLE 2.3   An Approach to Ethical Dilemmas

1. List the relevant facts (separating the irrelevant details from the central issues).
2. Identify the precise moral question to be answered.
3. List and think about the moral principles that might be used to support the positions that could be taken.
4. Make and explain your decision (i.e., your morally permissible course of conduct).
5. Justify your conclusions using positive reasons and ethical principles in support of your decision, anticipating and addressing contrary views.

EVALUATING ETHICAL DILEMMAS

Ethical dilemmas can be difficult when a swirl of facts obfuscate the central issue to be decided. It is important to approach ethical problems systematically. Regardless of the situation or the dilemma, your approach should be the same. A recommended approach is outlined in Table 2.3.

First, it is important to list the relevant facts (to separate them from facts that are not germane to the ethical decision). For example, if a person is drowning, and you are deciding whether to save her or him, the status of that person as a current or former lover is not relevant to your ethical decision. Second, it is crucial to identify the precise underlying moral question to be decided by separating it from other facts of the case. Third, it is important to understand the principles on which the ethical decision might be made. By the end of Chapter 4, you will have an understanding of the three major ethical schools of thought, their central principles, and how they are applied in practice. Fourth, it is important to explain your decision (i.e., the precise course of conduct you believe necessary). Fifth, you must justify your actions based on valid and applicable ethical principles, and you should anticipate contrary views and why your decision is superior in ethical terms to alternate choices.

ETHICS IN BOOKS

Ethics is everywhere, even in the books we read, which sometimes are written without ethics specifically in mind. Here is a summary of a book that looks at actions that affect others, followed by questions that ask you to reflect on the ethical connections.

WHY CAN'T WE BE GOOD?

Jacob Needleman
(Tarcher/Penguin, 2007)

Jacob Needleman is a professor of philosophy at San Francisco State University, who writes about a fundamental question of ethics (and also of criminal justice):

"Why do we not do what we know is good?" If we agree on major principles for behavior, taken from the Socratic, Jewish, Christian, and other major philosophical and religious traditions, why do so many of us not act consistently in accord with these principles?

A quote from the Torah is used by the author to express the simple basis for good behavior, summarizing it in one sentence: "What is hateful to you, do not do to your neighbor." In the Jewish tradition, Christianity, and other perspectives, the "golden rule" is a central, organizing theme, and "all the rest is commentary" on this basic principle. Therefore, we might expect adherence to this principle to be more universally practiced.

According to the author, good actions are preceded by good thoughts, and he turns to the philosophy of Socrates, Marcus Aurelius, and Epictetus as well as classroom techniques that involve thinking and listening while taking a specific action. The objective of these efforts is to identify the secret for transforming good ideas and thoughts into good actions, "which underlies the hypocrisy that haunts our lives, enabling us to go on and on betraying our ethical ideals while at the same time believing that we are doing what is good—or, in any case, that we are doing all that we possibly can."

Needleman uses the film *Obedience* as an example of how individuals justify immoral acts when told to do so by an authority figure (the film depicts the application of electric shocks for wrong answers to questions). He finds it difficult to explain the disjunction between widely held moral beliefs and the common instances we see of injustice, disrespect, and violence.

Needleman believes that the transition between thought and action "between what we are in our deepest heart and what we actually do and say" is what he calls "remorse of conscience." That is to say, only when we see in full consciousness our capacity (weakness) in avoiding doing the good, that we are able to cross the threshold from moral thought into moral action. Needleman believes that clear awareness of our (in)capacities when crossing between the "two worlds" of thought and action is what gives us the strength to act in accord with our principles.

QUESTIONS

1. If good ideas alone are not enough to produce good actions, are there practical ways to encourage desirable actions (e.g., reporting crimes, acting as a good Samaritan)?
2. How would Aristotle evaluate the linkage between moral virtues and actions? Would he see a similar separation between moral thought and action?

ETHICS IN THE MOVIES

Movies seek to entertain and inform the audience about a story, incident, or person. Many good movies also hit upon important ethical themes in making significant decisions that affect the lives of others. Read the movie summary here (and watch the movie if you haven't already), and answer the questions to make the ethical connections.

RETURN TO PARADISE

Joseph Ruben, Director
(1998)

Vince Vaughan (Sheriff), Joaquin Phoenix (Lewis), and David Conrad (Tony) are three friends on a five-week vacation in Malaysia who use and possess drugs for recreational use while there. Two of the friends return to the United States, and they all go their separate ways.

Two years later a young lawyer, Beth Eastern (Anne Heche), tracks down the two friends in the United States, informing them that the third (Lewis) has been jailed for the last 2 years in Malaysia and faces a possible death sentence there for drug possession. A few days after they had left Malaysia from their vacation, police had raided their camp and found large quantities of hashish. Lewis was still residing there, so he was held responsible. He is scheduled to be put to death in 8 days, and the only way the charges can be decreased is if the two friends come back to "paradise" and take their share of the responsibility. If they do, they both will spend 3 years in prison. If only one does, he will spend 6 years behind bars.

The film centers on the agonizing decisions of Sheriff and Tony in deciding if they should go back to Malaysia in the hopes of saving their friend. *Return to Paradise* poses one of the ultimate ethical dilemmas: Should you sacrifice your freedom for a friend, when you have at least partial responsibility for his predicament?

In a subplot, a journalist (Jada Pinkett) gets wind of the story of the pending execution in Malaysia and wants to write a story about it, but she is begged by the lawyer not to write about it because Malaysia is very sensitive about American criticism of Malaysian justice, and a critical story might endanger the agreement to reduce Joaquin Phoenix's death sentence. The journalist must make the decision to either sit on the story because it might affect the outcome of the case, or to print it because it is an important story.

QUESTIONS

1. Would you return to face 6 years in prison to spare a friend's life in a similar situation? What is your ethical rationale?
2. What are the ethical considerations of the journalist in deciding whether to publish the story, and what should her conclusion be?

Discussion Question

Why is moral virtue a habitual behavior?

Critical Thinking Exercises

All ethical decisions affect others (by definition) and, as Aristotle points out, ethical decision making is achieved consistently only through practice. Given the outline of virtue ethics provided by Aristotle (i.e., seeking the real goods via the moral virtues), evaluate the moral permissibility of the conduct in question in each scenario.

Important note on method: *Critical thinking requires the ability to evaluate viewpoints, facts, and behaviors objectively to assess information or methods of argumentation to establish the true worth or merit of an act or course of conduct. Please evaluate these scenarios, first analyzing pros and cons of alternate views,* before *you come to a conclusion. Do* not *draw a conclusion first, and then try to find facts to support it—this frequently leads to narrow (and incorrect) thinking.*

To properly evaluate the moral permissibility of a course of action using critical thinking skills

1. *Begin with an open mind (no preconceptions!),*
2. *Isolate and evaluate the relevant facts on both sides,*
3. *Identify the precise moral question to be answered, and*
4. *Apply ethical principles to the moral question based on an objective evaluation of the facts, only then drawing a conclusion.*

2.1 A Parole Fugitive at Princeton

A Princeton University student with a satisfactory school record was discovered to be a parole fugitive from Utah for crimes of theft and fraud. This case occurred during the 1990s; the fugitive used false documentation and a false name to obtain admission to the university, but on admission he performed well as a student. His identity was ultimately discovered by Princeton.[27]

- What action should the university take?

  (*Hint*: There are two parts here. Your answer requires an assessment of the moral permissibility of the student's actions first, then an assessment of the university's options under the guidelines provided by virtue ethics.)

2.2   Misrepresentation at MIT

The dean of admissions at the Massachusetts Institute of Technology (MIT) offered her resignation after confessing to résumé fraud. Marilee Jones was highly regarded on campus for her efforts to reduce the pressure on students applying to prestigious colleges, and she had coauthored a popular book on the subject.

Questions surfaced about her résumé after she received a promotion, and she later admitted that she had never graduated from college. "I misrepresented my academic degrees when I first applied to MIT 28 years ago," she wrote in a statement, "and did not have the courage to correct my résumé when I applied for my current job or at any time since."[28]

Faked personal history appears to be a growing phenomenon: In 2001, professor Joseph J. Ellis, a Pulitzer Prize–winning historian, was suspended for a year without pay from Mt. Holyoke College after the *Boston Globe* discovered that he was telling students personal stories about his combat experience in his course on Vietnam, when in fact he had never served in Vietnam. In 2002, Sandra Baldwin, president of the United States Olympic Committee (USOC), was forced to leave after it was discovered that she had never finished her degree.

"Holding integrity is sometimes very hard to do," Ms. Jones of MIT wrote in her book, "because the temptation may be to cheat or cut corners."

- What is the appropriate moral course of action for the university to take in this case?

  (*Hint*: One way to approach scenarios like this is to find, for example, the strongest argument in favor of the moral permissibility of MIT's actions and the strongest argument against the moral permissibility of MIT's action.)

2.3   Presidential Exit Ethics

There appears to be a pattern of controversial, but legal, decisions that occur as presidents leave office. As Bill Clinton left office, it was disclosed that $190,000 in last-minute gifts

had been accepted. Although accepting the gifts was legal, questions of propriety were raised.

In the last month of George H. W. Bush's presidency, he pardoned Caspar Weinberger, former defense secretary, and several other former White House officials who had been indicted for allegedly lying and withholding information from Congress and federal investigators in an investigation of secret U.S. arms sales to Iran and aid to the Nicaraguan Contra rebels. Although they were legal, these pardons thwarted an ongoing investigation.

As Ronald Reagan left office, he had a multimillion-dollar house financed by a "friend." This raised questions regarding the source of the funds and whether it represented repayment for past or future favors.[29]

- Assess the moral permissibility of these decisions.

2.4   A Large Contribution

Stanley Ho is an 85-year-old millionaire known as the "King of Gambling" in Macau (a Chinese territory). He is a major casino developer, and father of seventeen children, who has been scrutinized and investigated for links to organized crime. He has said that "these reports only say I know some Triad members. Well, maybe you have come across some. To be associated with or to know someone is completely different."[30] Ho has never been charged with a crime.

Ho made a gift to Oxford University in the amount of $5 million, which will be used to pay for university initiatives in Chinese studies. He was approved by Oxford's ethics committee to make the gift, one of the largest individual donations ever made to the university.

- Should Oxford accept the gift from a person whose background has been questioned?
- Are there any circumstances under which a university should not accept a monetary gift from an individual or organization?

2.5   The Ethics of Brain-Booster Drugs

There's a growing debate both in scientific circles and among the general populace: Should adults be using so-called "brain-boosting" drugs—normally intended to treat serious medical conditions—to improve concentration and performance? Some college students, of course, have been using stimulants for years: They take such things as modafinil, Adderall, and Ritalin (euphemistically known on campuses as "vitamin R") to enhance their memories for exams or to stay up all night and press out a term paper. By one estimate, at least 10 percent of American college students use prescription drugs as study aids.

Now the general adult population is turning to the pills, too—often illegally—to boost productivity and enhance their mental prowess on the job. Some experts laud the development: They think it's time to consider making the stimulants legal for brain-boosting functions.

But critics worry it will accelerate a slide toward a drugged society. In an era when people take everything from Viagra to enhance their romance to steroids to enhance their baseball statistics, they argue that the addition of so-called "cognitive enhancement" drugs will only make us more dependent on the pill bottle.

In an online poll in the British science journal *Nature*, answered by 1,400 people in sixty countries, one in five said they had used drugs for nonmedical reasons "to stimulate their focus, concentration, or memory." Only about half had a prescription for the drug they were using. A third had bought the drugs over the Internet. And even though about half reported unpleasant side effects, four out of five "thought that healthy adults should be able to take the drugs if they want to," *Nature* reported. Critics argue that more time is needed with the petri dishes and field testing before the drugs are used as mind enhancers. "The reality [is] that there is very little research to document whether [these drugs] are universally beneficial, whether they could be detrimental, what are the long-term outcomes, what are the side effects," says Nora Volkow, director of the National Institute on Drug Abuse, a U.S. government agency. "There's really very, very limited knowledge."[31]

Nearly everyone talking about brain-boosting drugs agrees that they ought to be both safe and effective before being widely used. But some worry about other problems they present. Would workers, for example, feel coerced to use enhancement drugs in order to win promotions or even simply to keep their jobs?

Advocates point out that humans already "enhance" their thinking in a variety of ways, from drinking beverages with caffeine (a known stimulant), to exercising to brighten their mood, to relying on a computer to increase knowledge, and to simply getting a good night's sleep before a big test. But for some, a caution light goes on when we're changing the way the brain works, particularly when so little is known about it.

- Evaluate the moral permissibility of taking "brain-boosting" drugs to enhance your performance (at work or play).

Key Concepts

Moral virtue *11*

Socratic method *12*

The Republic *12*

Nicomachus *12*

Hierarchy of goods *13*

Real goods *13*

Apparent goods *13*

Stoicism *14*

Hedonism *14*

Egoistic hedonism *14*

Cardinal virtues *16*

Notes

1. Mortimer Adler, *Desires Right and Wrong: The Ethics of Enough* (New York: Macmillan, 1991), p. 1.
2. For an account of Socrates' trial and death, see Plato, *Last Days of Socrates, The Euthyphro; The Apology; Crito; Phaedo* (New York: Penguin Classics, 1993).
3. Plato, *The Republic* (ca. 370 B.C.) (New York: Oxford University Press, 1994), Book II.
4. Aristotle, *What Is the Essence of Life?*, www.nahc.org/NAHC/Val/Columns/SC10–2.html (accessed January 30, 2005).
5. Aristotle, *The Nicomachean Ethics* (330 B.C.E.) (New York: Oxford University Press, 1998), p. 6.
6. Aristotle, *Nicomachean,* p. 14.
7. Aristotle, *Nicomachean*, p. 21.
8. Epictetus, *The Discourses of Epictetus* (105 A.D.) (New York: Everyman's Library, 1995), p. 5.
9. Henry Dwight Sedgwick, *The Art of Happiness: Or, the Teachings of Epicurus* (Manchester, NH: Ayer Publishing, 1970), p. 42.
10. John Watson, *Hedonistic Theories: From Aristippus to Spencer* (1895 edition) (Bristol, UK: Thoemmes Press, 1996), p. 112.
11. "Do the Right Thing," *USA Today* (March 5, 1991), p. 1D; Rummana Hussain, "Faulty ATM a Windfall for Drivers," *Chicago Sun-Times* (March 6, 2004), p. 3; "Customers Flock to Get That Little Bit Extra," *Falkirk Herald* (United Kingdom) (January 27, 2005).
12. Aristotle, *Nicomachean*, p. 29.
13. Aristotle, *Nicomachean*, p. 35.

14. Aristotle, *Nicomachean*, p. 45.

15. Judith A. Ross, *Ethics for Life* (Mountain View, CA: Mayfield Publishing, 2001), p. 410.

16. Thomas Aquinas, *Summa Theologica, I–II* (Grand Rapids, MI: Christian Classics, 1981); Plato, *The Republic*, Books I–IV.

17. Michael S. Josephson, *The Power of Character* (San Francisco: Jossey-Bass, 1998), pp. 11–12.

18. Adler, *Desires Right and Wrong: The Ethics of Enough*, p. 106.

19. Adler, *Desires Right and Wrong: The Ethics of Enough*, p. 181.

20. Aristotle, *Nicomachean*, p. 61.

21. Kennon M. Sheldon, Andrew J. Eliot, Youngmee Kim, and Tim Kassar, "What Is Satisfying about Satisfying Events: Testing 10 Candidate Psychological Needs," *Journal of Personality and Social Psychology*, vol. 80 (February 2001), pp. 325–339.

22. Daniel Goleman, *Emotional Intelligence* (New York: Bantam Books, 1995).

23. Amitai Etzioni, *The New Golden Rule: Community and Morality in a Democratic Society* (New York: Basic Books, 1998), p. 33.

24. Six Pillars of Character, www.charactercounts.org/defsix.htm (accessed October 24, 2004).

25. Boy Scout Oath, www.usscouts.org/advance/boyscout/bsoath.html (accessed October 24, 2004).

26. Rushworth M. Kidder and Jo Spiller, *Shared Values for a Troubled World: Conversations with Men and Women of Conscience* (New York: John Wiley & Sons, 1994).

27. "A Timeline of James Hogue's Life," www.mileendfilms.com/cm_timeline.html (accessed October 1, 2004).

28. "An Admissions Officer's Credentials," *The Chronicle of Higher Education*, vol. 53 (May 18, 2007), p. 4.

29. "Curious Clinton Ethics," *USA Today* (February 6, 2001), p. 3.

30. Dominic Kennedy and James Doran, "Oxford Takes Gambling King's Cash," *The Times* (London) (May 26, 2007).

31. Gregory M. Lamb, "Pill Wars: Debate Heats Up over 'Brain Booster' Drugs," *The Christian Science Monitor* (May 10, 2009).

CHAPTER 3

Formalism
Carrying Out Obligation and Duty

Learning Objectives:

- To understand the nature of deontological ethics.

- To recognize the centrality of duties versus inclinations in Kantian ethics.

- To increase the ability to isolate the categorical imperative from any set of facts presented in an ethical dilemma.

- To distinguish the categorical imperative from the practical imperative and hypothetical imperatives.

- To understand why lying is never permitted using the ethics of formalism.

The hardest part is not knowing what's right—but doing it.

—Michael Josephson (1998)

You are in your car at night on a poorly lit road. The car ahead of you appears to strike a lone pedestrian walking close to the side of the road, then the car speeds off without stopping. You immediately stop to help the injured man, dragging him off the side of the road, afraid he will be hit again in the darkness. As it turns out later, however, your movement of the victim caused him permanent paralysis—a terrible result to a well-meaning act.

Sometimes our actions produce bad results—even when our intentions are good. So how does one determine an ethical act? Emmanuel Kant sought to provide clear ethical guidance for difficult situations such as the one previously described.

KANTIAN ETHICS

Emmanuel Kant (1724–1804) developed an entirely different way of determining ethical conduct by focusing on obligations and duties. In his influential books *Grounding for the Metaphysics of Morals* and *The Critique of Practical Reason*, Kant argued that ethical conduct should be based on reason drawn from simple, unbending rational premises.

Kant searched for the appropriate rules to guide ethical conduct. His approach is a nonconsequentialist approach, known as formalism, or **deontological ethics**, meaning that the morality of an action is determined by whether it conforms to (or violates) a moral principle. The potential consequences of the decision are not relevant in this view. The key is to find the proper moral principle to guide ethical action.

In searching for this general moral principle, Kant believed that if a rule is morally valid, it must be of absolute necessity and apply in all circumstances. He uses the example "thou shalt not lie," for which he believes there should be no exceptions. Individuals are affected by many influences in decision making, and Kant was looking for a "supreme principle of morality."

Kant argued that nothing is good without qualification, except goodwill. Even good characteristics, such as self-control and moderation in emotions and passions, can describe a cat burglar as well as the good person. It was argued even in Kant's time that clear thinking guided by reason is all that is needed to be ethical, but Kant did not believe that reason alone was sufficient because people too often are influenced by subjective conditions. Therefore, objective principles are needed to guide decisions.

In looking at individual actions, Kant distinguishes between **duties and inclinations**. Inclinations have no moral worth because persons who find pleasure in spreading joy would do it anyway (i.e., it lacks moral content). Duty, however, connotes a person's moral obligation. It is what a person *ought* to do, regardless of whether it is convenient or popular or results in an unforeseen outcome. Therefore, duty should always be followed, and duty is fundamental to Kant's view of ethics.[1]

Kant is also emphatic in arguing that the moral worth of an action does not lay in its expected outcome or consequences. This is because consequences can be the result of luck, coincidence, or the actions of third parties over which you have no control. Therefore, morality is determined by a priori principles that prescribe an action using an established rule, rather than on an expected result.

THE CATEGORICAL IMPERATIVE

The centerpiece of Kant's philosophy is the **categorical imperative**, which guides all conduct. It states that a person should never act in a way in which the rule behind an action (maxim) should not become a universal law. Stated in another way, an act is morally right if and only if its maxim (i.e., the rule behind it) is universalizable.[2] For example, a person might say, "I don't want to pay my taxes because the government misspends money and won't miss my contribution anyway." Even if this statement was factually true, it would make a bad universal rule; therefore, it cannot be defended ethically.

Following the categorical imperative, it is wrong to make a promise you have no intention of keeping, even if it is a trivial promise (e.g., "I'll call you tomorrow" or "I'll pay you right back"). It is important not to make promises without intending to keep them because there may be many circumstances in which it is not advantageous to keep a promise (e.g., you don't have the money right now, you got a better offer, you're too busy doing other things, and so on). Duty, therefore, has nothing to do with potential consequences. Indeed, personal needs, feelings, and inclinations often work against keeping promises so, according to Kant, you do not want a person making decisions entirely on what might happen. Instead, decisions should be made based on duty.

Writing in 1785, in an apparent reference to Aristotle, Kant states that it is not difficult "to become doubtful at times whether any virtue is actually to be found in the world."[3] He believed that people often became shrewder as they got older and fell away from the idea of moral duty. People make excuses and rationalizations as a result of inclinations and perceived needs.

Kant quotes one of the Gospels where Jesus says, "Why do you call me (whom you see) good? None is good except God (whom you do not see)."[4] Kant believes that God is used in this passage as the highest example of moral goodness. What Kant is trying to make clear is the moral principle which underlies that goodness for people (connecting a priori principles with the rational free will of humans).

Kant distinguishes between hypothetical and categorical imperatives. **Hypothetical imperatives** are means to obtaining something else (similar to Aristotle's apparent goods). For example, a person who goes on a diet will lose weight. The diet is an optional method (i.e., exercise would work as well) of achieving an optional end (losing weight). A categorical imperative is an action objectively necessary in itself without reference to another end (analogous to Aristotle's real goods). There is no moral duty to diet or lose weight, so it is not a categorical imperative.

Another example of a hypothetical imperative is "Do God's will and you won't go to hell!" It uses God's will as a means to achieve some other end. In Kant's view, the categorical imperative is "Do God's will!" If this is a categorical true statement, it is necessary in itself and not as a means toward some other end (i.e., go to heaven or avoid hell). Kant shows the superiority of the categorical imperative because it is a universal law that is a moral duty that stands on its own, requiring no further justification. An example Kant uses as a hypothetical imperative is medical skill. The medicines and skills needed by a physician to make his patient healthy, and those needed by a poisoner to kill his victim, may be the same because they each serve to bring about their purpose effectively. Medical skill is, therefore, not a categorical imperative because it has value only as a means to some other end.

In another apparent reference to Aristotle, Kant states that it is impossible to determine what will make a person truly happy. Kant finds the concept of happiness indeterminate. The elements needed for happiness are empirical (from experience) and cannot be controlled by an individual. Kant declares, "even though everyone wishes to attain happiness, yet he can never say definitely and consistently what it is he really wishes or wills."[5] Kant believes it would require "omniscience" to know what would make you happy, a point on which he and Aristotle clearly disagree. Kant focuses on duty and obligation at the moment, whereas Aristotle focuses on virtuous conduct that leads to happiness in the future.

THE PRACTICAL IMPERATIVE

The second guiding principle in Kant's philosophy of formalism is the **practical imperative**, which states that you act in such a way that you treat humanity, yourself or another, always the same—as an end and never simply as a means. Therefore, a person can never be used as a means to an end. For example, you can never kill someone to save the life of another under Kant's philosophy because that would make a bad universal rule (violating the categorical imperative) and it uses another person as a means to an end (violating the practical imperative).

Kant's practical imperative is sometimes used as a basis to claim universal or natural rights. For example, the Declaration of Independence states: "We hold these truths to be self-evident, that all men are created equal, that they are endowed by their Creator with certain unalienable Rights, that among these are Life, Liberty and the pursuit of Happiness." This statement affirms the equality of all persons in legal terms based on Kant's more fundamental assertion that they are equal in moral terms as well. Of course, all rights imply some obligation on the part of others to observe and not violate those rights, and this is another thrust of the practical imperative: Individuals are to be treated as ends in themselves and not as means to some other ends.

Kant believed his theory of ethics, captured largely in the categorical and practical imperatives, is a superior way to make ethical decisions. Kant criticizes the Golden Rule (i.e., do unto others as you would have them do unto you), for example, as lacking a moral principle. The Golden Rule has been expressed in similar forms in virtually all religious traditions, including Judaism, Christianity, Islam, Buddhism, and Hinduism.[6] However, the Golden Rule doesn't describe what your duties to self or others *should* be. Under this rule, according to Kant, a criminal could argue successfully with a judge about any possible sentence or a masochist could argue that everyone should enjoy pain.[7]

Kant describes a "**kingdom of ends**" as an ideal state in which rational beings are united through common, objective universal laws that apply to everyone (and no one is used as a means by others). In this situation, reasonable people accept the rules for themselves whether they are giving or receiving the action. This would be the circumstance if all decisions were made in accord with the categorical and practical imperatives.

Given the scenario at the beginning of this chapter, it is clear that your conduct in dragging the hit-and-run victim off the road was morally permissible. In fact, Kant would say you performed your moral duty because your action was universalizable (the categorical imperative). We would want all people to do what you did, given the circumstances of the incident. Also, your action follows the practical imperative because you are treating the victim as an end in herself or himself, not as a means to some other end (e.g., getting your name in the newspaper as a hero). However, as discussed in the next chapter, your action could be reasoned in a different way, which might lead to a different result.

Consider the contemporary practice of buying counterfeit goods. A reporter for the *Miami Herald* newspaper went to New York City's Chinatown and was taken by local

ETHICS CHECKUP
Punishment for Lying

Five federal employees were investigated for misconduct, and they denied the charges when they were first asked about them. When it was discovered they did engage in the misconduct, they were given extra punishment for lying to the investigators. The U.S. Supreme Court upheld this extra punishment, concluding that an employee has no right to make false statements, and when asked about wrongdoing, a person has two legal choices: Tell the truth or say nothing.[8]

On what ethical principles is this decision based?

"guides" to three secret showrooms where she bought counterfeit handbags, which were tucked into a green-black garbage bag so they would not be seen upon leaving the premises. The reporter ultimately spent $195 on six luxury counterfeit purses, which would have cost $3,000 retail for the real thing. In a subsequent newspaper article on her Chinatown adventure, she noted in a sidebar that the counterfeit trade supports Asian mafias, steals the names and business from legitimate manufacturers, avoids millions of dollars in taxes, and is conducted without any controls over the use of child labor or banned chemical products. But the reporter went on to say that, even though police target the makers and sellers of counterfeits, "Casual buyers are unlikely to be busted," and she proceeded to give tips about how to buy the highest-quality fake purses.

There was a great deal of reader outrage over this article when it appeared, because it condoned buying illegal merchandise and supported illegal business activity. As a critic of this article and the counterfeit purchases said later, "I don't shop for counterfeit goods anymore. The actual quality is poor, and the feeling of having something fake is worse. I hadn't thought of the Chinese mafia angle until I read it in some of the reader's comments." [9]

In this case, both the original reporter and the critic justified their behavior on its potential outcomes: The reporter focused on the low cost and likelihood of apprehension, whereas the critic focused on product quality, owning fake merchandise, and helping the mafia. Their opposite conclusions (to buy it or not) focused entirely on their assessment of future consequences. Kant's formalism would assess the conduct in a different way, which permits only one course of conduct. Using the categorical and practical imperatives, the buying of counterfeits is both a bad universal rule and it uses others (specifically, legitimate manufacturers, businesses, and the illicit sellers) as a means to your personal goal of obtaining inexpensive purses. Therefore, buying counterfeit property cannot be justified under formalism (which is also the position taken under American criminal law), regardless of the likelihood of being caught, product quality, impact on organized crime, or how you might feel about it afterwards. Kant sees all of these considerations as irrelevant to making a moral decision, because they are mere after-the-fact rationalizations. Moral decisions must be made *a priori* under formalism, after considering both the categorical and practical imperatives and ignoring any subsequent impact your conduct may or may not have. It can be seen that formalism is reflected in criminal law that prohibits buying and selling counterfeit goods and stolen property, which are both illegal under all circumstances, regardless of any impact the conduct may have on oneself or others.

LYING AND CRITICISMS

Kant's formalism has been criticized for not being flexible. For example, a person might lie about the whereabouts of another when he or she knows the questioner has plans to kill that person. Kant believes the person should always tell the truth because "a lie always harms another, if not another human being, then it does harm to humanity in general" (i.e., it violates the unspoken social contract between people, rendering moral duties uncertain). Also, you cannot control consequences or outcomes, so you never know what the consequences of your lie will be. Therefore, potential consequences of your truthfulness should never be used as a **justification for lying**. Kant concludes, "Truth is not a possession, the right to which can be granted to one person but refused to another... it is an unconditional duty which holds in all circumstances." [10] Therefore, even a lie that looks like it will not result in dire consequences is not permitted under formalism because consequences are never known for certain and lying conflicts with your moral duty.

Kant's philosophy does not allow for exceptions, and some believe that this contradicts common experience. It seems that some morally good actions are done out of goodwill, benevolence, sympathy, or other laudable notions other than duty. It also does not distinguish duties toward others in family and love relationships from duties to all rational beings. It appears that the categorical imperative would be difficult to apply in some family, love, and friendship situations. At the same time, the categorical imperative has appeal in other relationships when expectations of conduct can be stated in more precise terms. As a popular book states, a "mature" (or perhaps "ethical") business philosophy is "Act in a way that you would want your employees to act if you were the employer," *and* "Employers should treat employees as they would want to be treated if they were the employees."[11] Therefore, Kant's ethics may have value in certain kinds of settings.

COMPARING FORMALISM AND VIRTUE ETHICS

Formalism and virtue ethics have few similarities and many differences. It is useful to compare these approaches by their goals, means, and how they judge ethical conduct. Table 3.1 illustrates this comparison.

The goal or object of ethical conduct is ethical happiness according to virtue ethics, and it is moral duty under formalism. These two very different objectives help to explain the major distinction between these approaches to ethical behavior. Virtue ethics links pursuit of the real goods and ethical happiness through the moral virtues, in which personal inclinations are relevant to assessing motivation. Formalism, however, portrays ethics as a duty that simply follows two universal imperatives without regard for personal inclinations because they are not seen as morally relevant. Judging ethical conduct requires an assessment of character according to virtue ethics, which involves patterns of conduct over time. Contrary to this approach, formalism looks solely at acts that correspond to the categorical and practical imperatives, regardless of outcome. This comparison helps to make clear the fact that virtue ethics is directed at developing a moral *person* through a pattern of moral conduct, whereas formalism seeks to develop moral *actions* regardless of where they lead.

TABLE 3.1 Comparing Virtue Ethics and Formalism

	Virtue Ethics	Formalism
Goal of ethical behavior	The life that is most desirable, achieved by pursuing real goods through virtuous action, results in ethical happiness.	Do moral duty.
Means to become ethical	Follow the moral virtues: "by doing just acts . . . the just man is produced."	Categorical imperative is the supreme principle of morality.
Judging ethical conduct	Good conduct cannot be prescribed. Individual acts can be misleading unless they come from "a firm and unchangeable character." Virtue is a mean that aims at the intermediate and avoids excess and defect.	Assess actions according to categorical and practical imperatives; consequences of acts do not bear on moral worthiness because other causes can result in the outcome, and personal inclinations have no moral value.

ETHICS IN BOOKS

Ethics is everywhere, even in the books we read, which sometimes are written without ethics specifically in mind. Here is a summary of a book that looks at values on a global scale, followed by questions that ask you to reflect on the ethical connections.

COSMOPOLITANISM: ETHICS IN A WORLD OF STRANGERS

Kwame Anthony Appiah
(W. W. Norton, 2007)

The author is a professor of philosophy at Princeton University and this, somewhat opaque, book for the average reader takes a provocative look at values in the globalized society of today. Appiah argues strongly against the common presumption that morals and ethics merely reflect local preferences, rather than universal truths. He argues for "cosmopolitanism," a term he traces back centuries, which he uses to mean "we have obligations to others . . . beyond those to whom we are related" or fellow citizens. In addition, the term means "we take seriously the value not just of human life but of particular human lives, which means taking an interest in the practices and values that lend them significance." Cosmopolitanism requires, therefore, "that each human being has responsibilities to every other," despite what local customs, culture, or loyalties might dictate.

He uses the example of crime prevention to illustrate his perspective: "If my interest is in discouraging theft, I needn't worry that one person might refrain from theft because she believes in the Golden Rule; another because of her conception of personal integrity; a third because she thinks God frowns on it." This is because the language of values that shapes a persons' actions will often differ, but if there is agreement on the type of action that needs to be done, differences in motivation and justification matter less. There are many common purposes that people in all societies of all kinds desire, but they seek them for different reasons that result from their history, customs, and habits. Cosmopolitanism focuses on these common purposes and values, because "it is easier to focus on values than to identify exceptionless principles," which are the focus of much of ethics.

Appiah notes that "people often recommend relativism because they think it will lead to tolerance," but he finds this to be essentially a cop-out, ignoring that we can learn from one another about what shared actions that are in the common best interest. Cosmopolitans, in his view, are committed to "pluralism" (there are many values worth living by) and "fallibilism" (knowledge is imperfect and subject to revision as new evidence is discovered). Appiah notes that cosmopolitanism's two ideals can sometimes clash: universal concern for others and respect for legitimate difference. Therefore, cosmopolitanism is "the name not of the solution but of the challenge."

QUESTIONS

1. With the establishment in recent years of the International Criminal Court and UN Conventions against Transnational Organized Crime and Corruption, it can be seen that international consensus is growing on global issues of criminal justice. Can cosmopolitanism help in bringing together countries on major issues of justice, while respecting individual differences?

2. Can you offer suggestions, based on a particular issue of justice (e.g., plea bargaining or trial and punishment or rehabilitation) that brings together the two ideals of universal concern for others and respect for legitimate difference?

ETHICS IN THE MOVIES

Movies seek to entertain and inform the audience about a story, incident, or person. Many good movies also hit upon important ethical themes in making significant decisions that affect the lives of others. Read the movie summary here (and watch the movie if you haven't already), and answer the questions to make the ethical connections.

HOTEL RWANDA

Terry George, Director
(2004)

Genocide occurred in Rwanda during a period of 100 days in 1994, and the world did not take notice. An estimated 1 million members of the Tutsi tribe were massacred by members of the Hutu tribe in a tragic case of ethnic rivalry and hatred. The movie *Hotel Rwanda* focuses not on the massacre, but tells the story of a hotel manager (Don Cheadle) who saved the lives of 1,200 people during the genocide. The manager, Paul, is a Hutu married to a Tutsi, bringing the tension to the personal level.

Rwanda was earlier ruled by Belgium, and during that period, Tutsis ruled and the Hutus were oppressed and many were killed. The Hutus are now in control, and the genocide consisted of armed troops prowling for and slaughtering Tutsis. The movie shows how the United Nations and the international community ignored the pending massacre and failed to intervene while it was occurring. A colonel (Nick Nolte), representing the United Nations as a peacekeeper, is portrayed in the film reporting the situation to his superiors and being ignored. Paul, the hotel manager, also informs his corporate headquarters of what is going on, but his hotel location is not a priority for them. These two men then act on their own to save as many lives as possible.

Rather than a film about wholesale killing, it is a film about how two people respond to tragedy when no one else does. It shows how they used finesse and guile to take on genocide and managed to save many lives in the process, even though the situation was an impossible one. Like other films before it that depict actual situations of gross injustice, such as *Midnight Express* (1978) and *In the Name of the Father* (1993), *Hotel Rwanda* raises important questions about human strength and weakness in the face of persecution.

QUESTIONS

1. What is the moral duty of someone aware of a possible genocide occurring in another country?
2. Are there circumstances under which it is not morally permissible to take action in such a situation?

Discussion Question

What does Kant see lacking in the Golden Rule?

Critical Thinking Exercises

All ethical decisions affect others (by definition). Given what you know about virtue ethics and Kantian ethics, evaluate the moral permissibility of the conduct in question in each scenario.

Important note on method: *Critical thinking requires the ability to evaluate viewpoints, facts, and behaviors objectively to assess information or methods of argumentation to establish the true worth or merit of an act or course of conduct. Please evaluate these scenarios, first analyzing pros and cons of alternate views,* before *you come to a conclusion. Do* not *draw a conclusion first, and then try to find facts to support it—this frequently leads to narrow (and incorrect) thinking.*

To properly evaluate the moral permissibility of a course of action using critical thinking skills

1. *Begin with an open mind (no preconceptions!),*
2. *Isolate and evaluate the relevant facts on both sides,*
3. *Identify the precise moral question to be answered, and*
4. *Apply ethical principles to the moral question based on an objective evaluation of the facts, only then drawing a conclusion.*

3.1 Lying to the Sick and Dying

A 46-year-old man comes to a clinic for a routine physical checkup as required by his insurance policy. He is diagnosed with a form of cancer that will likely result in death within 6 months. There is no known cure. Chemotherapy might extend his life a few extra months, but it will have side effects the physician does not believe are warranted in this case. The physician also believes that such therapy should be reserved for patients with a chance for recovery or remission. The patient has no symptoms, appears healthy, and plans to take a short vacation in a week.[12]

- Should the physician tell the patient what he has learned, or should he conceal it?
- If he tells the patient, should he tell him about the chemotherapy and why he opposes it in this case?
- If he tells the patient, should he wait until after the vacation?
- Should the physician encourage every last effort to postpone death?

  (*Hint*: If a scenario appears complicated, remember to follow these steps: (1) List the relevant facts [separating the irrelevant details from the central issues]. (2) Identify the precise moral question to be answered. (3) List and

think about the moral principles that might be used to support the positions that could be taken. (4) Make and explain your decision [i.e., your morally permissible course of conduct]. (5) Justify your conclusions using positive reasons and ethical principles in support of your decision, anticipating and addressing contrary views.)

3.2 Lies of Public Officials

The mayor of a large city is running for reelection. He has read a report recommending that he remove rent controls from city apartments after his reelection. He intends to do so but believes he will lose the election if his intention is known. When he is asked at a news conference 2 days before the election about the existence of such a report, he denies knowledge of it and reaffirms his strong support of rent control. In the mayor's view, his reelection is very much in the public interest, and the lie concerns questions that he believes the voters are unable to evaluate properly, especially with such short notice.

Is the mayor's lying morally permissible? (Answer this question given the five-part method in Exercise 3.1.)

3.3 Is a Good Deed Required?

Five-year-old Alexis Papa went shopping with her mother at a local supermarket in Richmond, Virginia. As Alexis hopped out of her family's minivan in the parking lot, she noticed a small zippered bag labeled "First Market Bank" lying on the ground. Inside the bag were two thick wads of cash.

Alexis said, "Who does this belong to? We have to give it back!" She and her mother walked into the First Market Bank, which was located inside the supermarket. A bank employee found a deposit slip and located the business customer who had dropped the bag of cash in the parking lot.[13] The business customer said, "A lot of people would have just kept it. They wouldn't have had the integrity to turn it in."

- Was Alexis morally required to turn in the cash she found?
- As it turned out, the bag contained only $150 in $1 bills. How does this amount affect the moral obligation on Alexis in this case?
- What is the moral obligation of the business customer to provide a reward to Alexis for returning the bag of cash?

3.4 Raising Awareness, Committing Crimes

In Kissimmee, Florida, outside Orlando, the police department has tried to improve citizen alertness and reporting crimes. They dressed officers as burglars and tried to create obvious burglaries to see if citizens would call the police under a program called "If you SEE something . . . SAY something."

They have entered houses through the side window and tried to forcibly open car doors in a Walmart parking lot. In the burglary incident, a neighbor called the police when he saw the burglar/officer moving electronic equipment from the house to an SUV in the driveway, but no one called police about forcibly entering a car, even after it was attempted several times. The officer was instructed to run for safety if an uncontrolled situation erupted or a citizen overreacted.[14]

- Evaluate the moral permissibility of the actions of the police in this effort to raise citizen awareness.
- Do you believe there are other ways to accomplish this goal that pose fewer risks?

3.5 Faith, Medicine, and Mandatory Cancer Treatment

The case of a missing Minnesota mother and her cancer-stricken son has rekindled the debate over parents who reject conventional medical treatments for their sick children because of religious beliefs. Authorities searched for Colleen Hauser and her 13-year-old son, Daniel, who has Hodgkin's lymphoma. The family refuses chemotherapy for Daniel, and the two disappeared, after a doctor's appointment and court-ordered X-ray revealed his cancer had grown. Mother and son did not show up for a court hearing.

"We've got to find this child, so we can get him into medical treatment," said James Olson, Brown County attorney. Brown County district judge John Rodenberg ruled the mother in contempt of court and issued a warrant for her arrest. He ordered that Daniel be turned over to Brown County Family Services and gave the agency the authority to consent to "appropriate and necessary" treatment. Authorities say a search has turned to Southern California, where mother and child were seen recently. Authorities said they believed the two were headed to Mexico.

The Hausers are Catholic, but also believe in the natural healing philosophy of the Nemenhah Band, a Missouri-based religious group that believes in methods advocated by some American Indians. Colleen Hauser testified in court that she believed chemotherapy is a form of poison and that she had been trying to "starve" Daniel's cancer with supplements, an organic and sugar-free diet and high-alkaline water. Hauser's cancer, according to medical experts, has a 90 percent cure rate if treated with chemo and radiation, but is almost invariably fatal if untreated.

In a separate case in Wisconsin, Leilani Neumann, 41, stood trial Wednesday, accused in the death of her 11-year-old daughter last year. The woman is charged with second-degree homicide in the death of Madeline Neumann, who died last year, as a result of untreated diabetes. (The girl's father is also scheduled for trial.) The Neumanns said they believed prayer would save Leilani.

A nonprofit group called *Children's Healthcare Is a Legal Duty* is tracking five criminal cases in the United States involving children denied health care because of religious beliefs. There are also cases in Oregon, Tennessee, and Pennsylvania. Since 1983, the group, which says it works to stop abusive religious and cultural practices, has tracked sixty-six cases. "It's a small number of children compared to the total problem of child abuse and neglect in this country, but they still deserve the right to live," said Rita Swan, the group's president. Swan, a former Christian Scientist, lost her son to meningitis in 1977 after forgoing medical care in favor of prayer. She left the church after her son's death and became an activist on the issue.

Most states have legal exemptions that provide some protection to parents who withhold medical care on religious grounds, Swan said. Those laws often discourage prosecutors from filing charges, she said. "They are hard to prosecute, too, for other reasons," she said. "These are grief-stricken parents, and they can be sympathetic defendants. They love their child, and they were doing what they thought was in their child's best interest."[15]

- Evaluate the moral permissibility of (1) the parents' decision to deny the recommended cancer treatment to their son and (2) the state's decision to force the parents to have the treatment administered against the parents' wishes.

Key Concepts

Deontological ethics *26*
Duties and inclinations *26*
Categorical imperative *26*

Hypothetical imperatives *27*
Practical imperative *27*

Kingdom of ends *28*
Justification for lying *29*

Notes

1. Immanuel Kant, *Grounding for the Metaphysics of Morals* (1785) (Indianapolis: Hackett Publishing, 1993).
2. Kant, *Grounding for the Metaphysics of Morals,* pp. 6, 24.
3. Kant, *Grounding for the Metaphysics of Morals,* p. 20.
4. Matthew 19:17; Mark 10:18; Luke 18:19.
5. Kant, *Grounding for the Metaphysics of Morals,* p. 27.
6. Wayne Dosick, "Love Your Neighbor," in M. Josephson and W. Hanson, Eds., *The Power of Character* (San Francisco: Jossey-Bass, 1998), p. 289.
7. Kant, *Grounding for the Metaphysics of Morals,* p. 37.
8. *LaChance v. Erickson*, 118 S.Ct. 753 (1998).
9. Edward Schumacher-Matos, "Fake-Brands Story Needed More Discretion," *Miami Herald,* (February 3, 2008); see also Rushworth M. Kidder, "Go Forth and . . . Shoplift?" www.globalethics.org/newline (accessed January 4, 2010).
10. Kant, *Grounding for the Metaphysics of Morals,* pp. 65–67.
11. Vincent Barry, *The Dog Ate My Homework: Personal Responsibility—How We Avoid It and What to Do about It* (New York: Andrews McMeel, 1998), p. 45.12; Sissela Bok, *Lying: Moral Choice in Public and Private Life* (New York: Vintage Books, 1999).
13. Rhea R. Borja, "Girl, Mother Do $150 Good Deed," *Richmond Times-Dispatch* (August 31, 2000), p. 3.
14. Elaine Aradillas, "Don't Shoot!: I'm Just a Cop Breaking into Your Home," *The Orlando Sentinel* (May 19, 2007).
15. Ben Jones and Emily Bazar, "Faith, Medicine at Odds in Chemo Refusal," *USA Today* (May 21, 2009).

CHAPTER 4

Utilitarianism
Measuring Consequences

Learning Objectives:

- To understand the nature of teleological ethics and its differences from deontological ethics.

- To recognize the centrality of the principle of utility in the ethics of John Stuart Mill.

- To develop an appreciation of why utilitarianism is sometimes called consequentialism.

- To increase the ability to distinguish objective ways to assess the total happiness produced by an action.

- To appreciate criticisms of utilitarianism as a way to judge ethical action.

Labor to keep alive in your breast that little celestial fire called conscience.

—George Washington (1732–1799)

The police in Nashville, Tennessee, paid $120,000 over a 3-year period to informants and prostitutes in an effort to impact the illicit sex trade. The police department paid informants "to touch and be touched" to gather evidence of prostitution. A police captain defended the practice by asking the question, "What is the greater good?" He continued, "It may be distasteful to some people, but it's better that we have those places shut down."[1] And, in fact, the city had closed more than thirty-five sex-related businesses, such as massage parlors and escort services. The money paid to informants came from seizures made in other prostitution and gambling cases. It was admitted, however, that a certain amount of sexual touching was usually necessary to show that the money being offered was clearly for the purpose of a sexual act.

Critics of these tactics included the county district attorney, who believed, "It is a little contradictory in letting the informant engage in the very act you're trying to stamp out." A city attorney acknowledged that as little contact as possible between informants and prostitutes is desirable, but "I'm reluctant to second-guess what the police have done so far because it's been so successful."[2]

Are such police tactics ethical? Without knowing it, the persons involved in this controversy were using the 200-year-old ethical concept of utility to determine the appropriateness of a police strategy. An understanding of this ethical theory helps resolve the dilemma posed by the police methods being used.

JOHN STUART MILL

John Stuart Mill (1806–1873) was born 2 years after Emmanuel Kant died. He developed the third of the three most influential ethical theories in history. Whereas Aristotle focused on virtue, and Kant on duty, Mill focused on utility. His approach is **teleological** because it decides ethical questions based on the good that results from an action. The morality of an act is determined, therefore, by the consequences it brings, compared with other alternative actions. In this view, ethical decisions result in the most good or happiness, whereas unethical decisions do not.

According to the central principle of **utility**, actions are right in proportion, as they tend to promote happiness, and wrong, as they tend to produce the reverse of happiness (pain). That is to say, goodness is determined by the consequences of an action.[3] It is the consequences of an action that determine its morality, making utility a teleological approach to ethics. The notion of utility, sometimes called **consequentialism**, was originated by Jeremy Bentham (1748–1832) and can also be found in the writings of Cesare Beccaria (1738–1794).[4] This ethical theory is based on the notion of hedonism, according to which all people are motivated by the pursuit of pleasure and avoidance of pain. Mill's exposition for determining the greatest happiness principle was a refinement of Bentham's ideas, which equated the morality of an act with the amount of happiness it produces.

Mill's notion of utilitarianism emphasized that "pleasure, and freedom from pain, are the only things desirable as ends."[5] Mill defines pleasure as happiness and the absence of pain. Pain is the absence of pleasure. He responds to the criticism that utilitarianism encourages people to act as hedonists by saying, "The accusation supposes human beings to be capable of no pleasures except those of which swine are capable." In other words, "Human beings have faculties more elevated than the animal appetites."[6] Mill recognizes that not all pleasures are equal and that clearly some are more valuable and desirable than others. Of course, those whose capacity for enjoyment is low have the greatest chance of being satisfied, but "it is better to be human being dissatisfied than a pig satisfied," or stated another way, "better to be Socrates dissatisfied than a fool satisfied."[7] Mill recognizes that some pursue sensual self-indulgence that is bad for their health, even though they are aware that health is the greater good.

PAIN, PLEASURE, AND HAPPINESS

An important question in Mill's ethical perspective is that if pain and pleasure are used to assess the happiness that conduct will bring, how does one determine which is the greatest pleasure or pain? Mill believes that general consensus of those with experience is the best indicator. The experience of those (all or most) who give a decided preference determines hierarchy of pleasures. This consensus of experienced people is to be used to determine which pleasures will truly bring happiness. It also is not important to distinguish personal happiness from social happiness according to utilitarianism. The *total* amount of happiness is how pleasure is to be judged.

There are those who believe that happiness in life is unattainable, but Mill finds this assertion "is at least an exaggeration." Clearly, a "continuity of highly pleasurable excitement... is impossible," but happiness is a widely shared experience by many people.[8] This experience is not often rapture, but many and various pleasures are experienced during life with fewer pains. Therefore, Mill believes happiness is attainable in the form of experiencing pleasure (versus pain).

Mill's utilitarian approach sees current affairs standing in the way of greater happiness. Writing nearly 150 years ago, he sounds like a commentator today: "The present wretched education, and wretched social arrangements, are the only real hindrance to [happiness] being attainable by almost all."[9] Mill believes there are two causes to an unsatisfactory life: selfishness and lack of mental cultivation. **Selfishness** is caring for nobody but oneself, which leads to unhappiness because it lacks both public and private affections that contribute greatly to happiness. A person with a **cultivated mind** is interested in everything, such as nature, art, poetry, history, and the future. Lack of mental cultivation leads to indifference to all these things and ultimately to unhappiness according to Mill. Selfishness and an uncultivated mind, therefore, are primary factors that hinder the achievement of happiness.

MOTIVATION VERSUS CONSEQUENCES

Utilitarianism does not view motivation as relevant in determining the morality of an action. For example, martyrdom is good only if it leads to greater happiness; it is not good in itself according to utilitarianism. This is because self-sacrifice through martyrdom is not an intrinsic good. "Self-sacrifice for the good of others is powerful, but the sacrifice, in itself, is not a good." Only the result is good, and Mill questions whether the sacrifice would be made "if the hero or martyr did not believe that it would earn for others immunity from similar sacrifices."[10] The motivation is not important in utilitarianism; it is the outcome that matters.

"Love your neighbor as yourself" is the Golden Rule, which Kant believed lacked moral content. Utilitarianism, however, requires a person to be a strictly impartial and disinterested spectator in assessing his or her own happiness versus that of others. Mill adds two conditions to the Golden Rule: (1) "The laws and social arrangements should place the happiness (the interest) of every individual...in harmony with the interest of the whole (as nearly as possible)" and (2) education and opinion should use their power over human character to establish in "every individual an indissoluble association between his own happiness and the good of the whole."[11] Therefore, Mill focuses on reconciling the happiness of the many with the happiness of the individual. The more a person sees his or her own happiness in ways that also enhance the happiness of others, the more likely it is that the greatest total happiness will be achieved.

Mill distinguishes utility from Kant's ethical perspective when he says, "ninety-nine hundredths of all our actions are done from other motives (other than duty), and rightly so done." He goes on to say, "the motive has nothing to do with the morality of the action."[12] Therefore,

ETHICS CHECKUP
Martha Stewart an Example?

Homemaking entrepreneur Martha Stewart was convicted for lying to investigators about a stock trade. She was sentenced to a short prison term. According to the U.S. attorney in Manhattan, the case will "send an important message that we will not, and frankly, cannot tolerate dishonesty and corruption."[13] Similar statements were made by other prosecutors of high-profile, white-collar, fraud-related charges in recent years against such companies as Enron, Worldcom, and Adelphia Communications.

What ethical perspective is assumed by the prosecutor? Are there alternative ethical arguments to support such perspectives?

motives are unimportant to utilitarianism, whereas they are central to formalism. For example, a person who saves someone from drowning is morally right under utilitarianism, regardless of whether his or her motivation is duty or a hoped-for reward.

Mill also addresses Aristotle's issue of good acts that might be committed by a bad person. Mill agrees that an action isn't bad because it is done by a bad person and that a proper action does not necessarily indicate a virtuous character. He also concurs with Aristotle in what determines a virtuous person: "I grant that . . . in the long run the best proof of a good character is good actions."[14]

CRITICISMS OF UTILITARIANISM

Utilitarianism has been criticized for not being practical or timely in weighing the consequences of one's actions prior to engaging in the conduct. Mill replies that if we wish to guide our conduct by Christianity, for example, there is no time to read through the Old and New Testaments before taking any action. Therefore, "the course of experience" helps guide actions in assessing probable outcomes.[15] There does not need to be a complex or prolonged weighing of likely consequences as a person gains experience with such decisions; there simply needs to be reflection based on past experience and the experience of others.

Utilitarianism has also been criticized because it is believed that people will weigh the consequences of their actions in a self-serving way, always ending up doing things in their own self-interest. Mill agrees that the intellect and virtue of individuals vary and that difficult decisions are unavoidable. "There exists no moral system under which there do not arise unequivocal cases of conflicting obligation. These are the real difficulties, the knotty points both in the theory of ethics, and in the conscientious guidance of personal conduct."[16] Nevertheless, it is possible to weigh alternative consequences objectively, and this is the only way to ensure ethical conduct.

Sometimes utilitarianism has been summarized in a shorthanded way, declaring that the **end justifies the means**, suggesting that as long as the outcome results in happiness, it is acceptable to use any means to obtain it. This is not necessarily true under the principle of utility because the end would have to result in greater total happiness to justify the use of means that might cause pain. This reasoning again draws a clear distinction from virtue ethics, which would not accept this rule because a morally good end cannot be served by means that are not themselves morally good. Aristotle would say that "the ends justify the means" is a maxim of expediency, not of virtue. If immoral means are used, the ends achieved are also morally impermissible.[17]

Ethical conduct is enforced according to utilitarianism by individual hope of favor (reward or pleasure) or fear of displeasure (penalty or pain) from others, or from God. Ultimately, a "society between equals can only exist on the understanding that the interests of all are to be regarded equally. . . . In this way people grow up unable to conceive as possible to them a state of total disregard of other people's interests."[18] For utilitarianism to work properly, therefore, individuals making decisions must weigh the consequences toward themselves and toward others equally and impartially.

SUMMARIZING ETHICAL THEORIES

Ending with the scenario that opened this chapter, utilitarianism provides one approach to assessing the ethics of police paying informants to solicit prostitutes, so they may be arrested. The good that results, of course, is the closing down of sex establishments and the incapacitation (at least temporarily) of prostitutes and purveyors in jail. If publicized, this police practice may also have a deterrent effect on future "johns" who might be tempted to solicit prostitutes. However, does this police strategy result in informants (who are often criminals) targeting other criminals (the prostitutes) with little impact on the general population? Will this police practice erode respect for police among citizens because they find it objectionable? Is the impact of this practice weak and only temporary (based on the minor sentences given to prostitutes and their customers)? Utility requires an objective weighing of these potential positive and negative impacts to determine the morality of the practice, whereas virtue ethics and formalism focus more closely on the practice itself, regardless of its outcome.

Table 4.1 provides a summary of the three major ethical theories. It can be seen that there are differences in the goals of ethical behavior, the means of becoming ethical, and how ethical conduct is to be judged based on virtue ethics, formalism, and utilitarianism.

TABLE 4.1 Summarizing Three Ethical Theories

	Virtue Ethics	Formalism	Utilitarianism
Goals of ethical behavior	The life that is most desirable, achieved by pursuing real goods through virtuous action, results in ethical happiness.	Do moral duty.	Seek the greatest total happiness.
Means of becoming ethical	Follow the moral virtues: "By doing just acts . . . the just man is produced."	Categorical imperative is the supreme principle of morality.	Maximize pleasure while minimizing pain.
Judging ethical conduct	Good conduct cannot be prescribed. Individual acts can be misleading unless they come from "a firm and unchangeable character." Virtue is a mean that aims at the intermediate and avoids excess and defect.	Assess actions according to categorical and practical imperatives; consequences of acts do not bear on moral worthiness because other causes can result in the outcome, and personal inclinations have no moral value.	Make individual decisions by weighing the consequences toward yourself and toward others equally and impartially. Individual motivation is not relevant; only the outcome matters.

All the ethical theories are internally consistent in the way they determine the goals, means, and criteria for judging conduct (the "what"), but there are large differences in the purpose or goal of ethical conduct (the "why"). These distinctions sometimes make the evaluation of ethical conduct difficult—but not impossible. When conduct is evaluated based on these three theories, applying one perspective at a time, it becomes easy to see the ethical path clearly by making visible the logical connections among means, goals, and the ways that ethical conduct is judged.

ETHICS IN BOOKS

Ethics is everywhere, even in the books we read, which sometimes are written without ethics specifically in mind. Here is a summary of a book that looks at actions that affect others, followed by questions that ask you to reflect on the ethical connections.

THE GOOD, THE BAD & THE DIFFERENCE: HOW TO TELL RIGHT FROM WRONG IN EVERYDAY SITUATIONS

Randy Cohen
(Broadway Books, 2003)

Randy Cohen writes a column for the *New York Times Magazine,* which is syndicated in many newspapers as "Everyday Ethics." It is a column where readers send in troubling questions and request an "ethical" response. Interestingly, Cohen is a professional writer; he is not an ethicist, has no training in the area, and discloses this in his book. The editors who hired him believed that ethics should not be a specialized field but "should comprise a set of questions every ordinary citizen can—must—address."

The book is a compilation of columns the author has written. Cohen defends his lack of knowledge of ethics saying, "Any discussion of ethics will come down to the values of the writer and how clearly and persuasively he can articulate those values and apply them to the particular scenario under discussion." Ethicists would disagree with this claim, and the ethical perspectives offered in this book, *Professional Ethics in Criminal Justice,* attest that there are objective standards developed over centuries of careful thought on which to evaluate actions for their moral permissibility.

The most interesting part of *The Good, The Bad & The Difference* is at the end where the author lists the ten most difficult questions he has been sent by readers.

They are summarized here:

1. Should you tell a good friend's wife about her husband's infidelity?
2. Should you continue to buy cigarettes for a 79-year-old friend dying of lung disease?
3. Should you accept a charitable donation from a businessman with ties to organized crime?
4. Should you leave the same amount of money in your will to your children, when one is very rich and the other is impoverished?
5. Should you lie and tell the judge you are opposed to capital punishment during jury selection at a murder trial (to possibly save the defendant's life)?
6. Should you say something to a mother who slaps her child for crying?
7. Should a physician maintain the confidentiality of a patient with a sexually transmitted disease, who asks that his wife be tested but not told of his extramarital affair?
8. Should an instructor who mistakenly gives credit for a wrong test answer deduct that credit when the student informs him of the error?

9. Should a wealthy person commission an artist to paint a reproduction of a more famous artist?
10. Should a person wear a motorcycle helmet as required by law, when he is only putting himself at risk?

These questions are all interesting: Some do not involve ethics, and a few others are not difficult in ethical terms, once you identify the precise issues of moral permissibility and obtain an understanding of the elements of ethical thought. This book, *Professional Ethics in Criminal Justice,* will help you understand and apply these ethical principles to a wide range of difficult decisions.

QUESTIONS

1. Choose any one of the ten questions listed in this box. What do you see as the most important consideration in answering the question?
2. Ethics is indeed for everybody, so what do you see as the primary purpose of teaching ethics at colleges and universities?

ETHICS IN THE MOVIES

Movies seek to entertain and inform the audience about a story, incident, or person. Many good movies also hit upon important ethical themes in making significant decisions that affect the lives of others. Read the movie summary here (and watch the movie if you haven't already), and answer the questions to make the ethical connections.

QUIZ SHOW

Robert Redford, Director
(1994)

Quiz Show recounts the true story of Charles Van Doren (Ralph Fiennes), the son of a famous academic and scholar, Mark Van Doren (Paul Scofield). It tells the story of a huge game show–fixing scandal that landed in the U.S. Congress.

Charles was a bright, handsome, and well-educated young man who had trouble earning the respect of his famous father. He was from a wealthy, well-connected family, and although he had a great deal of talent (he was a college professor), it was difficult for him to distinguish himself in his very accomplished family. Charles decided to try out for a television quiz show that, like *Jeopardy,* asked many difficult questions and required knowledge on a number of topics. Charles did well on the show and the ratings were very high, given his name, good looks, and success on the program.

The reigning champion of the show was Herb Stempel (John Turturro), who was not seen by the show's producers (and sponsors and the network) as handsome or as appealing as Charles, even though Herb was quite a good player. The show's producers wanted to keep Charles playing and have Herb lose, so they separately made offers to Charles to give him the questions in advance, and for Herb to "take a dive" by knowingly giving a wrong answer in the head-to-head match with Charles. Both Charles and Herb agreed to do so, despite misgivings.

Pressure was subsequently put on Charles from a congressional investigator looking into "fixed" game shows, but Charles eventually comes forward on his own and testifies before an investigating committee of Congress that he knew the answers to the questions in advance on the quiz show. In the end, he was humiliated, especially given the prominence of his family, and he was also fired from his job as professor. *Quiz Show* was nominated for the Academy Award for Best Picture in 1994.

QUESTIONS

1. If you were on a game show, and were offered the answers in advance, is it morally permissible to take them, knowing "it's only a game show"?
2. What is the moral permissibility of the show's producers, sponsors, and the network in trying to get the most appealing person to win (even if that person might not be the most talented)? Do you see any parallels to the television show *American Idol?*

Discussion Question

What is the purpose of ethical conduct, and on what criteria would you evaluate your conduct?

Critical Thinking Exercises

All ethical decisions affect others (by definition) and, as Aristotle points out, ethical decision making is achieved consistently only through practice. Given the outline of virtue ethics provided by Aristotle (i.e., seeking the real goods via the moral virtues), evaluate the moral permissibility of the conduct in question in each scenario.

Important note on method: *Critical thinking requires the ability to evaluate viewpoints, facts, and behaviors objectively to assess information or methods of argumentation to establish the true worth or merit of an act or course of conduct. Please evaluate these scenarios, first analyzing pros and cons of alternate views,* before *you come to a conclusion. Do* not *draw a conclusion first, and then try to find facts to support it—this frequently leads to narrow (and incorrect) thinking.*

To properly evaluate the moral permissibility of a course of action using critical thinking skills

1. *Begin with an open mind (no preconceptions!),*
2. *Isolate and evaluate the relevant facts on both sides,*
3. *Identify the precise moral question to be answered, and*
4. *Apply ethical principles to the moral question based on an objective evaluation of the facts, only then drawing a conclusion.*

4.1 A Flexible Expense Account

Clyde, a businessperson, catches a plane to Seattle to meet an important client. When he arrives in Seattle, it is pouring rain. He doesn't have his raincoat with him, and he can't go to the meeting soaking wet, so he buys a raincoat in the hotel men's shop and puts it on his expense account ($300).

A few weeks later, the company's accounting office calls him and says "You can't put a $300 raincoat on your expense account. We're returning your paperwork."

When he gets the form back from the accounting department, he crosses out "raincoat," writes in "dinner with client," and resubmits the form.

Clyde defended the change saying, "An expense account is a convenience for the company where I advance the company money to perform my job. I spend it, and they pay me back...slowly. Many times, I am charged a month's interest on the credit card before I get reimbursed. I bought the raincoat in order to represent the company effectively. I didn't do it just for the hell of it! Also, there are minor expenses I never bother to claim. So I figure the company comes out ahead anyway. Everybody in the company does it this way, and our competitors are known for padding their expense accounts in order to gain an unfair advantage in attracting clients!"[19]

- Evaluate the moral permissibility of Clyde's conduct.
- Later, Clyde's expense account submission is noticed by the company comptroller who attempts to have Clyde fired for submitting a false expense account record. Clyde argues the same points noted previously, but he adds that because he never received the

reimbursement for the raincoat expense submission, he should not be punished. What do you think?

4.2 The Bad Samaritan

David Cash and Jeremy Strohmeyer were friends and 18 years old. They were hanging out at a casino on the California–Nevada border at 3:00 a.m. At one point, Jeremy entered a women's restroom at the casino. He entered a stall and struggled with a 7-year-old girl. Jeremy was nearly 6 feet tall, and the girl weighed 50 pounds. David entered behind him and tapped Jeremy on the head, knocking his hat off in an effort to get him to stop. He could not get Jeremy to stop, so he left the restroom.

About 30 minutes later, Jeremy reappeared and told David he molested and killed the girl. The victim was found stuffed into the toilet bowl about 5:00 a.m. By this time, the two boys had already left the scene.

Jeremy was ultimately caught and charged with murder, and David is now a sophomore at the University of California at Berkeley. David was not charged with a crime because he simply failed to come to the aid of the victim. He said, "I have done nothing wrong." Most states do not require a witness to a crime to report it or offer aid.

A protest at Berkeley was organized in the hope of getting David expelled from the university, but the chancellor said there would be no expulsion because, although outrageous, his conduct violated no law.[20] Many students ostracized David and would not talk to him, angered by his being in the position to save a life yet choosing not to.

- Evaluate the moral permissibility of David's conduct.
- Is the decision of the university chancellor morally permissible?

4.3 The Ring of Gyges

Following is the story of the Ring of Gyges, which, when turned on your finger, makes you invisible. Glaucon makes an argument to Socrates about what would happen if someone had such a ring.[21]

Gyges was a shepherd in the service of the king of Lydia; there was a great storm, and an earthquake made an opening in the earth at the place where Gyges was feeding his flock. Amazed at the sight, Gyges descended into the opening, where, among other marvels, he beheld a hollow brazen horse, having doors, at which he, stooping and looking in, saw a dead body of stature, as appeared to him, more than human, and having nothing on but a gold ring. This he took from the finger of the dead and reascended. Now the

shepherds met together, according to custom, that they might send their monthly report about the flocks to the king. Into their assembly Gyges came with the ring on his finger. As he was sitting among them, Gyges chanced to turn the collet of the ring inside his hand, whereupon instantly he became invisible to the rest of the company and they began to speak of him as if he were no longer present. He was astonished at this, and again touching the ring he turned the collet outward and reappeared; he made several trials of the ring, and always with the same result—when he turned the collet inward, he became invisible; when outward, he reappeared. Whereupon he contrived to be chosen as one of the messengers to be sent to the court. As soon as he arrived, he seduced the queen, and, with her help, conspired against the king, slew him, and took the kingdom. Suppose now that there were two such magic rings, and the just put on one of them and the unjust the other; no man can be imagined to be of such an iron nature that he would stand fast in justice. No man would keep his hands off what was not his own when he could safely take what he liked out of the market, or go into houses and lie with anyone at his pleasure, or kill or release from prison whom he would, and in all respects be like a God among men. Then the actions of the just would be as the actions of the unjust; they would both come at last to the same point. And this we may truly affirm to be a great proof that a man is just, not willingly or because he thinks that justice is any good to him individually, but of necessity, for wherever anyone thinks that he can safely be unjust, there he is unjust. For all men believe in their hearts that injustice is far more profitable to the individual than justice, and those who argue as I have been supposing will say that they are right. If you could imagine anyone obtaining this power of becoming invisible, and never doing any wrong or touching what was another's, he would be thought by the lookers-on to be a most wretched idiot, although they would praise him to one another's faces and keep up appearances with one another from a fear that they too might suffer injustice.

- What would Aristotle, Kant, and Mill each do if they had such a ring?
- What would *you* do with such a ring?

4.4 *CSI:* Effect on Offenders?

The proportion of rape cases that go unsolved is increasing, and some believe it is the result of television portrayals. Although the rate of cases solved by arrest rate for violent crimes overall has remained about the same (45 percent), the rate of rapes solved by police has dropped by about 10 percent in the last decade (from 51 to 41 percent).

Some observers have speculated that this drop in the clearance rate might be due to more sophisticated offenders who are leaving less evidence at the scene. They argue that television shows like *CSI:* are informing offenders about the power of DNA evidence and that offenders are making victims shower or bathe and taking other measures to reduce evidence left at the scene. Other observers are not convinced that this change in the behavior of offenders is actually taking place, and note the general decline in the total number of rapes over the last decade, even though unsolved cases are growing.[22]

- If it were to be proven that television shows like *CSI:* help criminals avoid apprehension, is it morally permissible to prohibit them?
- Do you have alternative suggestions for addressing the possibility raised in this scenario?

4.5 Ethics and Pirates

The battle with pirates off the coast of Somalia came to a head with reports of two rescue efforts. One was a complete success. In the other, a hostage died. Were both—or either—ethically correct? The success came when a team of U.S. Navy Seals rescued Richard Phillips, the captain of a U.S.-flagged ship, from a lifeboat where he was being held by three Somali pirates. Navy sharpshooters killed his captors, after U.S. negotiators had refused the pirates' offer to free Capt. Phillips in return for their own freedom.

The less successful venture came when French soldiers stormed a 41-foot yacht seized by pirates 5 days earlier. The soldiers freed four French hostages and killed or captured the five pirates on board, but the yacht's owner was killed during the attack. French government officials repeatedly had warned the two families aboard the yacht, which was headed for Zanzibar, not to sail through the Gulf of Aden, where the attack took place.

Behind these events lie several premises on which we probably can all agree:

- Premise: Piracy is criminal, with no moral justification.
- Premise: Maintaining sea-lanes free from piracy is essential to international trade.
- Conclusion: Nations should take vigorous steps to eliminate piracy, by force if necessary—but under what circumstances?

Should nations put the needs of the whole community above the safety of their own citizens? Or should they refuse to put at risk the lives of noncombatants, that is, innocent people who have not signed up for military service? Should hostages be sacrificed in order to convince criminals that no effort will be spared to eradicate piracy? Or should the life of each citizen be more valued than preserving international trade?[23]

- Evaluate the moral permissibility of the two incidents: of the French soldiers to attack, even though it resulted in a death, and for the Navy Seals to attack despite the fact that it turned out well (i.e., if Capt. Phillips had died, would the attack have been morally wrong?)

Key Concepts

Teleological *37*
Utility *37*
Consequentialism *37*

Selfishness *38*
Cultivated mind *38*
End justifies the means *39*

Enforce ethical conduct *39*

Notes

1. Ian Demsky, "Police Defend Prostitution Tactic," *The Tennessean* (February 2, 2005), p. 1.
2. Demsky, *The Tennessean*, p. 1.
3. John Stuart Mill, *Utilitarianism* (1863) (Amherst, NY: Prometheus Books, 1993), p. 16.
4. Jeremy Bentham, *The Principles of Morals and Legislation* (1822) (Buffalo, NY: Prometheus Books, 1988); Cesare Beccaria, *An Essay on Crimes and Punishments* (1764) (Indianapolis, IN: Branden Publishing, 1992).
5. Mill, *Utilitarianism,* p. 17.
6. Mill, *Utilitarianism,* p. 18.
7. Mill, *Utilitarianism,* p. 20.
8. Mill, *Utilitarianism,* p. 23.
9. Mill, *Utilitarianism,* p. 24.
10. Mill, *Utilitarianism,* p. 27.

11. Mill, *Utilitarianism,* p. 28.

12. Mill, *Utilitarianism,* p. 29.

13. Jonathan D. Glater, "Prosecutors Send a Message: Are Executives Listening?" *New York Times* (March 14, 2004), p. A11.

14. Mill, *Utilitarianism,* p. 31.

15. Mill, *Utilitarianism,* p. 35.

16. Mill, *Utilitarianism,* p. 37.

17. Mortimer Adler, *Desires Right and Wrong: The Ethics of Enough* (New York, NY: Macmillan, 1991), p. 127.

18. Mill, *Utilitarianism,* p. 45.

19. Sam Grace, "The Theory and Practice of Expense Accounting," *Esquire* (August 1997), p. 109; Anne B. Fisher, "Expenses: Fiction, Maybe, but a Crime?" *Fortune* (October 16, 1995), p. 42; T.F. Gautschi, "Survey Uncovers Possible Lack of Workplace Ethics," *Design News* (March 25, 1996), p. 170.

20. Cathy Booth, "The Bad Samaritan," *Time Magazine* (September 7, 1998); see also Alan Gomez, "Witness to an Assault: Must You Report It?" *USA Today* (October 29, 2009).

21. Plato, *The Republic* (ca. 370 B.C.) (New York, NY: Oxford University Press, 1994), Book II.

22. Audrey Dutton, "More Rape Cases Go Unsolved," *Newsday* (New York) (September 19, 2006).

23. Rushworth Kidder, "The Next Great Moral Test," *Ethics Newsline* (April 13, 2009).

CHAPTER 5

Crime and Law
Which Behaviors Ought to Be Crimes?

Learning Objectives:
- To understand the differences between the consensus view and conflict view of criminal law.
- To appreciate the ethical issues posed by "quality of life" offenses.
- To distinguish the major perspectives on crime causation: classical, positivism, structural, and ethical.
- To develop an appreciation for the linkage between Kohlberg's theory of moral development and ethics.
- To increase understanding of Gilligan's ethics of caring.

The problem with the rat race is that even if you win, you're still a rat.

—Lily Tomlin (b. 1939)

In ethical terms, conforming to the law is not enough. People who act ethically do so because of principles that go beyond the law. Nevertheless, there exists a moral force behind the law that varies in strength depending on the conduct in question. For example, the laws against assaults (e.g., murder, rape, aggravated assault) merely reinforce a widely held belief that such conduct is unacceptable. If the laws against all forms of assault were abolished tomorrow, for instance, it is unlikely that assaults would skyrocket because of the independent moral force that exists even without such laws. So in the case of assaults and violence, the criminal law merely reinforces a strong, unwritten moral law.

However, theft is illegal in all of its forms (e.g., larceny, robbery, embezzlement, fraud), yet it is committed about ten times more often than are assaults. If the laws against theft were abolished tomorrow, it is unlikely that theft would become epidemic, but the incidence of theft would probably rise. This is because, although there is a moral force behind the laws against theft that recognizes its wrongfulness, it is not as strong as the moral force that keeps people from committing assaults.

Taking it one step further, it is illegal to park on many city streets during business hours. The existence of parking laws is made clear by street signs only 20 feet apart along the streets. There is no moral force behind parking laws (i.e., there is nothing inherently wrong—and no intrinsic harm—in illegal parking, for instance, unless one blocks a fire hydrant or building exit), so it is likely that people would park along every street in town if the police would only stop writing tickets. This difference in the declining moral force of the laws against crimes of violence, crimes of theft, and parking prohibitions shows how laws can only reinforce existing moral beliefs of citizens; laws do not develop independent moral forces on their own.

THE OUTER LIMITS OF MORALITY

Police in Russia's Belgorod region began an initiative in 2004 that imposed fines of up to $50 on those caught swearing in public. The money collected from the fines was used to support a campaign against foul language. The law, classifying use of foul language in public as a form of hooliganism, targeted young people. About $50,000 was collected in a matter of months from 2,500 violators. A police department official said, "We will continue the campaign for a long time . . . we want Russian [language] to remain as pure as the great classics." A young man told a Russian newspaper, "The cops have gone crazy."[1]

This is an interesting case where the boundaries of the criminal law were expanded to include foul language, something not normally against the law. Is this a good idea? It raises this question: "What is the outer limit of morality? Is it possible for a law to go beyond ethical boundaries?"

There are a number of historical examples of laws that exceeded ethical boundaries, which inevitably resulted in disaster. The Spanish Inquisition permitted by law the torture of citizens holding different religious views from the king; Nazi Germany permitted the enslavement and killing of Jews for no reason other than their religious beliefs; and during World War II, the United States forced Japanese Americans to give up their property and placed them in internment camps until the end of the war. In each instance, the law was based on religious, ethnic, or racial prejudice, and in each case, once the government was no longer able to enforce its unethical laws, the arbitrariness of the laws was publicly recognized, and the laws were overturned. It can be seen that there are limits on laws, and laws that exceed moral boundaries ultimately are unsuccessful, once the fear or paranoia subsides regarding the group or behavior being targeted.

In general terms, the criminal law can be said to arise as a result of consensus or conflict. The **consensus view** holds that the criminal law reflects society's consensus that a behavior is harmful enough to merit government prohibition. Émile Durkheim (1858–1917), a founder of sociology, stated in 1893 that an act is criminal "when it offends strong and defined states of the collective conscience."[2] Clearly, crimes of violence and theft possess a strong social consensus regarding their harmfulness. The **conflict view** holds that a behavior is criminalized only when it serves the interests of those in positions of power. According to this view, the law protects the property and personal interests of those running the government. Using these terms, it can be argued that the laws permitting the torture and internment during the Spanish Inquisition, Nazi Germany, and World War II had no consensus behind them and were only passed because they reflected the views of those in power who also had at their disposal the means to enforce these laws. When laws are routinely violated, or selectively enforced, it is useful to ask the question whether the laws have social consensus behind them regarding their harm to society or whether they exist to serve the interests of only a few.

CHOOSING WHAT TO CRIMINALIZE

The separation between what is immoral and what is illegal is blurred as legislatures pass broad laws encompassing more kinds of behaviors. For example, a number of states have passed laws that require motorcycle riders to wear helmets. However, some states do not require helmets. Is there an ethical position here, or does such an issue lack moral content?

On the one hand, it is important to protect motorcyclists from head injuries to the extent possible. Those injured would incur major medical bills and perhaps become permanently disabled, making it difficult for them to support their families, perhaps resulting in government support of them or their dependent family members. On the other hand, cannot adults decide for themselves whether they want to wear helmets? Do laws mandating helmets infringe on the rights of adults to make their own personal safety decisions? If you use ethical reasoning (i.e., virtue ethics, formalism, utilitarianism) to evaluate the helmet issue, it can be seen how there is moral content involved in the decision, which can be used to justify a mandatory helmet law.

The law should not be seen as the highest aspiration of morality but instead as its minimum requirement. When law is viewed as the highest aspiration of conduct, self-discipline and self-responsibility break down, and people show more concern for what is technically legal than with what is right, or, stated in another way, what they can get away with rather than what they ought to do. The more legalistically people frame their decisions, the narrower the established spectrum of self-responsibility is, which then becomes an excuse to act "in accord with the law" rather than according to what ethics demands.[3]

New York City experienced a remarkable drop in the crime rate that began during the late 1990s, a trend that later emerged in other major U.S. cities. The decline in crime was attributed in part to aggressive police tactics against minor offenses that affect the quality of life: drinking in public, playing loud music, urinating in public, jumping subway turnstiles, and loitering. It turned out that many of those arrested for these minor **quality of life offenses** were also wanted by police for more serious crimes. These aggressive police tactics involved stopping people on the street and requesting identification, conducting drug sweeps of entire neighborhoods, and frisking people. The tactics drew considerable criticism because they necessarily created at least temporary infringements of the privacy of many innocent persons. As one neighborhood organizer said, "In the beginning we all wanted the police to bomb the crack houses, but now it's backfiring at the cost of the community. I think the cops have been given free rein to intimidate people at large."[4] Police were alleged to be pulling people out of cars at gun point, roughing up those who didn't speak English, frisking citizens for no clear reason, conducting searches in an abusive manner, selectively harassing minorities, and using force without provocation.

Complaints against police grew considerably in New York, Pittsburgh, Charlotte, Washington, D.C., and other cities, alleging overly aggressive police tactics in the effort to reduce crime. These charges reflect a dilemma that lies at the heart of the U.S. criminal justice system: What is the best way to balance the rights of individuals to be left alone with the community's interest in apprehending criminals? And it begs the larger questions of what should be criminalized and how far should society go in making existing laws apply in practice.

This dilemma is most evident in the case of police because of their continual interaction with the public. But the balance between individual and community interests must also be struck in the decision to formally charge a person with a crime, the determination of guilt or innocence at trial, and in sentencing and parole release decisions. The entire criminal justice system is designed to provide a mechanism for achieving this balance in a just manner.

In the case of minor quality of life offenses, is there a moral boundary between what is criminalized (the offenses such as drinking in public, playing loud music, and loitering) and the rigor with which these laws should be enforced? The utilitarian position argues for balancing the consequences of aggressive enforcement of minor offenses in producing more total pain than pleasure. The pain consists of discriminatory law enforcement against certain kinds of individuals, fully enforcing laws against first-time offenders rather than giving them warnings, citizen complaints about aggressive enforcement, and loss of confidence in police decisions. Pleasure (happiness), however, is produced by reducing serious and minor crimes and by increasing public safety in general through full enforcement of minor offenses. The utilitarian position would determine the morality of the enforcement policy, therefore, by weighing the consequences that result.

Formalism would assess the morality of such enforcement in a completely different way. Because it is impossible to know what the consequences will be in advance, Kant believed that relying on consequences to make ethical decisions is not a valid or reliable way to make ethical decisions. Instead, formalism would determine the morality of such quality of life enforcement of minor crimes by the categorical imperative: Is such a policy of aggressive enforcement a good universal rule? Furthermore, such a policy must also not violate the practical imperative that individuals not be used as a means to some further end; people must believe that minor offenders deserve the police action against them, including any legal penalty, regardless of any larger social good that may result. Formalism would assess the ethics of such a policy by asking the question: "Do we want police to enforce quality of life offenses aggressively at all times?" If the answer is "yes," such a policy is morally permissible. In addition, formalism requires that the policy be ethical and serve the ends of justice on its face and not "use" individuals and arrests for some larger social purpose, such as general deterrence of future offenders (practical imperative).

Virtue ethics would examine aggressive enforcement of offenses in light of the motives and characteristics of each incident. Virtue ethics would hold that the enforcement policy is not ethical or unethical on its face, but it might be implemented unethically in particular instances that violate the moral virtues. Its objective is clearly a real good—trying to improve the civil peace (if accomplished without undue restraints on the real good of liberty)—but each instance of enforcement would have to be evaluated for the motive of the police officer (unbiased, prejudiced, etc.) and the circumstances of the incident (i.e., treating similar situations in similar fashion). Therefore, it can be seen that a policy of aggressive enforcement of minor quality of life offenses can be viewed differently, depending on the ethical perspective taken. Nevertheless, an ethicist would argue that this discussion of ethics should occur before such a policy is enacted to make clear the assumptions involved so that people are not surprised when unpopular incidents occur and people should understand the assumptions either as anticipated "costs" of such a policy or as a risk that society is unwilling to take.

VIOLATING LAW ON MORAL GROUNDS

It is important to understand that society forfeits some liberties to protect itself. Police are allowed to stop and search people and property under certain circumstances, for example, to protect society from criminals that may prey on them. Italian writer Cesare Beccaria observed in his influential book *An Essay on Crimes and Punishments* (1764) that people only give up *some* liberties to the government and entrust the government to intervene in the lives of citizens (and to punish law violators) only in cases where it is absolutely necessary. Beccaria's views were very influential on the founding fathers of the United States, and many of his principles found their way into the U.S. Constitution. Hence, very specific thresholds are established for arrest and search (probable cause), conviction (proof beyond reasonable doubt), and other important decisions to ensure that proper restraint is placed on the power of the government over the liberty of the less powerful citizen.

As a citizen, a person has a tacit or expressed "oath of fidelity" to the government, inasmuch as they agree to abide by the laws of the country in which they live. It is important that those laws (legal rules) are specific, however, for as Beccaria stated, "there is nothing more dangerous" than considering the "spirit of the law" because it results in "a torrent of opinion." The meaning and application of the law must be clear and not left up to "the good or bad logic of the judge [which] will depend on his good or bad digestion...and on all those little circumstances...[resulting in] the judge who mistakes the vague result of his own confused reasoning for the just interpretation of the law."[5] Beccaria takes a utilitarian position regarding the prevention and adjudication of crime, declaring that "pleasure and pain are the only springs of action in beings endowed with sensibility."[6] He also believed that honor and virtue are uncertain because they can change from age to age, a view contrary to Aristotle, who believed that real goods and the moral virtues were the same for everyone at all times. Nevertheless, legal rules must be specific, certain, and clear so that the obligations of citizens and the government are not subject to interpretation. This is important to ethics as well, so that the moral rules that guide conduct are not selectively applied, resulting in uncertain and questionable ethical decisions.

ETHICS CHECKUP
Beeper Ban

Alabama, among other states and cities, has adopted laws and policies to prevent youngsters from carrying electronic beepers and cell phones without written adult permission. Proponents say these devices are used by drug dealers, distract students, and disrupt classes while in school, whereas opponents see an unnecessary privacy intrusion, and some parents worry about the need to keep tabs on their children.[7]

Consider this proposal from the three different ethical perspectives. On what principle(s) would you base your vote on this issue?

THE ETHICS OF CRIMINALS

A 19-year-old dropped a 22-pound piece of concrete off a highway overpass, either to see it simply smash into pieces or perhaps to hit a passing car. When he dropped it, the concrete block hit a car, smashing through the windshield and killing the driver, who happened to be a professor at the University of Alabama.[8] There was no question that the teenager committed the act; he pleaded no contest to the charges against him (second-degree murder—death caused by gross recklessness). Although the act was stupid and pointless, could ethical thinking on the part of the offender have prevented the incident? Was dropping the concrete block in accord with any moral virtue? Would it have made a good universal rule? Was it pursuing the greatest total happiness (weighing potential pain and pleasure)? The answer to each of these questions is clearly "no." This tragic incident shows how ethical thinking can be used to avoid criminal consequences because, as in this case, the teenager had no intention of killing anyone, but unethical conduct caused a death. The teenager was sentenced to 21 years in prison.

In a related way, the abuse of prisoners at Abu Ghraib Prison in Iraq by U.S. military personnel was similarly avoidable. The abuse included naked prisoners kept in total darkness, male prisoners forced to wear women's underwear, and prisoners humiliated in other ways.[9] The United States had no policy of abuse, and the simple application of individual ethics may have prevented the abuse that occurred. Applying virtue ethics, formalism, and utilitarianism objectively reveals that this incident was as ethically avoidable as dropping the concrete block onto a highway. It is amazing how originally "small" or low-visibility decisions can become headline news when they are not thought through in ethical terms.

In contemporary society, a growing theme you hear is "don't sweat the small stuff" and the claim that "it's *all* small stuff."[10] This perspective on life encourages people not to take themselves or their actions seriously. It is not difficult to see how individuals use this viewpoint to justify self-serving, unethical conduct, such as stealing newspapers from vending machines, disabling parking meters, and eating grapes in the supermarket without paying for them. Defining decisions as "small stuff" makes it difficult to draw the line between moral and immoral conduct, and it "becomes a rationale for living without guidelines."[11]

Criminals often think in similar ways, rationalizing their decisions by minimizing the rights and interests of those they victimize. It can be argued that noncriminals and criminals are thinking alike when the attitude of "looking out for number one" attempts to make selfishness into a virtue and self-gratification a moral imperative. We become self-absorbed, seeking personal advantage, often with disregard for others or the costs that such self-absorption incurs. It supports a very narrow and self-serving view of what our own best interest is. "Looking out for number one" can be used to justify cheating and stealing because it defines everyone else as a threat to our own self-gratification.[12]

AN ETHICAL EXPLANATION OF CRIME

Those studying the causes of crime have not found a uniform explanation for it. Some have argued that a single explanation should be able to account for all criminality, whereas others believe that different explanations are required for different types of crime and offenders.[13] Explanations of crime can be grouped into four major types: classical, positivistic, structural, and ethical.

The **classical school** of thought in criminology sees crime as the result of the conscious exercise of an individual's free will. Classicists see people as hedonists: People pursue pleasure while attempting to minimize pain. Two of the best-known classicists, Cesare Beccaria and Jeremy Bentham, wrote during the eighteenth century and outlined the principles of classicism in criminal law.[14]

Classical thinking, sometimes called the free-will school, dominated criminal codes during the nineteenth century because the law assumed that all people were equal in their capacity to guide their conduct rationally. If the law was violated, the punishment was based on the violation committed, rather than on the type of person who committed it. This punishment was designed to deter future misconduct by the offender and other members of society. Recent exponents of the classical explanation include Michael Gottfredson and Travis Hirschi, who believe that crime is a course of conduct chosen by individuals with low self-control, who are unable to defer immediate gratification of their desires.[15] Empirical studies continue to test the ability of classical explanations to account for the commission of crimes, but the results are inconsistent.[16] Dissatisfaction with the classical school first appeared toward the end of the nineteenth century. Crime was still seen as a growing problem, and punishment of violators apparently was not deterring people from committing criminal acts—a perception that remains widespread today, more than a century later. The 1800s also witnessed the rise of the scientific method and the beginnings of social science. Charles Darwin (1809–1882) developed his theory of evolution through natural selection, publishing it in his famous work *The Origin of Species*.[17] Émile Durkheim observed differences in rates of suicide in different regions of France. He used these observations to develop a theory of social factors in suicide.[18] Both Darwin and Durkheim were pioneers in the use of the scientific method, in which knowledge is advanced through observation rather than by theorizing without first gathering data. This scientific approach to explanations gave rise to the positivist school of criminology.

According to **positivism**, human behavior is determined by internal and external influences. Positivists maintain that these influences, which include biological, psychological, and social factors, determine individual behavior. Rather than seeing crime as the product of the rational exercise of free will, as classicists do, positivists see crime as largely determined by a variety of internal and external influences on a person. In many ways the positive school in criminology emphasizes "nurture" (i.e., factors in the individual's environment), whereas the classical school emphasizes "nature" (i.e., a presupposed "natural" state of seeking pleasure and avoiding pain).

Positivists believe that there are fundamental differences between criminals and noncriminals based on these internal and external influences, which may include personality imbalances, family role models, and peer group pressure, among many others. From the positivist perspective, all people are not equal because the criminal act is seen as a symptom of an underlying problem rather than as the problem itself, as the classicists see it. Instead of punishment, therefore, positivists believe reform or rehabilitation of the offender is the best way to prevent future crime, either by changing the influences on an individual or by changing how he or she reacts to them.

The earliest positivists saw the roots of criminal behavior in biological attributes, an approach known as biological determinism. Cesare Lombroso (1835–1909) took body measurements of offenders in Italian prisons and concluded that there were "born criminals" with distinctive body measurements and skull sizes. On the basis of his measurements, Lombroso developed a theory of atavism that suggested that "born criminals" were biological throwbacks to an earlier stage of human evolution.[19] However, in 1913, an English physician, Charles Goring, published the results of his measurements of 3,000 English convicts, which had been compared to similar measurements of a group of nonconvicts. Goring found no evidence of a distinct physical criminal type, thereby discrediting Lombroso's theory of atavism.[20] A panel on the understanding and control of violent behavior of the National Academy of Sciences concluded that biological studies have "produced mixed results, suggesting at most a weak genetic influence on the chance of violent behavior."[21] Nevertheless, there is continuing interest in the interplay between biological predispositions and social influences on behavior.

Psychological explanations of crime look inside the human psyche (or internalized controls) for the causes of crime. Instead of examining human physiology, psychologists consider how the human mind operates.

Sociological explanations of crime are more common than any other type. They arose largely from the inability of biological and psychological explanations to account for many types of crime that appeared to be "normal" reactions of people raised in dysfunctional families or neighborhoods. Unlike biological or psychological explanations, which examine problems *within* the individual (whether physiological abnormalities or personality conflicts), sociological explanations consider *environmental* influences that affect the way people behave. Sociological explanations can be grouped into three types: those based on learning, those resulting from blocked opportunity, or those preventing a social bond to conventional society.

A third approach to explaining crime focuses less on individual behavior and more on the behavior of law. That is to say, social, political, and economic conditions cause certain behaviors to be defined as criminal. These conditions also cause the law to be applied in certain ways. As a result, a great deal of "marginal" criminal behavior is defined as crime by the powerful as a way to control people who are perceived as "undesirable." Laws against gambling, loan-sharking, and vagrancy are examples of the way law is employed as a tool of social control, rather than as a means of protecting society from harm.

According to the **structural or conflict view**, the crime problem has deeper roots than the immediate environment or the pursuit of pleasure. The criminal law reflects the will of those in power, and behaviors that threaten the interests of the powerful are punished most severely.[22] This rationale is used to explain why prisons are filled largely with poor and powerless people, rather than with middle- and upper-class wrongdoers. Conflict theory sees little consensus within society on basic values, so the interests of the powerful are imposed through the criminal law and the manner in which it is enforced.[23]

The **ethical view** sees crime as a moral failure in decision making. Simply stated, crime occurs when a person fails to choose the proper course of conduct because of a failure to appreciate its wrongfulness, rather than a failure to appreciate the possibility of being caught as the classicists suggest. According to the ethical view, the positivist and classical views are inadequate. In their place, the following set of principles are proposed:

1. External factors play a role in influencing some people to engage in crime, although these factors by themselves do not cause criminal behavior (as positivists suggest).
2. A freely willed decision lies at the base of virtually all criminal behavior, but there is no hedonistic tendency to engage in crime that is controlled only through the possibility of apprehension (as classicists suggest).
3. Crime is caused by failure to appreciate the wrongfulness of criminal conduct (i.e., failure to appreciate its long-term impact on the offender and on the community or victim).

In this view, crime results when criminal acts bring pleasure rather than guilt. The key to understanding crime causation lies in discovering *how* people make noncriminal choices. Stated another way, "Where do people learn to make decisions in accord with legal and ethical principles?"

Most people are incapable of thinking through decisions in ethical terms because ethical principles are rarely included in the educational process.[24] Lacking education or experience in ethical decision making, people often do what comes naturally: They base decisions on self-interest rather than on the greater interest of the community; they are concerned primarily with the short-term consequences of their decisions; and they confuse competing values, such as honesty and loyalty. This is illustrated by individuals who derive pleasure from shortchanging a store clerk, shoplifting, participating in gang crimes, vandalizing property, and committing other crimes, rather than feeling guilt over the wrongful behavior and empathy for the victim. For example, a study of college students and prison inmates found that the students were much more likely to feel bad or stressed about committing a crime, whereas the prison inmates were more likely to feel exhilarated or proud.[25] This suggests that appreciation of the wrongfulness of conduct (the basis for ethics) may be a bulwark against criminal behavior.

The ethical approach would redirect the positivist focus on external conditions and the classical focus on penalties to a focus on *individual responsibility*. When ethical principles are internalized, criminal conduct is prevented because pleasure is no longer derived from crime and because of the understanding and value placed on the crime's wrongfulness and its impact on the victim.

Table 5.1 summarizes the major features of each of the four basic explanations of crime. The relationships between the identified causes and the prescribed solutions are highlighted.

Efforts by Lawrence Kohlberg and Carol Gilligan have attempted to provide answers to how ethical decisions are learned. Kohlberg (1927–1987), a psychologist, looked specifically at the reasons why a person might break a law for a higher good. He interviewed children of different ages and had them respond to ethical dilemmas such as the following:

TABLE 5.1 Four Approaches to Explaining Criminal Behavior

Approach	Primary Cause of Crime	Prescribed Remedy
Classical	Free-will decision guided by hedonistic tendency to maximize pleasure and minimize pain.	Deterrence through threat of apprehension and punishment.
Positivist	Internal or external factors (e.g., biological, psychological, social, economic).	Rehabilitation or reform by changing these internal or external conditions, or changing an individual's reaction to them.
Structural	Political and economic conditions promote a culture of competitive individualism in which individual gain becomes more important than the social good.	More equitable distribution of power and wealth in society so that all individuals have a greater stake in a better society.
Ethical	Free-will decision guided by ethical principles. Illegal conduct fails to bring pleasure because of its wrongfulness and empathy for the victim.	Education and reinforcement in ethical decision making from an early age. Reduction of external factors that promote unethical decisions.

Heinz's wife was near death and her only hope for living was a drug being sold by a pharmacist for an excessive price. The drug cost $200 to make but was being sold for $2,000, and Heinz was only able to pay $1,000. He offered this sum to the pharmacist but his offer was rejected. Heinz said he would pay the rest later but still the pharmacist would not accept his offer. Now desperate, Heinz considered stealing the drug. Would it be right for him to do that?

Dilemmas such as this one were used to evaluate how moral decisions were made. These studies resulted in **Kohlberg's theory of moral development**, which holds that people progressed in their moral reasoning (i.e., their ability to act ethically) through a series of stages. Kohlberg believed that there were three two-step levels, moving from an emphasis on self-interest, to conformity to social rules, to internalizing ethical principles and personal conscience. Kohlberg claimed that these stages are universal to all people, that they operate in sequence, and that they are not reversible.[26] These stages are summarized in Table 5.2.

TABLE 5.2 Comparing Theories of Moral Development

Kohlberg's Stages of Moral Development	Kohlberg's Theory of Moral Development	Gilligan's Stages	Gilligan's Ethics of Caring
Preconventional morality	Hedonistic self-interest, maximizing pleasure/minimizing pain; ultimately building toward reciprocity—you help me, I'll help you.	Orientation toward self, personal survival	Personal needs trump moral considerations; building toward awareness of responsibility for the well-being of others.
Conventional morality	Conformity to social rules, considering consequences affecting others; building from pleasing those in personal relationships to following social rules for greater social approval.	Goodness as self-sacrifice	Taking care of others (especially family) more important than personal needs (self-sacrifice); building toward realizing the necessity of caring for self while also caring for others.
Postconventional morality	Universal moral principles internalized beyond what society requires; building from respecting the rights of others beyond what is required to acting in accord with universal principles of justice, reciprocity, quality, and respect.	Caring for self and others	Care as a universal obligation, requiring embracing principles of nonviolence, nonexploitation, and avoiding hurt more generally (i.e., morality is equated with caring).

Carol Gilligan (b. 1936) began as a research assistant to Kohlberg. She noticed differences in the ways in which males and females made ethical decisions and determined that Kohlberg's model did not adequately explain the moral development of women. Gilligan conducted interviews of males and females on her own and concluded that women see moral decisions in terms of care and responsibility, as opposed to men, who focus on justice and rights.[27] So, whereas men often see fairness and impartiality as primary factors in making moral decisions, women focus more on the needs of others and ways to maintain relationships in making these decisions. According to **Gilligan's ethics of caring**, there is a gender difference in how moral thinking develops, but she does not believe that the caring approach is exclusive to women. Her approach to moral decision making simply may be more commonly found among females. Standing on its own, Gilligan's perspective offers an alternative view to Kohlberg's competing theory of moral development. Table 5.2 summarizes Gilligan's and Kohlberg's theories side by side, and their similarities and differences can be compared. Both theories include a progression from hedonistic self-interest to greater personal and social responsibility in one's conduct, but they differ in the process of this development (right and justice versus caring and responsibility).

Empirical support for Kohlberg's and Gilligan's explanations of moral development is mixed. Other researchers have attempted to apply them to groups of businesspeople, offenders, and other groups of different ages and mixed gender. Several studies have been unable to validate their explanations in a way that distinguishes the moral reasoning of people of different ages and genders.[28] This suggests that other influences may be at work in the way that individuals learn to make ethical decisions.

Moral behavior can be learned in ways other than through a process of psychological development. For example, studies have found that ethical behavior can be learned simply by imitating the examples of others. In interviews with corporate auditors, Donald Cressey found that "every one of these financial executives said that the ethical behavior of company personnel is determined by the example set by top management."[29] The same situation was discovered by Marshall Clinard in interviews with middle managers in corporations.[30]

Interviews with the former president of Lockheed Corporation, A. Carl Kotchian, revealed that significant business decisions were made considering only economic factors. He agreed to make covert, but legal, payments to Japanese officials to sell large civilian airplanes there. In justifying his actions, Kotchian argued (accurately) that competitors were making similar payments, Lockheed was "asked" to make the payments as a criterion for consideration, and the ultimate sale (totaling more than $430 million for twenty-one future aircraft) "would provide Lockheed workers with jobs, and thus redound to the benefit of their dependents, and local communities and stockholders of the corporation."[31] Since that time, payments such as these have been made illegal under U.S. law, but it can be seen that the line between acceptable, unethical, and illegal conduct is not clear in this case. What is needed is an assessment of what *ought* to be done in situations like these, knowing that international business increasingly finds itself in situations where acceptable local practices vary considerably. Such anticipation of ethical dilemmas that will arise will make it clear to corporate executives, stockholders, regulators, and the general public what issues are at stake and how they were rationally (rather than expediently) considered.

In the infamous case at Love Canal, tons of toxic waste were buried. The area later became the site of homes and schools. Many residents of the area became ill and some died. In this case, it appears that the corporate disposer, Hooker Chemical, informed the Niagara Falls School Board in writing and through onsite inspections of the danger of the area. Nevertheless, the board obtained the property, later selling it to developers and putting storm sewers directly through the sealed canal bed where the chemicals were buried.[32] This case provides a remarkable example of how Hooker Chemical attempted to carry out its ethical duties in spite of pressure from the school board. In both the Lockheed and Love Canal cases, however, expediency overcame ethics, and there are victims still paying the price as a result. In neither case did any official ever claim to be motivated by what *should* happen. Instead, there was usually an a priori economic determination made, and the path of least resistance was followed. Clearly, the example of others is not always an appropriate way to inculcate ethical principles.

In the arena of white-collar crime, there exist a growing number of examples of well-educated people making business and professional decisions that violate the law.[33] The principles of ethical decision making are rarely made explicit because the educational process implicitly assumes that knowledge of facts implies knowledge of what to do with them. Given the pressures of the market place, "procriminal" definitions that may exist within industry, and the wide availability of techniques to neutralize or rationalize conduct, how is it that many choose to conduct business honestly and fairly, then, whereas others are not able to resist the pressures to "succeed" at all costs?

What is the process by which people choose to deny themselves an immediate gain for an ethical principle? Given the fact that most people have no education or experience in prioritizing values when they are placed in difficult situations, they often do what becomes second nature in the business community: They operate quickly, efficiently, and always in the best interests of the company. Therefore, shortcuts are chosen, safety is secondary, and the law is ignored when it comes between profit and self-interest.

The methods by which ethical principles are taught and internalized can vary, but most people are not taught or trained to think through a business or governmental decision in ethical terms. As James Coleman has observed, "Any effort to deal with the problem of white collar crime on this level must be aimed at changing the 'ethical climate' within the corporations and the government."[34] Ethics courses are now in vogue in many schools, but this approach, by itself, fails to integrate ethical considerations in all decision making. Management, personnel, public administration, financial, and political decisions all involve ethical questions with ethical solutions. These principles are often omitted in most educational programs on these subjects today.

A commitment to ethical decision making would make people liable for their bad decisions without the continual recriminations and debate over "who" or "what" was responsible for their behaviors. Individuals would be responsible for their own poor decisions with the knowledge that they did *in fact* know better. This approach is distinguished from the positivist approach in its focus on individual responsibility for personal or corporate decisions rather than external influences. It is distinct from classical approaches in that it focuses not on the certainty of apprehension or on punishment but rather on the "pleasure" portion of the pain–pleasure principle. That is to say, crime would be avoided more often because of its failure to bring pleasure (by applying the principles of ethics) rather than because of the fear of pain through apprehension and punishment.

White-collar crimes are especially amenable to this approach because they involve planning, rationality, and status. Street crimes are more random, more often committed in an emotional or drug-influenced state, and more often committed by persons not thinking rationally.

Attempts to inculcate ethical principles find a more receptive audience among those who contemplate their actions, consider the consequences, and have a degree of social status by nature of their employment and connection to legitimate society.

ETHICS LAWS

The conduct of public officials has gained increasing scrutiny in recent years because of instances of gross misconduct. The Watergate scandal was the primary motivation for better accountability of public officials during the past 40 years. That scandal involved illegal, covert surveillance and a cover-up of these activities by the president's staff during the 1972 presidential reelection campaign, resulting in the resignation of President Nixon and the conviction of a number of his staff members on charges of obstruction of justice and perjury.[35] The demand for more accountability for the decisions and conduct of government officials has led to the creation of the independent counsel (or special prosecutor), campaign finance reform, executive orders on government ethics, and the creation of the Office of Government Ethics.[36] Since Watergate, however, conditions have not necessarily improved. Critics contend that a "culture of scandal" has poisoned U.S. politics, the press is interested primarily in gossip and humiliation, and ethical standards have gotten worse.[37]

The U.S. House of Representatives Ethics Committee (consisting of five members from each party) has the authority to reprimand members in written reports or letters, admonish them before the entire House or, in the most extreme cases, expel them by a two-thirds vote of their peers. In 2004, the House Ethics Committee concluded that majority leader Tom DeLay's (R–TX) conduct "created an appearance" of favoritism when he mingled at a golf outing with energy company executives just days after they contributed to a political organization associated with DeLay. The firm was seeking help with legislation, which was at a critical stage of House–Senate negotiations. DeLay also raised "serious concerns" by contacting the Federal Aviation Administration to help locate Democratic lawmakers who were leaving Texas in an effort to stop state Republican legislators from passing a redistricting plan developed by DeLay. In an interesting response, DeLay told the ethics committee that he was working to advance his party's legislative agenda, but the committee responded, "The fact that a violation results from the overaggressive pursuit of one's legislative agenda simply does not constitute a mitigating factor."[38]

It is useful to examine DeLay's conduct from the perspectives of utilitarianism, formalism, and virtue ethics. Clearly, DeLay's justification suggests a utilitarian rationale that more good than harm would come from his actions (although he does not demonstrate that more *total* good came from his actions as required by utilitarianism—beyond his own personal benefit). The Ethics Committee took a Kantian approach, concluding that the conduct is evaluated based on whether it is a good universal rule regardless of the results. The committee's rejection of DeLay's justification attests to this view. Virtue ethics first would ask what real good was behind DeLay's actions (a difficult question in this case). Second, virtue ethics would ask whether the behavior was conducted in accord with the moral virtues (with justice, prudence, and ambition being the most relevant in this case). It appears that DeLay's conduct would not be ethical according to this view. Therefore, it can be seen that questionable conduct can be evaluated effectively in ethical terms by applying ethical principles to the conduct in question.

Questions have arisen in recent years about the means by which ethical violations are investigated. In 1934, Congress passed a law that made it a crime to lie to federal officials. This "false statements" statute was intended to keep managers and executives in industry from lying to government regulatory agencies about their compliance with the law. Since then, the law has increasingly been used against persons who have committed no crime yet who lied about their actions to a federal official. For example, Henry Cisneros, former U.S. Secretary of Housing and Urban Development, admitted during his background investigation for the job that he had given money to his ex-mistress (not a crime). He lied to the Federal Bureau of Investigation (FBI) about the amount and duration of the payments. He is the first person ever prosecuted on charges of lying on a background check. Cisneros resigned from his cabinet post and faced a possible prison term. Legal scholar Paul Rothstein observed, "It smacks of entrapment to ask people questions about their sex lives and then, when they lie, prosecute them for the lie."[39]

Ronald Blackley, a high-ranking official in the U.S. Department of Agriculture, was sentenced to 27 months in prison for lies he told about $22,000 he received from former business associates who had dealings with the Department of Agriculture. Blackley was not charged with taking the money; his crime was failing to disclose the income and lying about it to investigators.

Linda Tripp, a Pentagon employee, wore a concealed microphone to tape record her conversations with her friend Monica Lewinsky in the independent counsel's investigation of President Clinton. It was reported that Tripp failed to reveal in her Pentagon background check that she had been arrested for shoplifting at age 19, even though the charges had been dropped. If she knowingly lied, she could be prosecuted for making a false statement to a federal official.

An independent counsel was appointed to investigate Bruce Babbitt, secretary of the interior to President Clinton, for lying to Congress about lies he told a lobbyist, even though lying to a lobbyist is not a crime. Former vice presidential chief of staff Lewis "Scooter" Libby was sentenced to 30 months in prison and fined $250,000 for lying to investigators about what he told reporters about a CIA operative's identity, which was leaked to the media. Libby was convicted of four counts in a five-count indictment alleging perjury, obstruction of justice, and making false statements to FBI investigators.[40] (The prison sentence was later commuted by President Bush.) As a former independent counsel observes, "You're seeing more and more prosecutions now of lies in which there is no underlying criminal conduct."[41]

The prosecutions based only on false statements raise the question, "Should there be limits on the extent to which individuals can be prosecuted for lying, when they are lying about noncriminal conduct?" Kant argued that all lies were equally impermissible because they violate the unwritten social contract between people, rendering moral duties uncertain. So truth is not a possession but an "unconditional duty" that holds in all circumstances. Therefore, according to Kantian ethics, there is no differentiation between lies about noncriminal conduct and more pernicious types of lies. Virtue ethics would consider whether there were any real goods sought in lying and whether they violated the moral virtues. Clearly, very few lies would be permitted under virtue ethics. Utilitarianism offers the most leeway in lying, but the consequences of the lies would have to be evaluated in objective terms to determine whether the total (not only the personal) happiness outweighed the pain caused by the lies. Prosecution solely for lying about noncriminal conduct is probably a low threshold for making a criminal case, but such lies would be morally impermissible in most situations applying the principles of ethics.

ETHICS IN BOOKS

Ethics is everywhere, even in the books we read, which sometimes are written without ethics specifically in mind. Here is a summary of a book that looks at values on a global scale, followed by questions that ask you to reflect on the ethical connections.

ETHICS FOR THE NEW MILLENNIUM

Dalai Lama
(Riverhead Trade, 2001)

Tenzin Gyatso, the fourteenth Dalai Lama, offers his wisdom in this book about how to guide our actions. The Dalai Lama is the leader of Tibetan Buddhism, and the term *Dalai Lama* is translated to mean "spiritual teacher." The People's Republic of China invaded the region of Tibet and took control in 1959. The fourteenth Dalai Lama fled to India and has since ceded temporal power to an elected Tibetan government in exile, while he seeks support for greater autonomy for Tibet.

Buddhism has been said to be a simplified version of Hinduism: The goal is to stop all selfish desire, purify thoughts, and reach state of Nirvana (a state of pure consciousness, free from earthly vices and shortcomings). Like the other Eastern philosophies, such as Confucianism and Taoism, Buddhism takes a more relative, less absolute, view of moral goodness than we find in Western ethics. The Dalai Lama believes that all religions share common themes and serve the needs of different people under different circumstances, and he looks to individuals to develop their personal ethics in accord with general principles that either stand on their own or can be practiced in accord with various religions. Looking at all the religious traditions as well as humanism, "all agree on the negativity of killing, stealing, telling lies, sexual misconduct, and speaking with malicious intent" as well as the "need to avoid hatred, pride, covetousness, envy, greed, lust, destructive ideology, and so on." Therefore, he sees great similarities among traditions, especially in views toward compassion for others.

The Dalai Lama's book on ethics hits on several overarching themes. First, goodness, happiness, and our relationship with others are inextricably bound together. "We survive here in dependence on others. Whether we like it or not, there is hardly a moment of our lives when we do not benefit from others' activities. For this reason, it is hardly surprising that most of our happiness arises in the context of our relationships with others. Nor is it so remarkable that our greatest joy should come when we are motivated by concern for others." Because every action we take has a "universal dimension" in its potential impact on the happiness of others, "ethics are necessary as a means to ensure that we do not harm others." The content of "genuine happiness" consists in those spiritual qualities of "love, compassion, patience, tolerance and forgiveness, and so on." All unethical conduct arises from "lack of inner restraint," according to the Dalai Lama, and "the more we develop concern for others' well-being, the easier it becomes to act in their interests."

At the center of the book is a call to surrender oneself and the preoccupation with our personal happiness and success, in favor of concern for others. Because our actions virtually always impact on others, we should have their interests at the center of our vision.

QUESTIONS

1. The Dalai Lama's approach is most similar in the Western tradition to the ethics of Aristotle. How are they similar in assessing moral conduct, and how are they different?

2. Can you explain how a contemporary issue of justice (e.g., diversion versus prosecution and restorative justice) tries to bring together the ideas of surrendering the interests of the individual to a larger concern for others?

ETHICS IN THE MOVIES

Movies seek to entertain and inform the audience about a story, incident, or person. Many good movies also hit upon important ethical themes in making significant decisions that affect the lives of others. Read the movie summary here (and watch the movie if you haven't already), and answer the questions to make the ethical connections.

ENRON: THE SMARTEST GUYS IN THE ROOM

Alex Gibney, Director
(2005)

Enron is a documentary based on a book of the same title by *Fortune* magazine reporters Bethany McLean and Peter Elkind. It documents the collapse of Enron Corporation in one of the largest business frauds in history. Enron, founded in 1985, was the seventh largest corporation in America. Through a series of self-serving business practices and financial manipulation, the corporation was driven into bankruptcy in 2001, while its executives took millions in payments to themselves.

Enron was a company that sold natural gas and electricity as a wholesaler, making profits between the generation of power and its sale to public utilities. The corporation's chairman, Ken Lay, and its CEO, Jeffrey Skilling, used an accounting method that permitted the reporting of potential future earnings as profit (even though these projections were suspect), making the company appear a lot more profitable that it actually was.

Inside the company, the personnel practices were also unusual. Top management took a Darwinian view with an employee evaluation process that guaranteed that 15 percent of company employees would be recommended for dismissal each year. This was "a brutal process" that produced cutthroat competition among employees and also toward the outside world of suppliers and customers. The compensation of top executives was heavily weighted toward Enron stock, so tremendous effort was put into pushing Enron stock prices higher and then selling their stock for large profits (called "pump and dump"). These strategies pushed Enron to take enormous risks, and it reported very high anticipated profits—when actual profits were not occurring.

For example, Enron built a power plant in India, but India could not afford the power it would generate. Enron lost $1 billion in this venture but paid bonuses to executives based on predicted profits that never occurred. In another instance, taped conversations show contempt for California blackouts during the 1990s and displayed ruthless profit-seeking behavior, as Enron traders transferred electricity out of the state for the purpose of selling it back when the price went up. During this period, Enron had electric-generating plants shut down for short periods to raise the price of electricity and increase profits. Financial analysts, auditors, and banks enabled Enron's conduct by uncritically endorsing and participating in profitable deals with the company.

When the company declared bankruptcy in 2001, 20,000 employees lost their jobs and $2 billion in their retirement funds were gone, because company employees had been actively encouraged to keep their Enron stock, while top executives sold theirs. Enron executives were described as "victims of their own hubris and greed."

Enron's top executives and auditors were convicted of fraud and related crimes and sentenced to jail terms and significant fines. Many former employees are still trying to seek compensation from banks and other companies that shared in Enron's profiteering and should have been aware of the underlying fraud. *Enron: The Smartest Guys in the Room* was nominated for an Academy Award for Best Documentary.

QUESTIONS

1. Describe why the conduct of Enron's top executives was morally impermissible from the perspectives of virtue, formalism, and utilitarianism.
2. Can you explain any connection between the personnel practices at Enron (how the company treated its employees) and how the company conducted its business operations?

Discussion Question

Why is the law not the highest aspiration of morality?

Critical Thinking Exercises

All ethical decisions affect others (by definition) and, as Aristotle points out, ethical decision making is achieved consistently only through practice. Given the outline of virtue ethics, formalism, and utilitarianism, evaluate the moral permissibility of the conduct in question in each scenario.

Important note on method: *Critical thinking requires the ability to evaluate viewpoints, facts, and behaviors objectively to assess information or methods of argumentation to establish the true worth or merit of an act or course of conduct. Please evaluate these scenarios, first analyzing pros and cons of alternate views,* before *you come to a conclusion. Do* not *draw a conclusion first, and then try to find facts to support it—this frequently leads to narrow (and incorrect) thinking.*

To properly evaluate the moral permissibility of a course of action using critical thinking skills

1. *Begin with an open mind (no preconceptions!),*
2. *Isolate and evaluate the relevant facts on both sides,*
3. *Identify the precise moral question to be answered, and*
4. *Apply ethical principles to the moral question based on an objective evaluation of the facts, only then drawing a conclusion.*

5.1 A Boat Ride with Some Close Friends[42]

The members of your group are all experienced boaters. You undertake a trip on the Atlantic Ocean, hoping to sail to Europe during summer vacation. Things proceed as planned until an unexpected and severe storm pushes you far off course.

The storm swamps your vessel and renders your communications equipment inoperable. The boat is sinking, and your group is forced to abandon ship on a lifeboat.

The storm subsides the next day after an entire night of tossing you around the ocean like a Ping-Pong ball. Your group is OK, but your small freshwater and food supply were washed overboard during the storm, and you have no communications equipment to call for help. After 2 days, you all realize that you were probably blown so far off course during the storm that any potential rescuers either believe you drowned along with your sunken ship or are looking for you someplace other than where you are. It also becomes evident that you are slowly starving to death.

You may be 1,000 miles from land; the only drinkable water is the occasional rain, which is not sufficient to prevent you from dehydrating; and you are unable to catch any fish to eat. After 7 days without food and very little water, the situation is desperate. One member of your group suggests that one of the group members be sacrificed to save the rest from starvation.

- Your group must decide on this issue and you are the only one who has taken an ethics course. (Remember you are starving to death, so time is of the essence.)
- Identify the important ethical considerations, and make a decision on the morally permissible course of action.

5.2 It Fell Off a Truck

Mark worked two jobs as a security guard in Cleveland, Ohio. He was walking outside the downtown building where he works at 7:45 A.M., when three 42-pound bundles of money fell out of an armored truck en route from the Federal Reserve Bank to Jacobs Field, home of the Cleveland Indians baseball team. The back door of the truck apparently was left ajar. Inside the bundles wrapped in plastic was a total of $646,000 in cash. Mark turned in the money to the FBI 2 days later. The FBI reportedly told him, "You're not getting a reward and you're lucky you're not going to jail," suspecting that Mark had planned to keep the money until he thought that some of the money contained marked bills. Mark said, "I froze for maybe a second," when he first saw the money, but his 2-day wait to return the money was caused by trying to figure out how to claim the $75,000 reward offered for the money's return.[43]

- Was Mark morally obligated to return the money?
- Should Mark be penalized for waiting 2 days to return the money?

5.3 Prostitution: Simply a Business?

An admitted call girl once said that prostitution is a profitable business if you market it correctly and properly screen your clients. The U.S. Department of Commerce claims that the underground economy (especially illegal gambling and prostitution) represents between 3 and 40 percent beyond the legal economy.

Fifi defends the right to sell sex between consenting adults and argues that a person has the right to use his or her body in any way that maximizes income. "We allow people to box professionally. So why do we allow people to beat the crap out of each other for a living, but prohibit people from being nice to each other (via sexual acts)?"

From the perspective of prostitutes, such as Fifi, "It's not the government's business. Should sex between consenting adults be a concern of the government at all? We allow prostitution in Nevada and in many other countries, so we're inconsistent as well. You mean to tell me that all those places are immoral? We do the same thing that a legal massage parlor does, only we do it on different parts of the body."

However, many former prostitutes say that most were drug addicts and many were molested as children or as young girls or boys. "When I first did it, I felt a tremendous sense of power," said Bula, "but that feeling quickly faded. Feelings of powerlessness, shame, and drug addiction ultimately followed, knowing that my prostitution was a continuing form of abuse, even though I made good money."[44]

- Evaluate the moral permissibility of Fifi's decision to be a prostitute.
- Evaluate the moral permissibility of Bula's decision to be a prostitute.

5.4 *24* and Depictions of Torture

The Fox television show *24* follows a unique formula where Jack Bauer, a U.S. counterterrorism agent, must stop a major terrorist conspiracy over the course of a season that encompasses a single 24-hour day (i.e., 24-hour-long episodes are needed to solve the case). Some argue the program encourages real-life interrogators to "go too far" when they question terrorist suspects, mimicking the actions of the fictional Jack Bauer.

The *New Yorker* magazine featured a story about Joel Surnow, the show's creator and a self-described "right-wing nut" and reported that Surnow and the story's creative staff were visited by U.S. Army brigadier General Patrick Finnegan, the dean of the United States Military Academy at West Point, who flew to Southern California to meet with the creative team behind *24*. Finnegan was accompanied by three of the most experienced military and FBI interrogators in the country. They came to voice their concern that the show's central political premise—that the letter of American law must be sacrificed for the country's security—was having a toxic effect. In their view, the show promoted unethical and illegal behavior and had adversely affected the training and performance of real American soldiers. "I'd like them to stop," Finnegan said of the show's producers. The show's graphic depictions of the torture of suspects were "hurting efforts to train recruits in effective interrogation techniques and is damaging the image of the U.S. around the world."

"People watch the shows, and then walk into the interrogation booths and do the same things they've just seen," said Tony Lagouranis, who was a U.S. Army interrogator in Iraq and attended the meeting.[45] The Parents Television Council reports that *24* is the number-one show in terms of showing torture.

- What is the issue of moral permissibility in this situation?
- How should the ethical issue be approached from the perspectives of virtue, formalism, and utilitarianism?

5.5 No Junkmail Delivery

Mailman Steven Padgett received a probation sentence for failing to deliver a year's worth of junk mail on his route in North Carolina. "Today you'll get credit for a life well lived," the U.S. District Court judge told Padgett. The judge could have sent Padgett to prison under federal sentencing guidelines; instead, he put him on 3 years' probation, fined him $3,000, and ordered him to perform 500 hours of community service. Padgett, age 58, apologized to the postal service and his family for the crime of delaying and destroying mail. The prosecutor said authorities had notified hundreds of Padgett's customers about the criminal proceeding, and only one responded. That single response, however, was in support of Padgett.

Padgett built up goodwill on his route by handing out treats to dogs, making sure packages were left on dry porches, and introducing himself to customers. Children called him "Mailman Steve." The U.S. Postal Service never received a complaint about the missing mail and didn't know anything was amiss until they were contacted by a utility worker who noticed the excess mail at Padgett's house in Raleigh. Postal inspectors went to the home this spring and discovered the third-class mail piled in his garage and buried in his yard.

Postal authorities don't think any letters, bills, or other type of first-class or second-class mail were among the hundreds of thousands of fliers at Padgett's home, some dating back 10 years. It wasn't a conscious stand against waste or a junk mail protest that spurred Padgett to hold onto the mailers.[46] Rather, it was the inability to meet the demands of a job in a growing part of the county while contending with heart problems and complications from his diabetes. Not sorting and delivering the third-class mailings became a way to save time and make sure other mail got delivered on time.

• Evaluate the moral permissibility of the mailman's conduct in failing to deliver junk mail on his route.

Key Concepts

Consensus view *48*
Conflict view *49*
Quality of life offenses *49*
Classical school *52*

Positivism *53*
Structural or conflict view *54*
Ethical view *54*

Kohlberg's theory of moral development *56*
Gilligan's ethics of caring *57*

Notes

1. "A Stupid @#!% Law," *The Washington Post* (October 4, 2004), p. 2.
2. Émile Durkheim, *The Division of Labor in Society* (New York, NY: Free Press, 1893), p. 80.
3. Vincent Barry, *The Dog Ate My Homework: Personal Responsibility—How We Avoid It and What to Do about It* (Kansas City, MO: Andrews McMeel, 1998), pp. 73–76.
4. Larry Reibstein, "NYPD Black and Blue," *Newsweek* (June 2, 1997), p. 67; Al Baker, "New York Minorities More Likely to be Frisked," *The New York Times* (May 12, 2010).
5. Cesare Beccaria, *Essay on Crimes and Punishments* (1764) (Boston, MA: Branden Publishing, 1992), pp. 23–24.
6. Beccaria, *Essay on Crimes and Punishments,* p. 28.
7. Victoria Coman, "Shelby Obeys, but Questions Phone Ban," *Birmingham News* (Alabama) (April 8, 2004), p. 5; Maria Sacchetti, "Wrentham Schools Hang Up on Cell Phones," *The Boston Globe* (January 13, 2005), p. B1.
8. "Teen Sentenced," *USA Today* (February 2, 2002), p. 3.
9. Louis Meixler, "Red Cross Says It Warned U.S. of Prisoner Abuse Last Year," *The Associated Press* (May 7, 2004).
10. Richard Carlson, *Don't Sweat the Small Stuff and It's All Small Stuff: Simple Ways to Keep the Little Things from Taking Over Your Life* (New York, NY: Hyperion, 1997).
11. Barry, *The Dog Ate My Homework: Personal Responsibility—How We Avoid It and What to Do about It,* p. 80.
12. Barry, *The Dog Ate My Homework: Personal Responsibility—How We Avoid It and What to Do about It,* p. 90.
13. Compare the conclusions of Don C. Gibbons, "Talking about Crime: Observations on the Prospects for Causal Theory in Criminology," *Criminal Justice*

Research Bulletin, vol. 7 (1992), pp. 1–10, with Michael R. Gottfredson and Travis Hirschi, *A General Theory of Crime* (Stanford, CA: Stanford University Press, 1990).

14. For excerpts from the writings of Bentham and Beccaria, see Joseph E. Jacoby, *Classics of Criminology*, 2nd ed. (Prospect Heights, IL: Waveland Press, 1994).

15. Gottfredson and Hirschi, *A General Theory of Crime,* pp. 90–91.

16. Augustine Brannigan, "Self-Control, Social Control, and Evolutionary Psychology: Towards an Integrated Perspective on Crime," *Canadian Journal of Criminology*, vol. 39 (October 1997), pp. 403–431; T. David Evans, Francis T. Cullen, Velmer S. Burton, Jr., R. Gregory Dunaway, and Michael L. Benson, "The Social Consequences of Self-Control: Testing the General Theory of Crime," *Criminology*, vol. 35 (August 1997), pp. 475–501.

17. Charles Darwin, *The Origin of Species* (New York, NY: Modern Library, 1936).

18. Émile Durkheim, *Suicide* (New York, NY: Free Press, 1951).

19. Cesare Lombroso and Gina Lombroso-Ferrero, *The Criminal Man* (Montclair, NJ: Patterson Smith, 1972).

20. Charles Goring, *The English Convict* (London, UK: Her Majesty's Stationery Office, 1913).

21. Jeffrey A. Roth, "Understanding and Preventing Violence," *National Institute of Justice Research in Brief* (February 1994), p. 8; Albert J. Reiss and Jeffrey A. Roth, eds. *Understanding and Preventing Violence* (Washington, DC: National Academy Press, 1993).

22. Jeffrey Reiman, *The Rich Get Richer and the Poor Get Prison: Ideology, Class, and Criminal Justice*, 3rd ed. (New York, NY: Macmillan, 1990).

23. Jeffrey Reiman, *. . . And the Poor Get Prison: Economic Bias in American Criminal Justice* (Boston, MA: Allyn & Bacon, 1996).

24. Jay S. Albanese, *Dealing with Delinquency: The Future of Juvenile Justice*, 2nd ed. (Chicago, IL: Nelson-Hall, 1993), pp. 61–64; Jay Albanese, *White Collar Crime in America* (Englewood Cliffs, NJ: Prentice Hall, 1995), pp. 105–109; Jay Albanese, *Organized Crime in Our Times*, 4th ed. (Newark, NJ: LexisNexis, 2004), pp. 68–72.

25. Peter B. Wood, "Nonsocial Reinforcement and Habitual Criminal Conduct: An Extension of Learning Theory," *Criminology*, vol. 35 (1997), pp. 335–366.

26. Lawrence Kohlberg, *The Psychology of Moral Development* (New York, NY: HarperCollins, 1984).

27. Carol Gilligan, *In a Different Voice: Psychological Theory and Women's Development* (Cambridge, MA: Harvard University Press, 1993).

28. J. Weber and D. Wasielski, "Investigating Influences on Managers' Moral Reasoning: The Impact of Context and Personal and Organizational Factors," *Business and Society*, vol. 40 (March 2001), p. 79; Patricia van Voorhis, "Restitution Outcome and Probationers' Assessment of Restitution: The Effects of Moral Development," *Criminal Justice and Behavior*, vol. 12 (1985), pp. 259–287.

29. Donald R. Cressey, "Employee Theft: The Reasons Why," *Security World* (October 1980), pp. 31–36.

30. Marshall B. Clinard, *Corporate Ethics and Crime* (Beverly Hills, CA: Sage Publications, 1983).

31. A. Carl Kotchian, *Rikkiedo Jiken* (Lockheed Incident), published in Japan, 1976; Albanese, White Collar Crime.

32. Jay Albanese, "Love Canal Six Years Later: The Legal Legacy," *Federal Probation Quarterly*, vol. 48, no. 2 (June 1984), pp. 53–58.

33. See James William Coleman, *The Criminal Elite*, 5th ed. (New York, NY: St. Martin's Press, 2001); Nancy Frank and Michael Lombness, *Controlling Corporate Illegality: The Regulatory Justice System* (Cincinnai, OH: Anderson Publishing, 1988).

34. James William Coleman, *The Criminal Elite: The Sociology of White Collar Crime*, 5th ed. (New York, NY: St. Martin's Press, 2001), p. 249.

35. Keith W. Olson, *Watergate: The Presidential Scandal That Shook America* (Lawrence, KS: University Press of Kansas, 2003).

36. George D. Brown, "Putting Watergate Behind Us— Salinas, Sun-Diamond, and Two Views of the Anticorruption Model," *Tulane Law Review*, vol. 74 (February 2000), p. 747.

37. Suzanne Garment, *Scandal: The Culture of Mistrust in American Politics* (New York, NY: Random House, 1992).

38. Larry Margasak, "Ethics Panel Rebukes DeLay Twice in a Week," *Associated Press Online* (October 6, 2004).

39. Paul Glastris, " 'False Statements': The Flubber of All Laws," *U.S. News & World Report* (March 30, 1998), pp. 25–26.

40. Matt Apuzzo, "Former White House Aide Scooter Libby Is Sentenced to 2½ Years in Prison in CIA Leak Case," *The Associated Press* (June 5, 2007).

41. Glastris, *U.S.News & World Report,* p. 26.

42. *Based on the case The Queen v. Dudley and Stephens*, 14 Q.B.D. 273 (1884).

43. "FBI Investigating Missing Money," *Associated Press* (February 8, 2001); "Report: Man Wanted to Claim Reward," *Associated Press* (February 11, 2001), p. 3.

44. See Elia Kacapyr, "Notes from the Underground," *American Demographics*, vol. 20 (January 1998), p. 30; Sydney Biddle Barrows with William Novak, *Mayflower Madam* (New York, NY: Arbor House, 1986); Annette Foglino, "Quitting the Streets," *Life* (November 1, 1998), p. 96; "Life off the Streets," *Time* (November 16, 1998), p. 16.

45. Tom Regan, "Does 24 Encourage U.S. Interrogators?" *Christian Science Monitor* (February 12, 2007); Edward Wyatt, "New Era in Politics, New Focus for '24'," *The New York Times* (January 8, 2009).

46. Sarah Ovaska, "Mailman Steve Gets Probation," *The News & Observer* (Raleigh, North Carolina) (November 19, 2008).

CHAPTER 6

Police
How Should the Law Be Enforced?

Learning Objectives:

- To understand how the Fourth and Fifth Amendments of the Bill of Rights provide the principles for police stops, searches, arrests, and interrogations.

- To appreciate the threshold of "stop and frisk" and its differences from probable cause in evaluating situations for police.

- To recognize the differences among nonfeasance, misfeasance, and malfeasance in assessing police decisions.

- To develop an appreciation for the different causes and circumstances of police corruption.

- To evaluate the relationship between codes of ethics and ethical principles in producing consistent conduct.

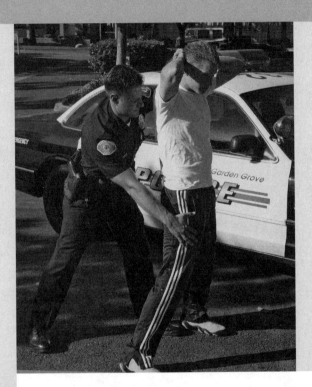

It is curious that physical courage should be so common in the world but moral courage so rare.

—Mark Twain (1835–1910)

In many ways, police are the gatekeepers of the criminal justice system. They are the representatives of the government that citizens are most likely to see and have contact. Police have the authority to intrude into the privacy and liberty of the public. Therefore, a great deal of attention is given to the police role in society in balancing the interests of the community in maintaining order and apprehending crime suspects with individual liberty and the right to be left alone.

THE SCOPE OF POLICE DECISIONS

Police observe behavior in the community and must make judgments about potentially criminal behavior to prevent crime and apprehend criminals. They make crucial decisions about whether individuals should be stopped, frisked, searched, arrested, or interrogated. This is a difficult task guided in legal terms by the Fourth Amendment to the U.S. Constitution, which offers only general direction using the standard of "probable cause."

Court decisions have been necessary over the years to interpret and apply the general Fourth Amendment standard in a changing world of automobile travel, drug trafficking, smuggling, and suspicious persons and activities that fall close to the probable cause threshold. In a similar way, the Fifth Amendment provides general direction for the conduct of interrogations by police, which also has required court interpretation to apply to contemporary situations. This chapter analyzes the ethical underpinnings of important legal standards and court rulings, which illustrate how constitutional principles written 200 years ago have ethical precursors.

INVESTIGATION AND SURVEILLANCE

The ethical difficulty faced by police is made evident in the case of terrorism. The role of police in antiterrorism efforts is a new one. Before September 11, 2001, antiterrorism efforts in the United States were the responsibility of the intelligence community. Parts of the Central Intelligence Agency (CIA), National Security Agency, Defense Intelligence Agency, and Federal Bureau of Investigation (FBI) were primarily responsible for gathering "intelligence," or information that might be important in protecting U.S. national security. Interest in intelligence gathering has now reached the local level because it has been recognized that local police can play a crucial role in gathering information at the neighborhood level about suspicious or unusual activity that is suggestive of criminal and possibly terrorist motives.

Intelligence gathering is a difficult task, however, because it takes a great deal of skill and experience to distinguish disjointed information from true intelligence. For mere information to become intelligence, it must be linked to particular individuals, locations, known groups, methods of operation, patterns of past conduct, or communications that raise the level of suspicion. Still, most intelligence work leads to dead ends, making it time-consuming and sometimes frustrating work. These issues are also characteristic of traditional criminal investigative work.

In the effort to develop information into intelligence, police are subject to criticism. They have been accused of "profiling" racial or ethnic groups by singling them out for scrutiny, unnecessary surveillance of suspects, following false terrorism tips that disrupt the lives of the subjects, and gathering intelligence without proper oversight. These criticisms are not to be taken lightly, but they are common any time police take on a new role. For example, when civil disorder and riots occurred in U.S. cities during the 1960s and 1970s, police were forced to respond to a new kind of investigative task, and abuses occurred.[1] With significant financial and training resources being devoted to the antiterrorism effort, it is hoped that fewer mistakes will be made. An obstacle, of course, is the elusive nature of terrorism and terrorist threats, which often are committed by small, unconnected groups that are difficult to identify in advance.

The fact that terrorism can involve a nebulous threat that is often difficult to isolate is problematic. The early experiences in the Unites States of setting threat levels (the red–orange–yellow–green terror alert system) caused many problems because no one was sure what changes in levels meant, and precise information was lacking to guide actions. Historically, police have been trained to act on specific information using established standards, such as probable cause, but the threat of terrorism appears to be much less specific, and it will require new skills to gather intelligence effectively in this area. This experience points to the need for specific guidelines for police actions in this area, which is a problem given the often nonspecific nature of terrorism and the need for intelligence.

One study of the terrorism response found that police and firefighters agreed "they do not know what they need to be protected against, what form of protection is appropriate, and where to look for such protection." Another study found that school resource officers believed that their schools were "soft targets" for terrorists and that most schools were not protected adequately.[2] This uncertainty points to the need for better information and police training on what are the most significant terrorist threats in the United States, what strategies and tactics are likely to be effective against these threats, and how antiterrorism enforcement activities and more traditional law enforcement tasks should be prioritized.

It is important to frame police decisions for surveillance and investigation not only in legal terms but also in ethical terms. For example, to achieve 100 percent security, some believe that all persons must be subject to searches and questioning, which is the procedure now in force at U.S. airports and around the world. Because air travel is seen as a privilege and not a right, passengers can simply choose not to travel by air if they object to the intrusive searches. But what if it is decided to extend those searches to all passengers boarding trains, buses, or boats? What about those entering taxis? Legislatures and courts can decide to make these searches legally permissible, but are they morally permissible? Would such a policy increase the greatest total happiness? Is it a good universal rule? Is it consistent with the moral virtues? Thoughtful consideration of ethical questions such as these will lead to more enlightened laws and fewer unanticipated consequences.

CURTAILING LIBERTY: STOP AND FRISK

Procedural law is a very important part of the criminal justice process because it specifies how people accused of crimes will be treated. Like substantive law, the provisions of criminal procedure are guided by the principles of the U.S. Constitution. The **Bill of Rights**—the first ten amendments to the U.S. Constitution—details many of the requirements for adjudication, such as arrests, warrants, searches, trials, lawyers, punishment, and other important aspects of criminal procedure. The purpose of the Bill of Rights is to protect the individual citizen against arbitrary use of power by the government.

For many years the police, the courts, and the public have been uncertain about the scope of a police officer's authority to stop a suspect when there are no grounds for arrest. Although it is common practice for officers to stop and question citizens, until 40 years ago, it was not clear whether the police actually had this right and, if they did, what its limits were. The case that established the legal authority and limits for a **stop and frisk** was *Terry v. Ohio*.[3] The case involved a Cleveland police officer who had been a plainclothes detective for 35 years and had patrolled a certain section of the downtown area for shoplifters and pickpockets for much of that time.

The officer saw three men repeatedly walk slowly past a store window and suspected that they were "casing" the store for a robbery. He identified himself as a police officer and proceeded to ask them several questions, to which they "mumbled something" in response. The officer then grabbed one of the men, turned him around, and "patted him down." He felt something in the man's left breast pocket and removed it; it was a .38 caliber revolver. He proceeded to pat down the outer garments of the other men and found another pistol on one of them. The men were charged with carrying concealed weapons in violation of the law.

In court, the men claimed that the officer had no probable cause to search them. Therefore, the search was illegal, and the guns should not be admitted as evidence against them. On appeal, the U.S. Supreme Court agreed that the police officer did not have probable cause to conduct a search, but the gun possession charge was allowed to stand.

The Court distinguished between a *stop* and an *arrest* and between a *frisk* and a *search*. A *frisk* was defined as a patting down of outer clothing, whereas a *search* is an exploration for evidence. Seizure of property occurs when there is some meaningful interference with the individual's possession of that property. The Court held that a frisk is essential to the proper performance of a police officer's investigative duties, for without it "the answer to the police officer may be a bullet, and a loaded pistol discovered during the frisk is admissible [as evidence]." As a result, the two men were convicted of illegally carrying concealed weapons. The Court concluded that the experienced officer's observations were "enough to make it quite reasonable to fear that they were armed; and nothing in their response to his hailing them, identifying himself as a police officer, and asking their names served to dispel that reasonable belief." The officer's actions were not

> the product of a volatile or inventive imagination, or undertaken simply as an act of harassment; the record evidences the tempered act of a policeman who in the course of an investigation had to make a quick decision as to how to protect himself and others from possible danger, and took limited steps to do so.[4]

According to the Supreme Court, frisks are limited to a search for weapons that may pose an immediate threat to the officer's safety. The Court concluded that cases such as these must be decided on the basis of their own facts, but, generally, police officers who observe unusual conduct that leads them to conclude that criminal activity may be involved, and that the persons may be armed and dangerous, are entitled to conduct "a carefully limited search of the outer clothing of such persons in an attempt to discover weapons" that might be used to assault them. Such a frisk was held to be reasonable under the Fourth Amendment, and any weapons seized may be introduced in evidence.

The decision in *Terry v. Ohio* lowered the standard for police to take action against a suspect. Prior to 1968, police could search only if they had probable cause. After *Terry*, police could conduct a frisk of a person's outer clothing to search for weapons if they had only "reasonable suspicion." Reasonable suspicion is a lower standard of evidence than probable cause, so the scope of the search permitted is less intrusive.[5]

Stop and frisk is now a common police practice. A survey asked citizens if they had been suspects in a police encounter in the past year. An estimated 4.4 million people reported having been questioned by police as possible suspects. Of this group, 740,000 (17 percent) had been patted down by police.[6] About 30 percent of those patted down by police were handcuffed, and nearly 40 percent of the encounters resulted in force being used or threatened.

The Supreme Court is still wrestling with the question of limits on frisks of suspects. For example, in the case *Illinois v. Wardlow*, decided in 2000, the Court ruled on a case from Chicago in which four police cars approached the sidewalk where Sam Wardlow was standing. Wardlow turned and ran down an alley. He was caught, and a gun was found in a frisk of his outer garments.

The issue in this case was whether the police had the requisite reasonable suspicion that criminal activity was afoot. In a 5–4 vote, a divided Supreme Court held that Wardlow's presence in an area known for heavy narcotics trafficking, combined with his unprovoked flight, justified the search.[7] This rule suggests that a suspect's flight at the mere sight of a police officer can be suspicious enough to justify a stop and frisk for weapons. Other cases decided by the Supreme Court reflect this tension between the need to stop and question suspects and the evidence needed to do so. For example, the Court held that a frisk that goes beyond a pat-down search is not permissible because of its limited purpose and scope. An officer felt a small lump in a suspect's pocket, which the officer then examined with his fingers and determined to be cocaine wrapped in cellophane. The Court held that once the officer concluded that the lump was not a weapon, the continued examination constituted a search without probable cause.[8] The search was disallowed because it was unrelated to the purpose of the frisk: to protect an officer's safety.

There are a dizzying number of cases decided by the courts that attempt to distinguish for the police and the public the line between legitimate police inquiry and the public's right to privacy. These cases involve automobiles, buses, drug courier profiles, traffic stops, and related circumstances in which police have suspicions, but not clear evidence, of a law violation.

How can ethics be of value in these circumstances? Ethics are useful because laws can never anticipate the innumerable variations in circumstances that police will face, so court decisions will necessarily be unending. Court decisions after the fact are of little value to police in making current decisions or to the public who are the subjects of stops and frisks. Ethics offers an objective standard by which individual officers and police departments may go a step further in following the law (because the law's application in future unanticipated circumstances cannot be known in advance). Ethics provides clear guidance in advance in cases where the law's application is still unclear, yet undecided, or unknown.

Under what circumstances *should* a suspect be stopped and frisked? Utilitarianism does not provide much guidance in these cases because it relies on consequences to determine morality. The outcome of a frisk is never known in advance, so the application of utilitarianism in these situations does not provide much assistance. However, formalism and virtue ethics guide ethical judgments without regard for consequences or outcomes. Given a particular set of circumstances, would conducting a stop and frisk be a good universal rule? That might be a good question for a police officer to ask himself or herself in situations where the law's application is unclear. Likewise, virtue ethics would ask whether a stop and frisk is prudent (not excessively cautious or carefree) and just (taking no more or less action than is due) under the circumstances. Training scenarios for police that involve situations in which existing law is vague provide an avenue to apply ethical principles when the law does not provide direction. In this way, ethics can offer some useful guidance in the changing situations faced in police work.

PLACING IN CUSTODY: ARREST AND SEARCH

Consider the case of former Olympic gymnastics star Olga Korbut. In 2002, she was caught for shoplifting $19 worth of groceries from a supermarket in Georgia.[9] You are the police officer called to the scene and recognize the suspect. You have always been a big fan of Olga Korbut, yet you are now faced with charging her with a misdemeanor shoplifting offense of stealing cheese, chocolate syrup, a box of tea, and seasoning mix. On the one hand, you would like her autograph and you would be willing to pay the $19 for the products taken. On the other hand, the law tells you that all persons are equal before the law and should be treated equally. Ethical analysis of this scenario illustrates that under any ethical perspective the outcome should be the same. Aristotle would find that failure to arrest for other considerations is not pursuing a real good (civil peace), and it also violates several moral virtues (it is self-indulgent and unjust). Kant would see a failure to arrest as violating both the categorical and practical imperatives (releasing her would be a bad universal rule, and you are considering using her release as a means toward your own ends—an autograph). Mill would weigh the consequences of your actions—would greater total happiness result from an arrest or a release in this situation? If the personal good here is self-indulgent (an autograph), it would not outweigh the good of enforcing the law uniformly.

Perhaps the most intrusive authority possessed by police is their ability to search citizens and their belongings and to seize their possessions. When a suspect is arrested, a search usually is conducted. Questions often arise regarding the scope of the authority to search, its limits, and the circumstances in which a search may or may not be appropriate. When these questions are raised in a particular case, we again refer back to the Fourth Amendment to the U.S. Constitution.

> The right of people to be secure in their persons, houses, papers, and effects, against unreasonable searches and seizures, shall not be violated, and no warrants shall issue but upon probable cause, supported by oath or affirmation, and particularly describing the place to be searched, and the persons or things to be seized.

Individuals thus are protected against searches and seizures conducted without a warrant specifying "probable cause." This provision goes back to the nation's early years. The ability of British soldiers to enter homes in America and seize property at will played a significant role in the colonists' movement toward independence. Without the protection of the Fourth Amendment, government agents could conduct searches in an arbitrary fashion, so the probable cause standard was developed.

Probable cause has been interpreted to mean a reasonable link between a specific person and a particular crime, given the "totality of circumstances."[10] It is a lower standard of proof than is required to convict at trial (proof beyond a reasonable doubt), but it is higher than the standard required to frisk a suspect (reasonable suspicion). If police have evidence that establishes probable cause, they write it in a sworn statement, a statement supported by "oath or affirmation." When a judge signs this statement, it becomes a warrant. Issuance of a warrant indicates that the judge agrees with the officers' assessment of the evidence. It also means that there is little chance of the evidence being thrown out of court at a later date because the judge approved the warrant prior to the search. Nevertheless, the courts have created exceptions to the warrant requirements over the years in circumstances in which it is not practical for police to obtain a search warrant in advance.

Problems arise (like they do for stop and frisk) in the limitless variety of circumstances that can test the boundaries of the probable cause standard. Consider the case of a bus en route from Florida to Michigan. Three plainclothes police officers were permitted to board the bus during a routine stop, and they displayed their badges and talked individually with passengers regarding their luggage in a "routine" search of illegal weapons and drugs. Passengers were permitted to enter and exit the bus as the officers spoke with the passengers. The officers approached two men and asked to search their luggage. Consent was given, and nothing was found. The officers then asked, "Do you mind if I check your person?" The two men agreed, and a patting down of their pants found packets that are sometimes used to carry drugs. A subsequent search found that both suspects had duct-taped bags of cocaine to their underwear. The men challenged their arrests on drug charges, arguing that their consent to the search was not voluntary. The U.S. Supreme Court held in this case, *U.S. v. Drayton*, that police officers are not required by the Fourth Amendment "to advise bus passengers of their right not to cooperate and to refuse consent to searches."[11] This finding is consistent with earlier decisions that do not require police notification of suspects of their right to refuse consent. It illustrates that the law regarding searches requires significant knowledge of the law of criminal procedure and that this procedure changes regularly in response to continuing court interpretations of the law as it applies to unanticipated circumstances.

Modern technology also poses new challenges in delineating where public space ends and private space (protected by the Fourth Amendment) begins. Based on suspicion that marijuana was being grown inside a home, a government agent used a thermal-imaging device to scan the house to see whether there was a high level of heat emanating from it—which would be consistent with the use of high-intensity lamps often used for growing marijuana indoors. The scan was done from the agent's car across the street, and it found that the walls of the home were substantially warmer than neighboring homes. Using this evidence, a search warrant was obtained, and an indoor marijuana-growing operation was discovered with more than 100 plants. The suspect challenged the use of the thermal-imaging device, claiming it constituted the equivalent of a search of his home without a warrant. The U.S. Supreme Court held that use of a thermal-imaging device aimed at a private home from a public street constitutes a search within the meaning of the Fourth Amendment. Therefore, the use of the imaging device without a warrant is unlawful under the Fourth Amendment because it involves obtaining, using sense-enhancing technology not in general public use, information about the interior of a home that could not otherwise have been obtained without physical intrusion into a constitutionally protected area (inside the house).[12] As technology improves, it is clear that there will be more cases attempting to draw the distinction between public space open to surveillance and searches and private spaces protected by the Fourth Amendment.

As these cases illustrate, legal rules alone are insufficient to guide police and inform the public on issues of search and seizure. No law can account for the many variations in circumstances that might occur. Ethics provide a useful framework to assess situations individually where the reach of the law is unclear. Ethics might also be a useful tool for judges who must make judgments in determining the application of the law. As society continues to change, the problems in balancing police authority with the rights of citizens are likely to become more difficult.

Consider the case of an unsolved murder in a small town on Cape Cod, Massachusetts. After 3 years, police had been unable to solve the murder of a female freelance writer, so, in an unusual move, police requested DNA samples from every man in the town (to attempt to match their DNA with semen found at the crime scene). The police sergeant said, "We're trying to find that person who has something to hide," and although the request for DNA is "voluntary," police say they will pay close attention to those of the 800 men in the town who refuse to provide a sample.[13] Although many residents cooperated, a number have not, making comments such as "I think it's outrageous," and "They're usurping my civil rights," or "It sounds like Stalin's secret police."[14]

Submitting to this general police request for DNA constitutes a "seizure" under law (because the samples are potential evidence in a criminal case), and although the courts have not yet ruled on the legality of this approach, ethics offer important guiding principles. The request for DNA samples has been defended on utilitarian grounds that potentially solving a murder contributes more to the total happiness than the inconvenience of providing a DNA sample. However, utility requires that consequences beyond the current case also be considered. There are many unsolved crimes in the United States, so why not take DNA samples from everyone to rule them out as potential suspects on a routine basis? Are there not limits to such requests that would make them undesirable? Consideration of the impact of more general testing must also be weighed objectively against the potential solution of a crime. Formalism would frame the question more directly and without regard to consequences, "Is requesting DNA samples from residents of a local community to solve a serious crime a good universal rule?" It is likely that formalism would say no because such a procedure uses people for some other purpose or end. Using large numbers of innocent people (via their DNA samples) in an effort to find a single guilty person (who may or may not be among those sampled) would be seen as violating the practical imperative, according to formalism.

Virtue ethics would look closely at the real good to be achieved (civil peace in this case) and whether it was being sought in accord with the moral virtues (i.e., Is such a general request for DNA samples for purposes of exclusion from a criminal investigation prudent and just? Is it giving people more or less than they are due?). Answers to these ethical questions help us to frame the desirability of this police decision.

As noted earlier, both formalism and virtue ethics provide guidance for individual decisions of search and seizure. Utilitarianism offers a framework to more appropriately assess the impact of a new legal rule that might be applied to a large number of cases—asking whether greater total happiness will be achieved with a new legal rule or whether counterbalancing harm will be caused? The critical thinking exercises at the end of this chapter provide practice in applying ethical principles to situations faced by police.

POLICE CORRUPTION

Forty-four police officers from northern Ohio were arrested on cocaine distribution charges—the largest number of officers ever arrested in a single day in U.S. history. More than 500 convictions resulted from federal investigations of police corruption in only 5 years.[15] Police corruption attracts a great deal of attention from the public. How common is police corruption, and why does it occur?

Every encounter between a police officer and citizen involves a decision. If the behavior is serious enough, the officer will arrest the offender. In the majority of cases, however, the officer has considerable discretion in choosing a course of action. Sometimes police are offered money or other inducements to take no official action or to release a suspect. If a police officer accepts money or favors in exchange for a specific legal duty, he or she has committed an act of corruption.

There are three forms of police corruption: nonfeasance, misfeasance, and malfeasance. **Nonfeasance** involves failure to perform a legal duty, **misfeasance** is failure to perform a legal duty in a proper manner, and **malfeasance** is commission of an illegal act. For example, an officer who sees a car swerving dangerously down the road can legitimately pull its driver over. If the driver hands the officer his license with a $50 bill clipped to it, and the officer takes it, does not write a ticket, and proceeds to search the driver by tearing off his clothes, the officer commits nonfeasance (in failing to write a ticket for a serious traffic violation), misfeasance (in conducting a search improperly), and malfeasance (in accepting a bribe).

Malfeasance is a form of corruption, whereas nonfeasance and misfeasance do not always constitute corruption. Many police departments set enforcement priorities and ignore petty offenses in favor of serious crimes. Under these circumstances, nonfeasance in certain situations represents department policy rather than an individual failure to perform a legal duty. Likewise, misfeasance is not always considered corruption. An officer's search in violation of legal rules may reflect improper understanding of the law rather than a willful attempt to circumvent it.

A general definition of police corruption thus should reflect the possibility of various types of official wrongdoing. **Police corruption** consists of illegal acts or omissions by police officers in the line of duty who, by virtue of their official positions, receive (or intend to receive) any gain for themselves or others. The important elements of this definition are the illegal acts or omissions, the fact that they occur while the officer is on duty, and the intent to receive a reward for these acts. Fundamentally, police corruption is misuse of authority for personal gain.

Explanations of corruption are of three types. Some explanations focus on individual officers, some on departmental problems, and others on problems external to the department.[16]

Individual explanations see the particular officer as the primary problem. If a few "rotten apples" were eliminated, police corruption would disappear according to this view. For example, some officers are seen as having "low moral caliber." They might feel underpaid, unjustly maligned by the public, and unrecognized for good work, which might make them corruptible. Another corrupt officer may misuse authority for selfish ends, thinking, "I might as well make the most of the situation," actively seeking opportunities for illicit payoffs and justifying this activity with a rationalization such as low pay or lack of recognition.[17] The case of Michael Dowd of the New York City Police Department is an example of a "bad apple." Dowd was found to be organizing raids on the apartments of drug dealers to steal cash and narcotics.[18] His behavior was featured in the Mollen Commission's investigation of corruption in New York City during the mid-1990s.

Explanations that focus on the individual officer are popular, but most experts reject the "rotten apples" explanation of corruption because it fails to explain how individual officers become corrupt or why police corruption is so widespread. Nor does it explain differences between departments or within a particular department over time. As one investigator concluded, if corruption is to be explained in terms of a few "bad" people, then some departments must have attracted a disproportionately high number of rotten apples over long periods.[19] Michael Dowd was one of nearly fifty officers who were arrested in New York City on charges of brutality, drug trafficking, extortion, and civil rights violations.[20] Another drawback to the "rotten apple" theory, noted by the Knapp Commission in its investigation of corruption in the New York City Police Department during the 1970s, is that it can become an excuse for command officers to deny that a serious problem exists.[21] This kind of thinking delayed FBI self-policing initiatives. The FBI disciplined 301 employees and fired thirty-two of them for sexual harassment, unprofessional conduct, misuse of their position, or theft of government property. Of those punished, 44 percent had previous recorded rule violations.[22]

A second type of explanation of police corruption is the "departmental" explanation. If corruption cannot be explained in terms of a few bad apples, then the barrel itself must be examined. An example of this approach is the deviant police subculture hypothesis. According to this view, small groups of officers within a department have similar outlooks regarding their commitment to the job and the support they receive from superiors. If these officers feel uncommitted and unsupported, their outlooks and values are reinforced by others in the group, which may lead to cynicism or lack of commitment to the job, thereby inviting corruption.[23] In New Orleans, for example, more than fifty police officers were charged with offenses including rape, assault, drug trafficking, and murder.[24] Group corruption suggests the existence of an organized subculture within the department that condoned illegal behavior.

Another version of this explanation focuses on loyalty and secrecy within the department. A questionnaire administered by William Westley revealed that three-quarters of the officers surveyed would not report their partners if they engaged in a corrupt activity. Moreover, officers would perjure themselves rather than testify against their partners. When he asked respondents for their reasons, Westley found that if the unwritten code of secrecy within the police organization was violated, an officer was regarded as a "stool pigeon," "rat," or "outcast," even though he or she reported illegal behavior.[25]

Departmental explanations have been investigated in several studies, which have shown that certain conditions within a department can be conducive to corruption.[26] As the Pennsylvania Crime Commission found in its investigation of corruption in the Philadelphia Police Department, "Systematic corruption does not occur in a vacuum. Officers succumb to pressures within the department," such as illegal conduct by fellow officers and failure by superiors to take action against "open and widespread violations" of the law and of department policy.[27] The Mollen Commission in New York City found that rather than merely overlooking the illicit behavior of other officers, groups of officers were acting as criminal gangs.[28] In 2000, a major police corruption scandal in the Los Angeles Police Department resulted in more than forty convictions being reversed as a result of planted evidence and false testimony. City officials estimated that civil damages for wrongfully convicted suspects could exceed $125 million.[29] A federal study of drug-related police corruption found a pattern of "small groups of officers who protected and assisted each other in criminal activities."[30]

A third explanation of corruption focuses on factors external to the department, especially government actions that make honest policing difficult. For example, laws prohibiting behaviors such as gambling, personal drug use, and prostitution are difficult to enforce, because there is no complainant except the government (represented by the police). As a result, police are mandated to enforce laws that neither the offender nor the "victim" wishes to have enforced. As a result, "the law enforcement system is placed in the middle of two conflicting demands. On the one hand, it is their job to enforce the law, albeit with discretion; on the other hand, there is considerable disagreement as to whether or not certain particular activities should be declared criminal."[31] In this situation police may "look the other way" or be paid to do so. Also, when arrests are made in gambling, drug, or prostitution cases and the offenders are treated leniently in the courts, it is easier for police to become corrupt because neither the public nor the criminal justice system appears to be serious about enforcing the law.

Another type of externally caused corruption stems from a weak or ineffectual local government. When government is unwilling or unable to oversee or manage its police force, the operation of the department becomes haphazard and corruption often results. In addition, corruption in the local government can spread to the police department through calls for the "protection" of illegal activities. A study of police corruption in three cities found that corruption was made possible by informal systems allowing politicians to influence personnel decisions within the police department. "By determining who will occupy key positions of power within a department, and by making as many members of the . . . department as possible obligated to the politicians, political leaders can impose their own goals on the department—including protection of vice for the financial benefit of the political party in power or of the party leaders themselves."[32]

Other investigators have found that corruption can result from the "political climate" of the city.[33] An example is the case of Chicago, where a new police chief was appointed after the previous chief was forced to resign when it was discovered that he had maintained a close friendship with a convicted felon. The Chicago Police Department faced accusations that police brutality was endemic, and officers had been charged with taking bribes and selling drugs. Despite a pervasive culture of corruption, the police union blamed local politicians for placing political interests above the law.[34] In a similar vein, Philadelphia appointed a new police chief to "improve the performance of a 7,000-officer force that has been troubled over the years by numerous accusations of brutality, graft and . . . ineptitude."[35] Both cities had long histories of political interference in department affairs and higher-than-average incidences of police brutality against citizens and corruption involving the vices.

Can ethics play a role in the extent and prevention of corruption? The most effective prevention strategies are those based on carefully identified causes. If corruption in a particular department involves only a few officers, several control strategies may be appropriate. Examples include close monitoring of complaints against the police to uncover early signs of unethical conduct, making all police hirings and dismissals more visible to serve as examples and deterrents and making sure police officers do not get into debt. Other, longer-term strategies include more exhaustive background checks of recruits, periodic retraining of all police, and

ETHICS CHECKUP
Dirty Harry

Clint Eastwood starred in a series of films during the 1970s and 1980s in which he played a cynical police detective named Harry Callahan. The first of these films was titled *Dirty Harry*, and it contained a sequence in which an unsympathetic criminal kidnapped a 14-year-old girl for ransom. Dirty Harry ultimately catches up to the criminal and shoots him in the leg as he tries to escape. Harry tortures the criminal, standing on the wounded leg, while asking for the location of the kidnapped girl.[36]

Dirty Harry gets the information, but the girl's body (she was already dead) and other evidence were subsequently excluded in court because of the method of the interrogation.

Can you defend Dirty Harry's conduct using any of the three major ethical perspectives?

measures aimed at enhancing professionalism by allowing leaves for study or specialized training. These sorts of strategies are likely to work because they attempt to improve the ethical commitment of individual officers to the ideals and values of a law enforcement career.

If corruption is found to be a result of problems in the department itself, a different set of control strategies would be appropriate. For example, establishing civilian review boards to hear complaints against the department and offer an ethical perspective from outside the department and enhancing career mobility within the department may help prevent hidden corruption. Likewise, procedures to ensure the fair and confidential hearing of personnel matters within the department and to guarantee that promotions are based on qualifications, rather than on patronage, can help prevent political considerations and unethical practices from inhibiting honest police work.

When corruption is the result of external, governmental factors, the most fruitful strategies improve police supervision and decision making. Supervision of officers can be improved by making sure that only qualified police and government officials are given supervisory responsibilities. Ethical conduct must be considered an essential qualification. Political reform through legislation may be needed to eliminate government interference with police department operations. Similarly, decriminalization of minor undesirable behaviors would eliminate opportunities for corruption by removing "victimless" crimes from police jurisdiction.

In its New York City investigation, the Knapp Commission found that the most important source of police corruption was control of the city's gambling, narcotics, loan-sharking, and illegal sex–related enterprises. The next most important source was "legitimate business seeking to ease its way through the maze of City ordinances and regulations."[37] In this case, changes in laws and regulations could have a substantial impact on police corruption. The Knapp Commission noted that "The laws against gambling, prostitution, and the conduct of certain business activities on the Sabbath all contribute to the prevalence of police corruption."[38] One expert concluded that without "a public commitment . . . to realistic vice laws . . . the elimination of police corruption will not occur."[39] The potential impact of police codes of ethics is discussed later in this chapter.

QUESTIONING: INTERROGATION OF SUSPECTS

Most Americans are familiar from television and movies that police must inform suspects of their legal rights before they are interrogated. This procedure was the result of the *Miranda* case in 1966, which held that a suspect's constitutional rights under the Fifth Amendment (protection against self-incrimination) are jeopardized when he or she is interrogated in police custody. Thus, the *Miranda* warning was invented.[40]

More recently, Congress enacted a law that challenged the *Miranda* ruling, claiming that admissibility of statements should be decided solely on whether they are voluntary—regardless of whether the *Miranda* warning was given by police. The U.S. Supreme Court ruled in *Dickerson v. United States* that as a constitutional decision of the Court, *Miranda* "may not be in effect overruled by an Act of Congress." Although Congress can modify or eliminate legal rules that are not constitutionally required, it cannot supercede U.S. Supreme Court decisions that apply and interpret the U.S. Constitution. In addition, the Court held that "Miranda has become embedded in routine police practice to the point where the warnings have become part of our national culture."[41] The Court appears to be correct in its assessment as both leading police administrators and the public favor the *Miranda* rule.[42] A Gallup poll found that 94 percent of U.S. citizens believe the police should be required to inform arrested persons of their constitutional rights.[43]

Nevertheless, the U.S. Supreme Court has decided many cases that provide exceptions to the *Miranda* rule. In *South Dakota v. Neville*, for example, the Court held that it is not "fundamentally unfair" to use a defendant's refusal to take a blood alcohol test as evidence of guilt. This refusal, if used as evidence, does not violate the protection against self-incrimination.[44] In *Oregon v. Bradshaw*, the Court held that if the accused waives the right to counsel, but then initiates further conversation, his or her statements may be used as evidence.[45] Roadside questioning of a motorist detained in a routine traffic stop was determined not to constitute a "custodial interrogation" for the purposes of *Miranda*, so the warning is not required in those situations.[46] In another case, police arrested a man for purchasing stolen firearms but questioned him about a murder. The Supreme Court held that "mere silence by law enforcement officials as to the subject matter of an interrogation is not 'trickery' sufficient to invalidate a suspect's waiver of *Miranda* rights." The constitutionality of the interrogation was upheld.[47]

These cases characterize the general direction of U.S. Supreme Court decisions, which has given police greater latitude to stray from the strict language of the original *Miranda* finding.[48] A host of conditions and exceptions to the *Miranda* rule has created uncertainty in its application. Uncertainty regarding confessions has prompted many police departments to videotape interrogations and confessions. Videotaping provides an objective record of the interrogation that can be used in responding to challenges from defense attorneys and in proving that confessions are voluntary. One study estimates that more than 60 percent of large police agencies in the United States videotape interrogations or confessions in at least some types of cases. About 85 percent of police departments surveyed believe that videotaping improves the quality of interrogations.[49]

So how can ethics be of assistance in the interrogation of crime suspects? Similar to the cases involving searches and seizures, the unending maze of court cases involving interrogations illustrate that the law in this area is difficult to apply in practice. There are infinite variations of scenarios that police and suspects might face, and law simply cannot foresee them all. Ethics offers the police objective rules to think through systematically scenarios where legal rules are not clear or do not yet apply.

Consider the case of a 16-year-old student in Arizona who was involved in a fight at school. His mother arrived after police questioned her son about the fight but then she had to leave for about 20 minutes to pick up a young daughter. She told the assistant principal that she wanted to be present for any further questioning. The assistant principal agreed that the mother or, if she did not return in time, an administrator would sit in on the interview. While the mother was gone, police discovered a sawed-off shotgun in the trunk of another student's car that was apparently connected to her son. When the mother returned, three officers were questioning him behind closed doors about the gun, and an officer refused to let her enter. Police said the boy had voluntarily waived his

Miranda rights against self-incrimination. Should police have let the mother be present during the son's interrogation?

Existing law did not address this situation, so police had to make a decision without a specific legal rule to guide them. Considering ethical principles, it would be clear that excluding the parent is a bad universal rule (formalism), the potential negative conclusions that might be drawn about the voluntariness of an interrogation involving three police officers and a 16-year-old might be severe (utilitarianism), and it is questionable whether such a decision is in accord with the moral virtues (especially temperance, prudence, and justice). Looking at the situation in ethical terms, therefore, may have helped the police see that their decision lacked an ethical basis.

As it turned out, the Arizona Supreme Court eventually heard this case and held that having a parent present could have helped authorities satisfy any question that the confession was voluntary because it makes it more likely that the juvenile was not coerced and understood the consequences of giving up the right to remain silent. According to the court, police may be justified in keeping a parent out in some circumstances if time is critical or when a parent is also a suspect or is threatening or disruptive. But when police do not have a good reason for excluding a parent, "a strong inference arises that the state excluded the parent in order to maintain a coercive atmosphere or to discourage the juvenile from fully understanding and exercising his constitutional rights."[50] The court was also troubled that there was no record that the boy received an age-appropriate version of the *Miranda* warning, there existed no signed acknowledgment of his waiver, and the boy's statements comprised virtually all of the evidence against him. Therefore, the police decision to exclude the mother was held to violate the boy's constitutional rights, and his conviction was overturned. It can be seen that the application of ethical principles may have prevented a reversed conviction in this situation where the law was not clear. Police officers conversant with the major ethical perspectives will be able to assess a given situation in ethical terms, which provides useful guidance for morally permissible conduct especially when legal rules are unclear or lacking.

LIES IN COURT

Police often play a pivotal role in court in testifying about the circumstances of the arrest and their version of the events surrounding a crime. Police have been accused of sometimes lying in court to buttress the cases against a suspect. In a Baltimore case, police obtained a search warrant to look for drugs and weapons in a car, but defense attorneys learned subsequently that the car was actually searched 3 hours before the search warrant was obtained—fraudulently using the evidence found from the illegal search to justify a search warrant application.[51]

The most common incidents of lying by police occur when it is seen as necessary to perform legitimate police actions, such as undercover operations where police must lie to maintain their "cover." Similarly, lying is often necessary in making arrests for prostitution, narcotics sales, and other vice crimes. Police are sometimes encouraged to lie during interrogations. For example, a suspect might be told that his accomplice has confessed (even though he has not) in order to secure a confession from the suspect.[52] When lies are unchecked, further lies are likely. As Skolnick and Leo observe, "When police are permitted to lie in the interrogation context, why should they refrain from lying to judges when applying for warrants, from violating internal police organization rules against lying, or from lying in the courtroom?"[53]

A survey of defense attorneys found that most believed that perjury by police in court occurs frequently.[54] Police officers have also reported that their fellow officers lie in court.[55] The rationale offered is that it is done because they know the offender is guilty. But this is the purpose of the adjudication process, and unchecked lies by police subvert the system.[56] Prosecutors, defense attorneys, judges, and superior police officers have a duty to check for credibility in search warrant applications, interrogations of suspects, and in court testimony especially when statements appear questionable under the circumstances.

Lying is sometimes considered "good police work" because it obtains the desired result, but it still is lying and, therefore, must be considered in ethical terms. For example, undercover "sting" operations necessarily involve lies in the effort to catch criminals, and some argue this deception may have the unanticipated consequence of tempting police to be untruthful in their court testimony as well.[57] Formalism sees all lies as unethical, whereas utilitarianism would weigh the harm to the suspect against the good produced by the evidence obtained from the lie. Virtue ethics asks the purpose of the lie to see if its objective and method was accomplished in accord with the moral virtues (especially justice, prudence, and the nature of the untruthful statement in seeking a real good). Therefore, both utilitarianism and virtue ethics would consider each situation individually to establish whether the lie was morally permissible.

CODES OF ETHICS

Codes of ethics for police have been developed in recent years as a mechanism to enhance police professionalism and reduce corruption. The International Association of Chiefs of Police (IACP) adopted a code of ethics in 1987. This was predated by the United Nations (UN) Code of Conduct for Law Enforcement Officials in 1979.[58] The eight articles of the UN code are as follows.

UN Code of Conduct for Law Enforcement Officials

1. Law enforcement officials shall at all times fulfill the duty imposed upon them by law, by serving the community and by protecting all persons against illegal acts, consistent with the high degree of responsibility required by their profession.
2. In the performance of their duty, law enforcement officials shall respect and protect human dignity and maintain and uphold the human rights of all persons.
3. Law enforcement officials may use force only when strictly necessary and to the extent required for the performance of their duty.
4. Matters of a confidential nature in the possession of law enforcement officials shall be kept confidential, unless the performance of duty or the needs of justice strictly require otherwise.
5. No law enforcement official may inflict, instigate or tolerate any act of torture or other cruel, inhuman or degrading treatment or punishment, nor may any law enforcement official invoke superior orders or exceptional circumstances such as a state of war or a threat of war, a threat to national security, internal political instability or any other public emergency as a justification of torture or other cruel, inhuman or degrading treatment or punishment.
6. Law enforcement officials shall ensure the full protection of the health of persons in their custody and, in particular, shall take immediate action to secure medical attention whenever required.
7. Law enforcement officials shall not commit any act of corruption. They shall also rigorously oppose and combat all such acts.
8. Law enforcement officials shall respect the law and the present Code. They shall also, to the best of their capability, prevent and rigorously oppose any violations of them. Law enforcement officials who have reason to believe that a violation of the present Code has occurred or is about to occur shall report the matter to their superior authorities and, where necessary, to other appropriate authorities or organs vested with reviewing or remedial power.

The UN code is an example of the mixture of kinds of statements found in codes of ethics. Codes of ethics for police and other professions vary widely and their contents often combine general principles with requirements. A complete version of the UN Code of Conduct as well as the ethics or conduct codes of other law enforcement and governmental organizations can be found in the Appendices at the end of the book.

Types of Statements Found in Codes of Ethics

- Statements of principles (aspirations, ideals)
- Statements of requirements (mandatory rules of conduct)

The UN code illustrates a mixture of these two types of statements. Article 1 reads like a requirement or mandatory rule ("shall at all times fulfill the duty"), whereas Article 2 is a more general principle or ideal ("shall respect and protect human dignity"). Read each of the other articles carefully to determine whether they are a principle or a requirement. Mixing these two kinds of statements in a single code can cause problems regarding expectations of the code and expectations of conduct from police officers.[59] Mandatory rules or requirements are often read by police and their supervisors like statutes to determine precisely whether conduct fits under the rule. This kind of judicial interpretation often defeats the purpose of a code of ethics. If you are looking for loopholes or very precise shades of meaning, a code of ethics should not be involved. Instead, a useful code of ethics should rely more on *principles* that officers should consider in making decisions. **Codes of ethics** are designed to promote thoughtful and professional conduct, not account for every possible situation a police officer might face.

Violations of codes of ethics can be dealt with in one of two ways: rewards for exemplary behavior and penalties for conduct that violates the code. Police work has not professionalized in the same way as law, nursing, accounting, and other professions have in that there is generally no lateral career mobility between departments because of lack of uniformity in education and training requirements throughout the United States. Uniformity in education and training requirements for other professions have made them more desirable careers, promoting loyalty to the *profession* rather than loyalty only to one's *employer*. Stronger allegiance to ethics is encouraged when individuals act and are treated as professionals rather than as mere employees.

Police work is a difficult task. As this chapter has made clear, police are faced with situations that cannot be anticipated by laws, so they are often left to make decisions without clear guidance—decisions that sometimes are later reviewed by courts. Police training places great emphasis on learning legal rules and court mandates that continually change, while offering generally only a few hours of ethics training on principles for decision making that never change. Ethics offers a practical way to assess scenarios objectively in situations where legal rules have unclear application, offering consistent principles to guide police conduct that impact real goods, such as liberty and civil peace.

ETHICS IN BOOKS

Ethics is everywhere, even in the books we read, which sometimes are written without ethics specifically in mind. Here is a summary of a book that looks at action that affect others, followed by questions that ask you to reflect on the ethical connections.

ON BULLSHIT

Harry G. Frankfurt
(Princeton University Press, 2005)

Harry Frankfurt, a moral philosopher and professor emeritus at Princeton University, opens his book with the statement, "One of the most salient features of our culture is that there is so much bullshit. Everyone knows this." His concern is that we are not clear about what it really is, why there is so much of it, and all its consequences. The serious, and ironically comic, formulation of this situation by the author resulted in tremendous popularity of this book and his appearances even on comedy shows.

The book does not consider the rhetorical uses of bullshit but focuses on "the realms of advertising and of public relations, and the nowadays closely related realm of politics, (which) are replete with instances of bullshit so unmitigated that they can serve among the most indisputable and classic paradigms of the concept." Frankfurt finds that bullshitting "involves a kind of bluff," and that "lying and bluffing are both modes of misrepresentation or deception." The difference is that lying involves clear falsity, whereas bluffing and bullshitting involve fakery or phoniness. For example, a counterfeited item often has the appearance of an exact copy, but the difference lies in how it was made.

The author quotes a novel in which a father tells his son, "Never tell a lie when you can bullshit your way through." This statement points to the subtle difference between lying and bullshitting. Lying misrepresents the speaker's beliefs about the state of affairs or about the state of affairs themselves, whereas the bullshitter's statements are not necessarily false, but the speaker misrepresents what he is up to ("misrepresentational intent"). So both the liar and bullshitter falsely claim to communicate the truth, but the liar is trying to deceive us on the facts, while the bullshitter does not care about the truthfulness of his statements. As Frankfurter summarizes, "It is impossible for someone to lie unless he thinks he knows the truth. Producing bullshit requires no such conviction."

Why is there so much bullshit? Frankfurter concludes that, "Bullshit is unavoidable whenever circumstances require someone to talk without knowing what he is talking about," where a person has obligations or opportunities "to speak extensively about matters of which they are to some degree ignorant." This situation is aggravated by citizens who feel it is their responsibility to have opinions about everything, when of course no one can have informed opinions about everything, thus producing large volumes of bullshit.

QUESTIONS

1. Many corporate and governmental scandals in recent years have involved lying about facts in an effort to hide the truth. Is this different from bullshitting, according to Frankfurt, and what is the difference in ethical terms?
2. Why do you believe that our general attitude toward bullshit is generally less negative that our attitude toward lying? Is this morally justified?

ETHICS IN THE MOVIES

Movies seek to entertain and inform the audience about a story, incident, or person. Many good movies also hit upon important ethical themes in making significant decisions that affect the lives of others. Read the movie summary here (and watch the movie if you haven't already), and answer the questions to make the ethical connections.

MINORITY REPORT

Steven Spielberg, Director
(2002)

Minority Report is set in the year 2054, and John Anderton (Tom Cruise) is chief of the Department of Pre-Crime in Washington, D.C. There has not been a murder there in 6 years, because of an operation Anderton supervises where three pre-cognitive humans ("pre-cogs") drift in a flotation tank and have their brain waves tapped by computers. These brain waves can pick up thoughts of premeditated murders, so the police can be warned and arrest the would-be perpetrators before they can kill (hence the "Department of Pre-Crime"). Of course, it is not as easy as this, because the pre-cogs can provide only the time and date of the murder, the murderer's name, and the victim's name—the other facts can be learned only by clues derived from the various images generated by the pre-cogs around the time of murder. The film is based on a short story by Philip K. Dick.

The pre-crime police strategy is going to expand nationwide, and there is personal and bureaucratic jealousy toward Anderton and the pre-crime unit. The movie focuses on a rare disagreement among the "pre-cogs" over a pending murder, and one of the pre-cogs apparently files a minority report disagreeing with the others. Normally, the minority report is disregarded, but the twist is that Anderton himself becomes a target for arrest as a predicted killer, and he is apparently warned of this by one of the pre-cogs.

Anderton then is chased by police, assisted by one of the pre-cogs named Agatha (Samatha Morton), and the futuristic police pursuit and search is interesting and compelling. For example, everyone is subject to retina scans, so Anderton has to get an eye transplant to hide his identity while being pursued. The story has several twists, and it raises important issues about the certainty of knowledge and how knowledge should be used.

QUESTIONS

1. If we were able to predict premeditated murders in the future by somehow scanning the minds of citizens, is this enough evidence to apprehend and take legal action against them? What would the major ethical perspectives say?
2. The accurate prediction of criminal behavior is not yet possible, but profiles are sometimes used by police for targeting suspects. Under what circumstances is the use of a profile to take police action morally permissible?

Discussion Question

Why are legal rules alone insufficient to guide police actions in the area of searches and seizures?

Critical Thinking Exercises

All ethical decisions affect others (by definition) and, as Aristotle points out, ethical decision making is achieved consistently only through practice. Given the outline of virtue ethics provided by Aristotle (i.e., seeking the real

goods via the moral virtues), evaluate the moral permissibility of the conduct in question in each scenario.

Important note on method: *Critical thinking requires the ability to evaluate viewpoints, facts, and behaviors objective-*

ly to assess information or methods of argumentation to establish the true worth or merit of an act or course of conduct. Please evaluate these scenarios, first analyzing pros and cons of alternate views, before you come to a conclusion. Do not draw a conclusion first, and then try to find facts to support it—this frequently leads to narrow (and incorrect) thinking.

To properly evaluate the moral permissibility of a course of action using critical thinking skills

1. *Begin with an open mind (no preconceptions!),*
2. *Isolate and evaluate the relevant facts on both sides,*
3. *Identify the precise moral question to be answered, and*
4. *Apply ethical principles to the moral question based on an objective evaluation of the facts, only then drawing a conclusion.*

6.1 Suicide by Cop

A 19-year-old college student and problem gambler was pulled over by police on the Long Island Expressway for driving erratically. He pulled out a toy handgun, pointed it at the officer, and was shot and killed. In a separate incident, a 45-year-old cancer patient was shot by Jersey City police when he entered a pizza shop in which two officers were eating and pulled a gun on them.

These incidents are difficult to explain because they do not appear to be random acts of passion, rage, or felony. As one officer put it, "Why would you point a gun at a police officer," unless you wanted to be shot?

Some experts believe incidents such as these are forms of "suicide by cop," where individuals force police to shoot at them in situations that normally would not involve threat or force. Studies have found that many of these shooting victims are white males in their 20s with a history of alcohol or drug abuse—a profile similar to suicide victims in general who are prone to suffer from depression, hopelessness, and deteriorating personal relationships.

The use of police to carry out a death wish is difficult to explain, but suicide is often difficult for a person to carry out, and using a police officer removes the burden from the individual. Also life insurance policies do not pay for suicide victims and most religions forbid suicide, making it more problematic for a person to consider. There are no statistics, but it is estimated that up to 10 percent of fatal police shootings are provoked by those actively seeking to die.[60]

- Evaluate the moral permissibility of "suicide by cop."
- To what extent is a police officer morally obligated to assess whether a person he or she shoots actually wants to be killed?

6.2 Abusive Speed Traps

Many motorists have stories of being stopped with out-of-state license plates in speed traps by a small-town police officer. It has been alleged that such speed traps are designed to raise revenue for the town or the police department rather than to protect public safety.

The problem has become so pervasive in Georgia that the legislature passed a law that restricts revenue from speeding tickets to a maximum of 40 percent of the police department's budget. The law is specifically designed to stop police departments from "using radar guns as fund-raising tools instead of safety devices."[61]

Opponents of such a restriction believe that funds are needed to support local police in small jurisdictions where the only alternative to ticketing would be tax increases. They also argue that strict traffic enforcement helps keep crime rates low.

You are the police chief in a small rural police department that sorely needs more funds to reach what you believe is a more reasonable police presence. Obtaining a local tax increase to support your efforts appears impossible.

- Is it morally permissible to assign your officers to set speed traps aimed primarily at out-of-state automobiles?
- Is it morally permissible to set speed traps for the sole purpose of raising needed revenue?

6.3 The Informants among Us

Police corruption in the United States is a much smaller problem compared to that in other nations where entire police forces may be corrupt. Nevertheless, instances of corruption in U.S. policing do occur and often have serious consequences. An important issue is the treatment of those who expose this corruption.

Those who blow the whistle, or become confidential informants for the FBI or other agencies, are often ostracized by their peers. In a New Jersey case, a local police officer contacted the FBI and wore a body wire for 18 months to tape bribery and corrupt activities (under the supervision of the FBI). It resulted in the largest police corruption investigation in the history of the state. A total of thirty-four people were indicted, including the police chief. The charges included taking bribes to protect prostitution, illegal gambling, and liquor sales, and extorting money from towing companies. Most of those indicted pleaded guilty.

The local officer who gathered the evidence was threatened by fellow officers, moved six times out of fear for his safety, and was fired from his job as a police officer. The department claimed that he was fired as a result of disciplinary charges, and the officer is suing to try to get his job back.[62]

- How ought coworkers treat those who inform authorities of illegal activities in the agency? Examine this question from the perspective of virtue ethics, formalism, and utilitarianism.
- In response to this case, former New York City police officer Frank Serpico said, "It's always worth it to be at peace with yourself." Does this imply reasoning from a particular school of ethical thought?

6.4 FBI Spy Powers Challenged

Congress first authorized FBI agents in 1986 to obtain electronic records without approval from a judge using "national security letters" to acquire e-mails, telephone, travel records, and financial information such as credit and bank transactions. In 2001, the Patriot Act eliminated any requirement that the electronic records belong to the suspected person, so an innocent person's records can be obtained if FBI field agents consider them merely relevant to an ongoing terrorism or spying investigation.

The Inspector General (IG) of the Justice Department conducted a review, authorized by Congress, that concluded the number of national security letters requested by the FBI skyrocketed after the Patriot Act became law in 2001. The IG found more than 700 cases in which FBI agents obtained telephone records through "exigent letters," which asserted that grand jury subpoenas had been requested for the data, when in fact such subpoenas had never been sought.

The FBI's failure to establish sufficient controls or oversight for collecting the information constituted "serious and unacceptable" failures, the IG told the committee. "We believe the misuses and the problems we found generally were the product of mistakes, carelessness, confusion, sloppiness, lack of training, lack of adequate guidance, and lack of adequate oversight."

In a review of headquarters files and a sampling of just four of the FBI's fifty-six field offices, the IG found forty-eight violations of law or presidential directives during between 2003 and 2005, including failure to get proper authorization, making improper requests, and unauthorized collection of telephone or Internet e-mail records, suggesting that "a significant number of . . . violations throughout the FBI have not been identified or reported."[63]

- Given the existence of many violations of these investigative powers in cases involving electronic records, is it morally permissible to eliminate these powers?
- Taken from another perspective, evaluate the moral permissibility of continuing these investigative powers in light of the findings of the Inspector General.

6.5 Internet Sex Stings

The use of undercover police working anonymously online (as bait in Internet chats) has become routine in some locations in order to trap those looking for underage sex online. The Indiana Court of Appeals ruled (2-1), however, that attempted sexual misconduct with a minor, a Class B felony, requires that the victim actually be a minor (and that an undercover officer doesn't count).

The Court used the same reasoning to reverse a conviction for sexual misconduct, leaving only a child solicitation conviction intact. The offender, age 48, was arrested after he showed up at an Indianapolis apartment with rope and condoms in his pockets after explicit online chats with an undercover investigator posing as 15-year-old "Samantha."

The dissenting judge in this 2-1 appellate case argued that all charges should stand against the suspect. "He did all he believed was necessary to complete the offense of sexual misconduct of a minor, and he failed to complete the offense only because it was not possible under the circumstances."[64]

Now prosecutors must rely on charges of child solicitation, a Class C felony charge that applies under Indiana law as long as the defendant merely believes the intended victim is at least 14 and younger than 16. The Class C felony carries a potential sentence of 2–8 years in prison, far short of the maximum 20-year penalty for attempted sexual misconduct.

Prosecutors argue that online stings protect teenagers by snaring likely perpetrators, though judges often give reduced sentences or even probation because there are no actual victims.

- Evaluate the moral permissibility of the Court's decision to limit the scope of online liability in undercover cases of sexual solicitation of minors.

Key Concepts

Notes

1. Irene Jung Fiala, "Anything New? The Racial Profiling of Terrorists," *Criminal Justice Studies*, vol. 16 (2003), p. 53; Jerry Berman and Lara Flynt, "Intelligence Oversight and Control for the Challenge of Terrorism," *Criminal Justice Ethics*, vol. 22 (Winter/Spring 2003), p. 2.

2. Philip Shenon, "Two Studies Cite Confusion on Terrorism," *The New York Times* (August 21, 2003), p. A3.

3. *Terry v. Ohio*, 88 S.Ct. 1868 (1968). (See also the related cases of *Sibron v. New York*, 88 S.Ct. 1902 [1968] and *Peters v. New York*, 88 S.Ct. 1904 [1968].)

4. *Saldal v. Cook County*, 113 S.Ct. 538 (1992).

5. *Alabama v. White*, 496 U.S. 325 (1990); see also *Ornelas v. United States*, 116 S.Ct. 1657 (1996).

6. Lawrence A. Greenfeld, Patrick A. Langan, and Steven K. Smith, *Police Use of Force: Collection of National Data* (Washington, DC.: Bureau of Justice Statistics, 1997), p. 13.

7. *Illinois v. Wardlow*, 120 S.Ct. 673 (2000).

8. *Minnesota v. Dickerson*, 113 S.Ct. 2130 (1993).

9. "Olympic Gymnastics Great," *USA Today* (February 2, 2002), p. 3.

10. *Illinois v. Gates*, 426 U.S. 318 (1982).

11. *U.S. v. Drayton*, 122 S.Ct. 2105 (2002); see Thomas W. Hughes, "Bus Interdiction by the Police: United States v. Drayton," *American Journal of Criminal Justice*, vol. 27 (Spring 2003), p. 197.

12. *Kyllo v. United States*, 121 S.Ct. 2038 (2001).

13. Pam Belluck, "To Try to Net Killer, Police Ask a Small Town's Men for DNA," *The New York Times* (January 10, 2005), p. A5; "DNA Dragnets," *USA Today* (January 19, 2005), p. 10A.

14. Belluck, "DNA Dragnets." p. 10A.

15. Warren Cohen, "The Feds Make a Cop Drug Bust," *U.S. News & World Report* (February 2, 1998), p. 36; Kevin Johnson, "Forty-Two Law Officers Arrested in Sting," *USA Today* (January 22, 1998), p. 3.

16. Mark Pogrebin and Burton Atkins, "Probable Causes for Police Corruption: Some Theories," *Journal of Criminal Justice*, vol. 4 (1976), pp. 9–16; Samuel Walker, *The Police in America* (New York, NY: McGraw-Hill, 1983).

17. Herman Goldstein, *Policing in a Free Society* (Cambridge, MA: Ballinger, 1977); Virgil Peterson, "The Chicago Police Scandals," *Atlantic* (October 1960), pp. 58–64; Howard S. Cohen and Michael Feldberg, *Power and Restraint: The Moral Dimension of Police Work* (New York: Praeger, 1991); Edwin J. Delattre, *Character and Cops: Ethics in Policing*, 2nd ed. (Washington, DC.: AEI Press, 1994); Steve Herbert, "Morality in Law Enforcement: Chasing 'Bad Guys' with the Los Angeles Police Department," *Law and Society Review*, vol. 30 (1996), pp. 799–817.

18. Gordon Witkin, "When the Bad Guys Are Cops," *Newsweek* (September 11, 1995), pp. 20–22; Mike McAlary, *Good Cop Bad Cop* (New York, NY: Pocket Books, 1994).

19. Walker, *The Police in America*, p. 181.

20. Witkin, "When the Bad Guys Are Cops." pp. 20–22; Tom Morganthau, "Why Good Cops Go Bad," *Newsweek* (December 19, 1994), p. 34.

21. Knapp Commission, *Report on Police Corruption* (New York, NY: George Braziller, 1972), p. 6.

22. Michael Hedges, "Lawbreakers among Law Enforcers," *Richmond Times-Dispatch* (August 10, 1999), p. 3.

23. John Kleinig, *The Ethics of Policing* (New York, NY: Cambridge University Press, 1996).

24. Witkin, "When the Bad Guys Are Cops." p. 22.

25. William A. Westley, *Violence and the Police* (Cambridge, MA: MIT Press, 1970); John Diedrich, "Wall of Silence Not Breaking: Police May Protect Their Own before They Testify against Them," *Milwaukee Journal Sentinel* (February 12, 2005), p. 3.

26. Albert J. Reiss, *Police and the Public* (New Haven, CT: Yale University Press, 1971); J. Roebuck and T. Barker, "A Typology of Police Corruption," *Social Problems*, vol. 21 (1974), pp. 423–427; E. Stoddard, "The Informal Code of Police Deviancy: Group Approach to Blue Coat Crime," *Journal of Criminal Law, Criminology, and Police Science*, vol. 59 (1968), pp. 201–213.

27. Pennsylvania Crime Commission, *Report on Police Corruption and the Quality of Law Enforcement in Philadelphia* (St. Davids, PA: Pennsylvania Crime Commission, 1974).

28. Morganthau, "Why Good Cops Go Bad." p. 34.

29. James Sterngold, "Police Corruption Inquiry Expands in Los Angeles," *The New York Times* (February 11, 2000), p. A16; "L.A. Mayor: Use Tobacco Funds to Pay Police Suits," *USA Today* (February 18, 2000), p. 3.

30. U.S. Comptroller General, *Informationon Drug-Related Police Corruption* (Washington, DC: U.S. General Accounting Office, 1998).

31. William Chambliss and R. Seidman, *Law, Order and Power* (Reading, MA: Addison-Wesley, 1971), p. 490.
32. Lawrence W. Sherman, *Scandal and Reform: Controlling Police Corruption* (Berkeley, CA: University of California Press, 1978), p. 35.
33. John A. Gardiner, *The Politics of Corruption: Organized Crime in an American City* (New York, NY: Russell Sage, 1970); Chambliss and Seidman, *Law, Order and Power*; Knapp Commission, *Report on Police Corruption.*
34. Dirk Johnson, "Popular Detective Will Head Chicago Police," *The New York Times* (February 19, 1998), p. 2.
35. B. Drummond Ayres Jr., "Former New York Official to Lead Philadelphia Police," *The New York Times* (February 19, 1998), p. 16.
36. Carl B. Klockars, "The Dirty Harry Problem," *The Annals of the American Academy of Political and Social Science*, vol. 452 (November 1980), pp. 33–47.
37. Knapp Commission, *Report on Police Corruption*, p. 68.
38. Ibid., p. 18.
39. Edward A. Malloy, *The Ethics of Law Enforcement and Criminal Punishment* (Lanham, MD: University Press of America, 1982), p. 45.
40. *Miranda v. Arizona*, 86 S.Ct. 1602 (1966).
41. *Dickerson v. United States*, 120 S.Ct. 2326 (2000).
42. William J. Bratton, "Miranda Protects the Public," *APBnews.com* (April 19, 2000).
43. "Supreme Court's Miranda Decision: The Public's Opinion," *Gallup News Service* (June 27, 2000).
44. *South Dakata v. Neville*, 103 S.Ct. 916 (1983).
45. *Oregon v. Bradshaw*, 103 S.Ct. 2830 (1983).
46. *Berkimer v. McCarty*, 104 S.Ct. 3138 (1984).
47. *Colorado v. Spring*, 107 S.Ct. 851 (1987); see also *Clabourne v. Lewis*, 64 F.3d 1373 (1995).
48. *Oregon v. Elstad*, 105 S.Ct. 1285 (1985); *Moran v. Burbine*, 106 S.Ct. 1135 (1986); *Colorado v. Spring*, 107 S.Ct. 851 (1987); *Illinois v. Perkins*, 111 S.Ct. 1121 (1990); *New York v. Quarles*, 104 S.Ct. 2626 (1984).
49. William A. Geller, *Videotaping Interrogations and Confessions* (Washington, DC.: National Institute of Justice, 1993).
50. Paul Davenport, "Conviction Overturned Because Parent Kept Out of Interrogation," *The Associated Press State and Local Wire* (April 23, 2004), p. 3.
51. Gregory Kane, "Getting to the Truth on Existence of Police 'Liars List,' " *The Baltimore Sun* (October 7, 2004).
52. Thomas Barker and David L. Carter, *Police Deviance*, 3rd ed. (Cincinnati, OH: Anderson Publishing, 1998).
53. Jerome H. Skolnick and Richard A. Leo, "The Ethics of Deceptive Interrogation," *Criminal Justice Ethics*, vol. 2 (Winter/Spring 1992), pp. 3–12.
54. N. G. Kittel, "Police Perjury: Criminal Defense Attorneys' Perspective," *American Journal of Criminal Justice*, vol. 11 (Fall 1986), pp. 11–22; Alan Dershowitz, *The Best Defense* (New York, NY: Vintage Books, 1983).
55. Thomas Barker, "An Empirical Study of Police Deviance Other Than Corruption," *Journal of Police Science and Administration*, vol. 6 (1978), pp. 264–272; Jessica Fargen and Peter Gelzinis, "Thin Blue Line: BPD to Cops: Tell Truth or Face Consequences," *Boston Herald* (September 27, 2009).
56. Larry Cunningham, "Taking on Testilying: The Prosecutor's Response to In-Court Police Deception," *Criminal Justice Ethics*, vol. 18 (Winter/Spring 1999), pp. 26–40.
57. Skolnick and Leo, *Criminal Justice Ethics,* p. 12.
58. Adopted by UN General Assembly resolution 34/169 (December 17, 1979).
59. Michael Davis, "Do Cops Really Need a Code of Ethics?" *Criminal Justice Ethics*, vol. 10 (Summer/Fall 1991), pp. 14–28.
60. Alan Feuer, "Drawing a Bead on a Baffling Endgame: Suicide by Cop," *The New York Times* (June 21, 1998), p. B1; Zlati Meyer, "Suicide-by-Cop Cases are Growing," *The Free Press* (December 13, 2009); Kris Mohandie, J. Reid Meloy, and Peter I. Collins, "Suicide by Cop among Officer-Involved Shooting Cases," *Journal of Forensic Sciences*, vol. 54 (March 2009), pp. 456–462.
61. Krista Reese, "What, No Speed Traps? Georgia Acts to Curb Abusive Traffic Stops," *U.S. News & World Report* (March 15, 1999), p. 32.
62. Alan Feuer, "Outcasts at the Blue Wall: Virtue Is Cold Comfort for Police Who Inform on Peers," *The New York Times* (December 30, 1998), p. B1; Peter Maas, *Serpico* (New York, NY: HarperCollins, 1997).
63. Michael J. Sniffen, "Lawmakers Threaten FBI over Spy Powers," *The Associated Press* (March 20, 2007).
64. Jon Murray, "Rulings Target Internet Sex Stings," *Indianapolis Star* (January 4, 2009).

CHAPTER 7

Courts

How Ought a Case Be Adjudicated?

Learning Objectives:

- To appreciate John Rawls' theory of justice and the "greatest equal liberty" principle.
- To recognize the importance of the Model Rules of Professional Conduct for prosecution and defense conduct.
- To understand what a "mob lawyer" is and the proper role of a defense attorney in criminal cases.
- To assess the scope of a prosecutor's discretion and its implication for ethical conduct.
- To evaluate the nature of plea bargaining and the ethical dilemma it creates.
- To understand the ethical underpinnings of sentencing decisions.

A man's habits become his character.

—Edmund Burke (1729–1797)

Everyone has a reason for what he or she does, and it is the task of the adjudication process to evaluate the acceptability of the reasons offered. Consider the case of former U.S. ambassador Joseph Wilson, who wrote an editorial in the New York Times criticizing President

George W. Bush for falsely linking Iraq to African uranium in his 2003 State of the Union speech. A few days later, the name of Central Intelligence Agency (CIA) agent Valerie Plame, Wilson's wife, was leaked to the press. It is a felony to reveal, and thereby endanger, the identity of a CIA agent. Wilson alleged that the exposure of his wife was retaliation by the Bush administration for his critical editorial. Journalists reported that Bush administration officials had revealed the CIA agent's identity, and after failing to learn the identity of the leak from government officials, the U.S. attorney general began issuing subpoenas to journalists contacted by Bush officials. Many of the reporters insisted that First Amendment guarantees of free press should protect them from such subpoenas, claiming their promises of confidentiality to sources are needed to protect those leaking information that serves the public good by making government more transparent and accountable. The judge disagreed, citing an earlier U.S. Supreme Court case that held, "We cannot accept the argument that the public interest in possible future news about crime . . . must take precedence over the public interest in pursuing and prosecuting those crimes." The judge ordered several reporters to serve jail time for refusing to testify before a grand jury investigating the matter, noting that "all available alternative means of obtaining the information have been exhausted, the testimony sought is necessary for the completion of the investigation, and the testimony sought is expected to constitute direct evidence of innocence or guilt."[1]

This case illustrates the need to carefully assess (and then adjudicate) the claims of the journalists in not revealing their sources. It must be determined whether the justification they offered is valid, which is the fundamental role of ethics in decisions affecting criminal justice. For example, the judge in this case is faced with balancing the goods to be achieved from solving the alleged leak of a CIA agent's identity versus protecting future journalistic sources from being revealed. The total possible happiness to be achieved from a short-term goal (solving this case) versus a long-term goal (protecting journalists' sources) points to the problem of utilitarianism in measuring and comparing different consequences because the possible outcomes and their impacts are not always apparent or predictable. Formalism would frame the decision as asking which is the better universal rule: "It is in the public interest to always protect a journalist's sources from being revealed" or "Journalists must reveal their sources in cases involving endangering a government agent, when all other avenues of investigation have been exhausted." Finally, virtue ethics would frame the judge's decision in determining whether a real good (knowledge or civil peace) is being pursued in accord with the moral virtues (especially prudence and justice). Would you make the same decision as the judge did in this case?

DOING JUSTICE

The criminal justice system is designed to enforce moral rules that have been written into the criminal law. Aristotle believed that justice consists of giving each person his or her due. The Preamble to the U.S. Constitution reads

> We the People of the United States, in Order to form a more perfect Union, establish Justice, insure domestic Tranquility, provide for the common defence, promote the general Welfare, and secure the Blessings of Liberty to ourselves and our Posterity, do ordain and establish this Constitution for the United States of America.

The real goods of civil peace and liberty are expressly mentioned, as is the moral virtue of justice, showing their centrality not only for individuals but for entire societies as well. Kant believed that justice does not specify what each person is owed, so he added that a just rule or law exists when reasonable persons would accept the rule for themselves.

John Rawls (1921–2002) was a twentieth-century philosopher who posited a **theory of justice,** stating that there are two principles of justice acceptable to all people: (1) Each person is free and worthy of respect, and liberty is restricted only out of respect for the liberty of others, and (2) social and economic opportunities must be open to all even though outcomes may be different. Inequalities should not unfairly burden any segment of society. Rawls's view implies a tension between freedom and equality, and he shows a concern for the social justice in society. He believes justice and fairness are different concepts. Justice applies to all people at all times, whereas fairness occurs when a person has the opportunity to decline (e.g., a school or a job). According to Rawls, the highest good is the "**greatest equal liberty principle**," which means that every person should have the right to liberties equal to those of everyone else having the same rights. Inequality is accepted only if it benefits the underprivileged.[2]

Crime and justice are linked in ethical terms in that conduct is criminalized to maintain social justice and order. Under ideal conditions, when everyone is acting justly, crime will not occur. In a similar vein, **James Madison**, fourth president of the United States, stated in the federalist papers in 1788, "If men were angels no government would be necessary and if angels governed, no controls on government would be necessary."[3] As this chapter describes, there is a long history of constitutional interpretation dealing with the balance to be struck between the public interest in apprehending and adjudicating crime suspects and the interest of private individuals to be left alone.

Public opinion is mixed regarding how this balance is achieved in practice. A Gallup poll asked an important question in 2000 and again in 2003.[4] The question and answers are presented in Table 7.1. There was a slight drop in citizen ratings of fairness of the criminal justice system (which includes police, courts, and corrections) from 2000 to 2003, but two-thirds (66 percent) of the public believe the system is fair in its treatment of those accused of crimes. This suggests that a clear majority of citizens believe that justice is occurring, but it is still troubling that one-third (32 percent) do not. Therefore, it is important that the meaning and application of justice in practice be considered carefully because public opinion, public confidence, and public support of the justice system are crucial in a democratic society. Consensus that criminal justice decisions are based on objective principles of ethics and justice is needed to defend and uphold confidence in the justice system when difficult or controversial decisions are at issue.

TABLE 7.1

In general, do you think the criminal justice system is very fair, somewhat fair, somewhat unfair or very unfair in its treatment of people accused of committing crime?

Year of Survey	Very or Somewhat Fair	Very or Somewhat Unfair
2000	67%	29%
2003	66%	32%

PROSECUTOR MISCONDUCT

Lawyers have bad reputations; they are always ranked among the lowest of the professions in terms of public confidence. As it turns out, they have had this image for a long time. Both Plato and Aristotle wrote disparagingly of advocates who misrepresented the truth, making the guilty appear innocent. In the modern era, the American Bar Association adopted **Model Rules of Professional Conduct** in 1983, recognizing that "virtually all difficult ethical problems arise from conflicts between a lawyer's responsibilities to clients, to the legal system, and to the lawyer's own self-interest in remaining an upright person while earning a satisfactory living." This excerpt from the Preamble to the *Model Rules* might be applied to *any* profession. Most ethical dilemmas involve balancing self-interest; duty to clients, customers, or colleagues; and responsibility to the profession. In a nod to the central importance of ethical principles, the *Model Rules* also state in the Preamble that difficult issues "must be resolved through the exercise of sensitive professional and moral judgment guided by the basic principles underlying the Rules."[5] It is those basic ethical principles that underlie the *Model Rules* and are the substance of ethics. The *Model Rules* merely attempt to apply those principles to law-related situations.

The conduct of some prosecutors before and during trial has generated a great deal of concern on ethical grounds. A well-known instance of clearly unethical conduct is from the case *Miller v. Pate*, in which the prosecutor concealed from the jury that a pair of underpants with red stains on it were stained by paint, not blood.[6] In other cases, prosecutors have tried to prejudice a jury against a defendant with deliberately inflammatory and untrue statements. For example, a prosecutor said in his summation, the defendant and his lawyer "are completely unable to explain away their guilt."[7] According to one prosecutor, the reason professional misconduct takes place is because "it works."[8] This utilitarian rationale assumes that the intended good that results (conviction) outweighs the possible negative consequences (misleading the jury, undermining the adversary process, and possible erroneous convictions). Therefore, even a utilitarian argument does not support the practice, and formalism and virtue ethics would reject it on principle, regardless of the outcome achieved.

The reason the practice of untruths in court "works" is because there is inconsistent enforcement of the legal and ethical rules of prosecutor conduct. In one case, a conviction was upheld, even though the appellate court found the prosecutor's comments to be "totally out of order," and the prosecutor was not penalized in any way.[9] An analysis of conflicting and inconsistent court decisions on this issue concluded that "they demonstrate the utter failure of appellate courts to provide incentives for the prosecutor to control his behavior . . . very little guidance is given to the prosecutor to assist him in determining the propriety of his actions. Clearly, without such guidance, the potential for misconduct significantly increases."[10] Appellate courts can correct or punish prosecutors with a warning, reversing the case, or by publicly naming the prosecutor. They cannot be fined, because the U.S. Supreme Court has held that prosecutors are not personally liable for misconduct in presenting a case.[11] Although some degree of immunity from liability is desirable, a complete shield from liability when misconduct occurs does nothing to prevent misconduct from continuing in the future.

These cases illustrate that professional misconduct sometimes has short-term rewards (e.g., convictions, personal popularity), but longer-term consequences are left for others to deal with (e.g., miscarriages of justice, low public regard for lawyers, declining public support for the criminal justice system). Without external checks through meaningful review of professional decisions, these important decisions can become self-serving, promoting only self-interest rather than public interest.

Of course, there are occasional cases where a prosecutor might intentionally lose a case when he or she believes the individual charged is innocent. These cases are normally handled by reducing charges or having the case dismissed, but in a New York City case an assistant district attorney (ADA) intentionally lost a case that his supervisor told him must be prosecuted. The ADA had to weigh the demands of ethics against his obligation to his office. He was ordered to take the case to course and let a judge decide it, even though his 2-year investigation of the facts led him to believe the suspects were innocent. The ADA helped the defense lawyers in the case in handling witnesses, and the suspects were ultimately freed.[12] This kind of case is rare, but it illustrates that both prosecution and defense must advocate for their clients (the public and the accused), but there is also a duty to seek the truth, which sometimes is lost in the workings of the adjudication process.

DEFENSE MISCONDUCT

Kevin Rankin was a lawyer for the Philadelphia Cosa Nostra organized crime group. He obtained statements and testimony that he knew were false on behalf of family members charged with crimes. He also paid off a corrections officer to perjure himself.[13] Rankin was ultimately convicted for his role as a participant in an organized crime narcotics conspiracy and was sentenced to 54 years in prison.

Bruce Cutler was the attorney for New York City Gambino family mob boss John Gotti and later for Gotti's son. Prosecutors successfully disqualified him from representing the Gottis in several cases, arguing that he had a conflict of interest because of his friendship with his clients and participation in some of the events that would be raised at trial. The prosecution claimed Cutler was "as integral a part of the Gambino family as any of its members."[14]

Frank Ragano spent 30 years representing alleged organized crime figures, such as Santo Trafficante of Florida, Carlos Marcello of New Orleans, and Jimmy Hoffa of the Teamster's Union.[15] After the deaths of Trafficante and Marcello, Ragano recounted in a book that he was seduced by the power and influence of these individuals and ultimately decided to leave his circle of clients. As a **mob lawyer,** Ragano confessed that "my gravest error as a lawyer was merging a professional life with a personal life. Ambition and aspiration for wealth, prestige, and recognition clouded my judgment. . . . Representing Santo and Jimmy was a shortcut to success—too much of a shortcut."[16] He admitted that he "crossed the professional line" when he became intimate friends with his infamous clients. He "gradually began to think like them and to rationalize their aberrant behavior. Their enemies became my enemies; their friends, my friends; their values, my values; their interests, my interests."[17] Ironically, an Internal Revenue Service (IRS) audit of his tax records was ordered soon after his successful defense of Trafficante, and Ragano was sentenced to a year in prison. Can you explain Frank Ragano's behavior as a mob lawyer in ethical terms?

In an effort to deter conduct such as that of Frank Ragano, the government has turned to forfeiture laws. Under forfeiture laws, the proceeds of organized crime-related activity may be forfeited to the government. Lawyers argue that if the fees paid to them by organized crime-linked defendants can be forfeited under this provision, attorneys will avoid representing this kind of client, which impacts on a defendant's right to counsel and due process.[18] If defense attorneys are required to ask their clients about the sources of their legal fees, would it set a poor precedent for "high-profile" defendants? Should their physicians and accountants be required to ask the same question? Some would say yes, whereas others see this as neither workable nor desirable, compromising the attorney–client privilege by making lawyers monitor the sources of their clients' funds.[19]

Defendants do not have a right to high-priced counsel, but should they have the right to use proceeds from crime to pay lawyer's fees or living expenses during court proceedings? Other countries permit defendants to use suspected illegal funds to defend themselves and for living expenses during trials, but the United States does not:

If a criminal robbed a bank and was caught holding the bags of cash taken from the vault, I think we would all agree that the money would be returned to the bank and the robber . . . not be entitled to use the proceeds of his crime to pay for lawyers to mount his defense. It should be no different for other types of crimes.[20]

The tension between a professional having to know the source of his or her client's funds and a defendant's use of alleged illegal funds for legal representation creates a difficult dilemma that deters some attorneys from taking organized crime cases. The ethical issues of representing a notorious client are compounded by the high personal cost such representation might entail. The government uses a utilitarian calculus to discourage representation of targeted clients by raising the possibility of adverse consequences for the defense attorney.

For all lawyers in prosecution, defense, or private practice, there is "no uniform or coordinated procedure" for federal, state, and local jurisdictions to exchange information regarding disciplinary problems with attorneys. Attorneys disciplined in one state, for example, "are not automatically scrutinized in other states where they may also be licensed to practice." There is also "no formal arrangement" where state bar disciplinary committees are notified of disciplinary actions or convictions against attorneys in federal court within or outside their state.[21] This allows attorneys to move to different jurisdictions and continue using unprofessional conduct. A system that does not consistently punish those who violate the law or the rules of professional responsibility tacitly promotes it. Therefore, defense attorneys, like prosecutors, need meaningful oversight of their decisions to ensure their congruence with public interest.

ISSUES AT TRIAL

Darrell Harris was placed on trial for killing three people and seriously wounding a fourth at a Brooklyn social club. It was the first capital punishment case to be tried after New York State had reinstated the death penalty. Harris was charged with robbing the victims of $200 and then killing them because he wanted no witnesses. His defense attorney claimed that Harris "lost control and snapped" during this incident because he suffered from posttraumatic stress disorder from the "combatlike" work conditions in the jails when he worked as a corrections officer.[22] In addition, Harris's attorney argued that Harris's mental health was affected by a chaotic and abusive childhood, spinal meningitis that caused brain damage, cocaine and alcohol abuse, and failure to hold a job. Two days before the homicides occurred, Harris was fired from his job as a security guard. He also had discovered his car had been towed. Previously, he had resigned from his job as a corrections officer after failing a drug test.

These claims bear little relationship to the charges filed, and they feed the perception that defense attorneys focus less on seeking truth than on exoneration of their clients at any cost.[23] Cases such as this one raise other questions as well: "What are the limits of proper representation, and what is the purpose of the adjudication process?"

In criminal cases, police and prosecutors attempt to establish criminal liability. This involves establishing the presence of the elements of the crime that subject the accused person to criminal penalties. Defendants, and defense lawyers working on their behalf, attempt to establish reasons why the act in question, the suspect's state of mind, or the circumstances of the incident establish a case for acquittal. In many cases, the defense will stipulate that the act and harm were both caused by the defendant but that there is a valid excuse for the defendant's conduct. In most cases, the defendant ultimately admits to the conduct in question, leading to the question: "Should a lawyer defend a guilty person?"

ETHICS CHECKUP

Justice versus Mercy

A scientist was sentenced to 5 years in prison for conspiracy to sell trade secrets worth $8 million from two pharmaceutical companies.[24] The scientist also had cancer and was expected to live only about 6 months longer. He told the judge, "I don't want to die in prison." But the judge said he had "no choice" and sentenced the scientist to the prison term.

On what principles(s) would you make a decision in this case, and what would your sentence be?

Some people wonder how defense attorneys live with themselves after they help a guilty person be exonerated, but this view overlooks the fact that defense attorneys represent only the *legal rights* of defendants, not their past, their personality, or their guilt or innocence. In fact, it is "not their job to decide who is guilty and not. Instead, it is the public defender's job to judge the quality of the case that the state has against the defendant."[25] According to the standards of the American Bar Association, "the defense lawyer is the professional representative of the accused, not the accused's alter ego."[26]

In a murder case that was appealed to the U.S. Supreme Court, a defense attorney did not permit his client to testify falsely about whether he had seen a gun in the hand of the victim. The defendant claimed that he was deprived of effective assistance of counsel because of his lawyer's refusal to permit the defendant to perjure himself. The Supreme Court disagreed and held that the defense lawyer's duty "is limited to legitimate, lawful conduct compatible with the very nature of a trial as a search for truth." As a result, "counsel is precluded from taking steps or in any way assisting the client in presenting false evidence or otherwise violating the law."[27] The **proper role of a defense attorney** is to represent a defendant in an honest way that seeks the truth in the case. The Code of Professional Responsibility prohibits false statements of fact or law in court; there is much "fiction weaving that customarily passes for argument to a jury."[28] As we have already seen in the case of prosecutors, there may also be a gap between the principles and the actual practice of criminal defense. It can be seen that several of Aristotle's moral virtues (i.e., justice, truthfulness, temperance, prudence, pride, ambition) are sometimes twisted and misapplied in an effort to pursue personal success over the public good. Objective review of these decisions by the participants themselves, and by outside bodies, can point to these ethical errors and serve as warnings to others.

DECIDING CASES WITHOUT TRIAL

Prosecutors have few limits on how they carry out their role. Consider the example of a Manhattan district attorney in New York City who established a narcotics eviction program. In response to complaints of tenants in poor neighborhoods, the district attorney asked landlords to begin eviction proceedings against tenants who were using drugs or allowing others to use their apartments to sell drugs. If the landlord did not act, the district attorney initiated eviction proceedings under New York's real estate law, which prohibits the use of any premises for the conduct of illegal activity. Police searches of the premises produced the evidence that supported allegations of illegal use. In one case, a 68-year-old woman was living with two daughters who were selling drugs. The judge allowed the mother to remain in the apartment but barred the daughters from returning there. In 6 years the program removed more than 2,000 drug users and dealers from both residential and commercial buildings.[29] This case illustrates the broad powers of prosecutors in both selecting prosecution targets and the nature of the prosecution itself.

The **prosecutor's discretion** is considerable in the manner in which the law can be enforced and adjudicated.[30] Prosecutors can set priorities, concentrate on certain types of cases, and avoid other cases entirely. In the case of an armed robbery, for example, police turn over the case to the prosecutor, who decides (1) whether the case will be prosecuted and (2) what charges will be pressed. In the case of armed robbery, for example, assault, larceny, and weapons charges could be filed in addition to the robbery charge (because they are lesser included offenses). After charges have been filed, the prosecutor can decide not to press the charges any further or to reduce the charge in exchange for a guilty plea. After a defendant has pleaded guilty or been convicted in court, the prosecutor usually recommends a particular sentence to the judge. Thus, the prosecutor has considerable discretion at virtually all important decision points in the criminal justice process: determining whether the police decision to arrest was appropriate, determining the charge, recommending bail, playing a role in whether a defendant goes to trial, and influencing the judge's sentencing decision.

The scope of a prosecutor's discretion continues to expand as the adoption of mandatory minimum sentence laws and truth-in-sentencing laws has reduced the judge's flexibility in sentencing choices. This shifting of sentencing authority away from judges to the prosecutors (in deciding on the charge to be prosecuted) has been criticized for placing too much power in the hands of one person.[31] Clearly, prosecutors have opportunities to misuse their discretionary powers because of the tremendous scope of their authority.[32] They have garnered the most criticism in the process of plea bargaining.

Plea bargaining occurs when a prosecutor agrees to press a less serious charge, drop some charges, or recommend a less severe sentence if the defendant agrees to plead guilty. Some prosecutors claim that plea bargaining is a necessary evil that enables them to handle large caseloads. Others claim that it is merely an administrative convenience. In either case, plea bargaining is the method of settlement for approximately 90 percent of all criminal cases.[33]

Defense attorneys provide legal protection to defendants by examining the evidence used to establish probable cause and questioning whether the evidence proves guilt beyond reasonable doubt. This role sometimes brings the defense counsel into conflict with police and prosecutors and with victims and witnesses who believe they are being "attacked" by the defense. An effective defense attorney, however, skillfully examines the reliability and validity of the evidence produced by the police, prosecutors, victims, and witnesses; the attorney should not attack anyone as an individual. Strong advocacy of the legal rights of a defendant can become blurred with the desire to win at all costs. But the role of a defense attorney is crucial because it increases certainty about outcomes in the adjudication process. Without high levels of certainty in findings of guilt or innocence, the public loses faith in the justice system and in the government it represents.

A plea bargain often results in a reduced sentence, and the prosecution will often recommend a longer sentence on the same charge after trial. Is it fair, just, or ethical to impose harsher penalties on someone found guilty after trial than on someone who agrees to plead guilty for a reduced sentence? Clearly, a trial is designed for a full airing of the facts, providing the opportunity for cross-examination of witnesses to assess the strength of the evidence offered. Plea bargaining replaces a trial with a guilty plea, which is a less reliable process.[34] In ethical terms, a sentence is a statement of the moral "worth" of the crime. Formalism sees the purpose of sentencing as retributive, so there is no justification for changing punishment based on whether it is a plea or trial. Similarly, virtue ethics would have trouble justifying different punishments based solely on the method of adjudication. Plea bargaining is justified entirely on utilitarian grounds: More good results from the plea bargain (an immediate and certain conviction and sentence) than harm (disproportionate sentences and facts not evaluated by a neutral party at trial). Do you believe plea bargaining is morally permissible on utilitarian grounds?

JUDICIAL DECISIONS

A judge in New Jersey ruled in 2004 that criminals may have their DNA samples destroyed after they complete their prison sentences. The judge ruled that "Once a felon has paid his or her debt to society and has fully resumed civilian life, the state's right to maintain that person's DNA withers."[35] This decision caused tremendous controversy because it apparently opened a large hole in an earlier law that required everyone convicted of a crime to submit a DNA sample. As the attorney general stated in his intention to appeal the judge's decision, the whole purpose of maintaining a DNA database is "to determine if a career criminal has done it again."[36]

This DNA case in New Jersey represents one of **two important kinds of judicial decisions** that judges are required to make: ruling on evidence and sentencing choices. These judgments are crucial because they involve a person's liberty, something that virtue ethics recognizes as a real good (i.e., an end to be desired in itself). The judge's argument in the DNA case is an interesting one, implying that if DNA is kept forever, isn't it the equivalent of holding someone under a lifetime term of providing DNA as evidence, when the sentence has already been served and debt to society been repaid? However, the attorney general makes a good point in noting that the purpose of the DNA database is to do just that—to determine DNA matches for unsolved crimes. The issue of balancing two competing social goods forms the utilitarian argument: Should a sentence end completely after the term is served, or should the DNA of an offender be stored forever to help solve future crimes? Both can be seen as desirable social goods with consequences that are not always easy to foresee. From the perspective of formalism, which of these is a good universal rule, and does either violate the practical imperative? Finally, virtue ethics asks whether the real good in sentencing (civil peace) is enhanced in accord with the moral virtue of justice (giving someone no more or less than they are due).

The answer to the utilitarian question depends on how you judge the two questions of social good in terms of the total happiness they might produce. Formalism would clearly reject keeping the DNA samples because the policy uses persons (via their DNA) as a means to another end. Virtue ethics would question the extent to which holding the DNA sample forever contributes to civil peace and whether holding a burglar's or embezzler's DNA in perpetuity, after he or she has served the sentence, is consistent with justice. Virtue ethics might find DNA databases for serious violent or repeat offenders more ethically justifiable than for less serious offenders. This ethical analysis illustrates the difficulties of judicial decision making because of the different ways that evidence can be considered and sentences justified.

Sentencing of offenders is assessed differently using different ethical perspectives. These are summarized in Table 7.2.

Utilitarianism looks toward the *future* in assessing the impact of alternate sentences on the future conduct of the offender and also within general society (i.e., potential consequences and deterrence). Formalism looks to the *past*, seeing that punishment can be based only in proportion to the seriousness of past conduct (retribution). Attempting to anticipate the impact of the sentence on the offender in the future, or on others in the future, cannot be known, and it unjustly uses the current offender as a means to an end. Virtue ethics looks at the *present*, focusing less on the act committed and more on the character of the person who committed it and how a sentence would work to achieve real goods in accord with the moral virtues. The differences between the major ethical perspectives are highlighted in the case of sentencing, and it illustrates how different ethical assumptions result in divergent sentencing philosophies. Sentencing is discussed in more detail in Chapter 8.

			Primary Sentencing Philosophy
	Focus of Sentence	**Direction of Vision**	
Formalism	On the act committed	*Past:* punishment based on seriousness of past conduct	Retribution
Utilitarianism	On the act committed	*Future:* look for best way to prevent new crime	Deterrence
Virtue ethics	On the character of the person	*Present:* achieve civil peace via moral virtues	Rehabilitation

TABLE 7.2 Ethical Underpinnings of Sentencing

ETHICS IN BOOKS

Ethics is everywhere, even in the books we read, which sometimes are written without ethics specifically in mind. Here is a summary of a book that looks at actions that affect others, followed by questions that ask you to reflect on the ethical connections.

ME TO WE: FINDING MEANING IN A MATERIAL WORLD

Craig Kielburger and Marc Kielburger
(Fireside, 2006)

Craig and Marc Kielburger are brothers and founders of the groups Free the Children and Leaders Today. Their book describes how they became involved with helping others on a large scale. They weave in many personal stories of both famous and unknown people who have performed acts of giving toward others and their motivations for doing so. The book attempts to show how a motivated individual of modest means can make (and have made) a difference in this world.

Free the Children was founded in 1995 and is the largest existing network of children helping children though education. Thus far, it has organized more than a million young people in education programs in 45 countries. It has also built more than 450 schools in the developing world. Leaders Today was founded in 1999 and provides leadership programs for 350,000 young people each year through community groups, schools, and international training opportunities.

The authors talk of the search for meaning and how it is often elusive: "many of us fall into a trap and work long hours because of a sense of responsibility to others, not being able to say no at work, or trying to provide 'only the best' for our family. We make these choices with good intentions, but in the end they are not the best for our family, or ourselves. We get sucked into a way of life that does not fulfill us." In traveling around the world with volunteers doing work in developing countries, the authors found that "many of the people with whom we worked had very little in the way of material possessions yet expressed a sense of happiness more powerful than anything we had experienced . . . empathy for others, a willingness to feel for the less fortunate and reach out to help. Happiness and joy in small things. Strength in community."

The "Me to We" perspective described by the authors looks for individuals to assess objectively their own situation: "in our current culture, we constantly receive messages that success is about the things we have," material goods, a competitive outlook, a preoccupation with the self or "Me." On the other hand, the "We" perspective focuses on gratitude for what you have, empathy for others, redefining happiness by aligning your goals with your values, and forging a stronger connection to others in the local and global community.

The book is filled with practical suggestions for actively living a life with meaning by focusing on "we" rather than on "me." Quoting Eleanor Roosevelt, they conclude,

"One's philosophy is not best expressed in words. It is expressed in the choices that we make, and those choices are ultimately our responsibility."

QUESTIONS

1. If a life of meaning is characterized by many little-noticed deeds, rather than a few immortal deeds, how can these small deeds make a difference in huge social problems such as educational opportunity, poverty, and injustice?
2. What would the major ethical perspectives (of Aristotle, Kant, and Mill) say about the desirability of performing small, unseen ethical acts? Are ethics more meaningful when practiced among the less fortunate?

ETHICS IN THE MOVIES

Movies seek to entertain and inform the audience about a story, incident, or person. Many good movies also hit upon important ethical themes in making significant decisions that affect the lives of others. Read the movie summary here (and watch the movie if you haven't already), and answer the questions to make the ethical connections.

A CIVIL ACTION

Steven Zaillian, Director
(1999)

Woburn, Massachusetts, is a small industrial town 12 miles north of Boston. A resident, Anne Anderson (Kathleen Quinlan), had been suspicious about the tap water in Woburn and what seemed like a large number of cases of serious illness, including twelve cases of leukemia in a small town. Based on the book by Jonathan Harr, *A Civil Action* recounts an actual case against Beatrice Foods and W. R. Grace, which owned a tannery that cured animal hides by pouring chemicals over the leather. The legal question was whether the chemicals were permitted to spill into the surrounding ground and water supply, contaminating the drinking water, causing illness in the town residents.

The attorney who took the case is Jan Schlictmann (John Travolta), who was a stereotypical "in-it-for-the-money" kind of civil attorney. But over the course of this case, he identified with the very sick victims in Woburn, and he looked for justice rather than profit.

As a civil case, the burden of proof is lower than in a criminal case, but it is still very difficult to prove the link among the chemicals and the existence and responsibility for seepage into the water, to the contact with victims and their subsequent illnesses. Numerous experts and conflicting testimony characterized the case, and the corporations spared no expense in attempting to prove their nonresponsibility.

Schlictmann refused a settlement offer from the corporations for a total of $24 million, believing he could obtain a fairer compensation at trial. The trial jury ultimately awarded $8 million, which was largely earmarked for the cleanup of the chemicals. The case bankrupted Schlictmann's law firm due to the very high expenses it incurred for a long-term case, paid experts, and legal assistance, and its failure to achieve a settlement large enough to cover its costs.

QUESTIONS

1. Evaluate the moral permissibility of Schlictmann's refusing the $24 million settlement offer in the hopes of a better outcome at trial.
2. If you were an attorney representing the victims in this pollution case, how would you determine what a "just" outcome should be?

Discussion Question

Do you believe that a judge's sentencing decisions should be focused on the past, present, or future?

Critical Thinking Exercises

All ethical decisions affect others (by definition) and, as Aristotle points out, ethical decision making is achieved consistently only through practice. Given the outline of virtue ethics provided by Aristotle (i.e., seeking the real goods via the moral virtues), evaluate the moral permissibility of the conduct in question in each scenario.

Important note on method: *Critical thinking requires the ability to evaluate viewpoints, facts, and behaviors objectively to assess information or methods of argumentation to establish the true worth or merit of an act or course of conduct. Please evaluate these scenarios, first analyzing pros and cons of alternate views,* before *you come to a conclusion.* Do not *draw a conclusion first, and then try to find facts to support it—this frequently leads to narrow (and incorrect) thinking.*

To properly evaluate the moral permissibility of a course of action using critical thinking skills

1. *Begin with an open mind (no preconceptions!),*
2. *Isolate and evaluate the relevant facts on both sides,*
3. *Identify the precise moral question to be answered, and*
4. *Apply ethical principles to the moral question based on an objective evaluation of the facts, only then drawing a conclusion.*

7.1 Butt Charge

The state of Maine proposed a new law requiring every filter-tipped cigarette sold there to carry a nickel surcharge.[37] The 5 cents would be refunded when the butt was returned, in the same way that cans and bottles carry deposits in some states. Butts would be returned to the same recycling locations that handle cans and bottles.

According to the proposal, cigarette manufacturers would place a mark on the filter of each cigarette sold in Maine, indicating the 5-cent deposit notice. If passed, this law would raise the price of a pack of cigarette by $1.

The law arose from problems caused by an earlier ban of cigarette smoking in most public places, forcing smokers outside and leading to the problem of used butts on the ground around the entrances to stores, public buildings, and parking lots. The law also seeks to provide a new source of revenue for the state while avoiding a general tax increase. If half of all butts sold were returned for a deposit, the state would gain about $50 million in unclaimed deposits.

Cigarette vendors and manufacturers did not support the proposed new law, arguing that it would push smokers to buy their cigarettes in other states. There was also the question of health concerns in handling used butts and the practical matter of counting the returned used cigarette butts.

- You are a smoker living in Maine. Is it morally permissible to enact such a law?
- How does your argument change if you are a nonsmoker?

7.2 Attorney Confidentiality of a Client's Criminal Plans?

In a Washington case, a defense attorney was told, both by a psychiatrist and an attorney for the client's mother, that his client's mental illness made him a threat to others. The attorney did not disclose this information at the bail hearing for his client. Eight days after his release, the client assaulted his mother and attempted suicide.

The appellate court held that the attorney was not legally obligated to disclose this information because the client made no threats in the presence of his attorney that he was going to harm someone. In addition, the mother was aware of the risk she faced.[38]

In forty states, an attorney is permitted to keep silent even after learning that a client plans to kill someone.[39] In these states, disclosure of a client's intention to commit a serious crime is entirely at the discretion of the attorney.

How does an attorney's dual responsibility to his or her client and as an officer of the court rank the interests of the client versus that of society? Is there a moral obligation involved to either the client or society?

The general rule of confidentiality in the attorney–client relationship states that "a lawyer may reveal such confidences or secrets to the extent the lawyer reasonably believes necessary to prevent the client from committing a crime." Most states do not distinguish serious from nonserious crimes, and it is easy for an attorney to justify nondisclosure on grounds that disclosure is "unethical."[40] This conclusion is possible by claiming that the attorney is an advocate for the client, so loyalty lies with the client. It might be argued that it is sometimes difficult to distinguish vague criminal threats from actual criminal plans. This can also be seen as an extension of the legal rule that strangers have no obligation to aid someone in distress.

There are practical reasons for confidentiality, the most important of which is that clients might withhold important facts if they were not certain that their attorneys won't disclose them to third parties. New Jersey is one of the ten states that require attorneys to disclose a client's stated intention to commit a homicide or other serious violent crime. A survey there found that about 9 percent of 786 attorneys responding had encountered at least one situation in which they believed their clients were going to commit such serious crimes, but only half of the attorneys disclosed that information to others.[41] Therefore, it appears that even the requirement of disclosure of planned crimes does not guarantee the attorney will do so. However, when a client discloses to his or her attorney the intention to commit a crime, can the attorney be viewed as an accomplice once the crime is committed?

- Do attorneys have a moral obligation, beyond that stated in the law, to protect others from what they believe to be a planned crime?

7.3 A Judge's Relations

A judge in Chicago was charged with violating ethics rules for having sex in his chambers with a court reporter.

Apparently, a physical relationship took place in the office, and the judge and court reporter had sex on multiple occasions during workdays. The judge argued in his defense that there is no rule specifying that consensual relations with another adult in the privacy of his chambers are prohibited.

It was charged that the sexual relationship with the court reporter "created an atmosphere of impropriety and is not in keeping with the dignity of a judicial officer," although no state rule has been found that addresses or prohibits consensual sex by a judge in his office.[42]

The judge was also charged with forcing kisses on two ADAs, repeatedly asking female prosecutors for dates and commenting on their appearances. But these charges were separate from the judge's challenge of his having consensual sex with a court reporter in his chambers.

- Assess the moral permissibility of the judge's conduct using the three major ethical perspectives.

7.4 The Duke Lacrosse Case

The attorney general of North Carolina dismissed all charges against three Duke University lacrosse players who had been charged a year earlier with raping a stripper at a party attended by team members. The attorney general publicly rebuked Michael B. Nifong, the district attorney of Durham County, as a "rogue prosecutor" and said the cases were "the result of a tragic rush to accuse and a failure to verify serious allegations."

The case had received tremendous national publicity and, early on, an assumption was made regarding the culpability of the lacrosse players, which was fueled by the prosecutor who gave approximately seventy media interviews. When the case was showing signs of weakness due to failure of any DNA match and problems in corroborating the victim's version of events, the charges were not dropped until defense attorneys publicized the lack of evidence and the attorney general took over the case. The case was also punctuated by Nifong's reelection as district attorney during these events.

Nifong was charged with an ethics violation for failing in his legal obligation to reveal favorable, exculpatory evidence to the defense. The North Carolina State Bar accused Nifong of illegally withholding DNA evidence favorable to the defendants, lying to a bar committee examining his conduct, and making false statements about evidence and systematically abusing "prosecutorial discretion."[43] Nifong was disbarred in 2007.

- Assume that Nifong had a strong belief that the defendants were guilty. How does this affect the moral permissibility of his conduct?

7.5 Criminals Testifying for the Prosecution

The federal government is relying on some serious criminals—murderers, drug dealers, and gang members—to make its case in a double death penalty trial in Baltimore's U.S. District Court. In exchange for leniency, at least six "cooperating witnesses," most of whom haven't yet been sentenced for their crimes, will testify against James Dinkins, and two co-defendants.

That's raised concerns among defense attorneys, who say the cooperators have a strong motivation to lie. They point to a recent study out of the University of Arkansas that suggests one in two people will perjure themselves if given an incentive to do so. "Their testimony is essentially bought and paid for," said John Wesley Hall Jr., president of the National Association of Criminal Defense Lawyers.

But prosecutors say the deals are necessary evils and the best way to get information about covert and illegal organizations. They work very hard with law enforcement agencies to "flip" people for just that reason. "Often the people who are in the best position to be witnesses in a case are the people who themselves have been involved in the criminal activity," said Maryland U.S. Attorney Rod J. Rosenstein.

If convicted, Dinkins, who is accused of murdering a federal witness, could be put to death. The U.S. attorney's office has made deals with other convicted criminals in exchange for testimony, ensuring that some of offenders will be released from prison much earlier in exchange for their testimony. As a result, there's a lot riding on the testimony of people with "reprehensibly low" credibility, according to one of the defense attorneys. "There's no DNA, no forensics, no bullet, no fiber, nothing to directly link the defendant to these murders, not a fingerprint," lawyer Jonathan Van Hoven told the jury during opening statements. There's "nothing but the testimony of people you are not going to be able to trust or believe."

One cooperating criminal pleaded guilty to second-degree attempted murder in state court with a recommendation that he serve 30 years, 15 of them suspended. He wasn't charged with any of the other crimes he confessed to, and he won't be—if he fully cooperates in this case. That gives him a strong incentive to say whatever the government wants to hear, defense attorneys said. Such witnesses are necessary, acknowledged defense attorney Hall. "The government needs them," he said. "Sometimes the defense needs them too, but we have nothing to offer. If we were to offer what the government gave, we'd be prosecuted for bribery."[44]

- Evaluate the moral permissibility of the prosecutor's decision to use convicted criminals, whose sentences are not yet final, to testify against another suspect.

Key Concepts

Notes

1. Susan Schmidt and Carol Leonnig, "Reporter Held in Contempt in CIA Leak Case," *The Washington Post* (August 10, 2004), p. A1.
2. John Rawls, *A Theory of Justice* (New York, NY: Clarendon, 1972).
3. James Madison, *The Federalist Papers* (#51) (New York, NY: Buccaneer Books, 1990), p. 20.
4. "Crime Poll: Topics and Trends," *Gallup News Service* (2003).
5. American Bar Association, *Model Rules of Professional Conduct*, 52 U.S.L.W. 1–27 (August 16, 1983).
6. *Miller v. Pate*, 386 U.S. 1 (1967). The defendant's conviction was upheld on appeal but overturned by the U.S. Supreme Court, holding that the prosecutor deliberately misrepresented the truth.
7. *United States v. Perry*, 643 F.2d 38 2nd Cir. (1981).
8. Bennett L. Gershman, "Why Prosecutors Misbehave," *Criminal Law Bulletin*, vol. 22 (March/April 1986), pp. 131–143; Jennifer Emily and Steve McGonigle, "Dallas County District Attorney Wants Unethical Prosecutors Punished," *The Dallas Morning News* (May 4, 2008).

9. *People v. Shields*, 46 N.Y. 2d. 764 (1977).

10. Gershman, p. 140; see also Bruce A. Green and Fred C. Zacharias, "Regulating Federal Prosecutors' Ethics," *Vanderbilt Law Review*, vol. 55 (March 2002), pp. 381–478.

11. *Imbler v. Pachtman*, 424 U.S. 409 (1976).

12. Benjamin Weiser, "Doubting a Case, a Prosecutor Helped the Defense," *The New York Times* (June 23, 2008).

13. President's Commission on Organized Crime, *Organized Crime Today: The Impact* (Washington, DC: U.S. Government Printing Office, 1987), pp. 228–229.

14. William Glaberson, "Effort to Oust Gotti Lawyer Reopens Debate on Tactics," *The New York Times* (May 4, 1998), p. B6.

15. Frank Ragano and Selwyn Raab, *Mob Lawyer* (New York, NY: Simon & Schuster, 1997).

16. Ragano and Raab, *Mob Lawyer,* p. 362.

17. Ibid.

18. President's Commission on Organized Crime, *Organized Crime Today: The Impact,* p. 253.

19. Katrina A. Abendano, "The Role of Lawyers in the Fight against Money Laundering: Is a Reporting Requirement Appropriate?" *Journal of Legislation*, vol. 27 (2001), p. 463.

20. Linda M. Samuel, "Restraining the Global Threat," in R. Broadhurst, Ed., *Transnational Organized Crime Conference: Proceedings* (Hong Kong Police Force, 2002).

21. President's Commission on Organized Crime, *Organized Crime Today: The Impact,* p. 253.

22. Patricia Hurtado, "Lost Control and Snapped: Defense Cites Stress in Social-Club Killings," *Newsday* (May 5, 1998), p. 7.

23. Stephen J. Morse, "The 'New Syndrome Excuse Syndrome'," *Criminal Justice Ethics*, vol. 14 (Winter/Spring 1995), pp. 3–15.

24. "Five-Year Sentence in Secrets Case," *Newark Star-Ledger* (July 13, 1991), p. 1.

25. Lisa J. McIntyre, *The Public Defender: The Practice of Law in the Shadows of Repute* (Chicago, IL: University of Chicago Press, 1987), p. 145.

26. American Bar Association, *Standards for Criminal Justice*, Number 4–1.1.

27. *Nix v. Whiteside*, 475 U.S. 157 (1986).

28. H. Richard Uviller, *Virtual Justice: The Flawed Prosecution of Crime in America* (New Haven, CT: Yale University Press, 1996), pp. 153, 155.

29. Peter Finn, *The Manhattan District Attorney's Narcotics Eviction Program* (Washington, DC: National Institute of Justice, 1995).

30. Richard Bloom, "Prosecutorial Discretion," *Georgetown Law Journal*, vol. 87 (1999), p. 103.

31. Steven R. Donziger, ed. *The Real War on Crime: Report of the National Criminal Justice Commission* (New York, NY: HarperPerennial, 1996), pp. 183–184.

32. Peter J. Henning, "Prosecutorial Misconduct and Constitutional Remedies," *Washington University Law Quarterly*, vol. 77 (Fall 1999), p. 201.

33. B. Boland, E. Brady, H. Tyson, and J. Bassler, *The Prosecution of Felony Arrests* (Washington, DC: Bureau of Justice Statistics, 1983); Gerard Rainville and Brian A. Reaves, *Felony Defendants in Large Urban Counties* (Washington, DC: Bureau of Justice Statistics, 2003).

34. Kenneth Kipnis, "Criminal Justice and the Negotiated Plea," in M. Leighton and J. Reiman, Eds., *Criminal Justice Ethics* (Upper Saddle River, NJ: Prentice Hall, 2001), p. 370.

35. Robert Schwanesberg, "Ruling Deals Blow to DNA Law," *NJ.com* (December 23, 2004).

36. Schwanesberg, "Ruling Deals Blow to DNA Law."

37. Freed Bayles, "In Maine, Five-Cent Butt Charge Targets Litter," *USA Today* (March 5, 2001), p. 5.

38. *Hawkins v. King County*, 602 P.2d 361 (Was. App. 1979).

39. Brendan W. Williams, "Some Secrets Are Not Worth Keeping: The Attorney's Duty of Confidentiality Versus Disclosure of Intended Client Crimes," *Criminal Law Bulletin*, vol. 34 (March–April 1998), pp. 97–117.

40. Steven R. Salbu, "Law and Conformity, Ethics and Conflict: The Trouble with Law-Based Conceptions of Ethics," *Indiana Law Journal*, vol. 68 (1992), pp. 101–130.

41. Leslie C. Levin, "Testing the Radical Experiment: A Study of Lawyer Response to Clients Who Intend to Harm Others," *Rutgers Law Review*, vol. 47 (1994), pp. 81–129.

42. John Flynn Rooney, "Ethics Rules Don't Apply to Judge's Case, Panel Told," *Chicago Daily Law Bulletin* (September 17, 1998), p. 1.

43. "Lacrosse Case Decision," *The Herald-Sun* (Durham, NC) (April 12, 2007), p. A2.

44. Tricia Bishop, "Testifying for the State: Criminals," *The Baltimore Sun* (May 28, 2009).

CHAPTER 8

Punishment and Corrections
What Should Be Done with Offenders?

learning objectives:

- To understand the distinctions among the four purposes of criminal sanctions: retribution, incapacitation, deterrence, and rehabilitation.

- To recognize the issue of disparity in sentencing, how sentencing guidelines were designed to reduce disparity, and the ethical issues involved.

- To assess the issue of correctional ethics and the situations in which ethical decisions become crucial in correctional settings.

- To understand how corporal punishment and innovative sentences can be evaluated from an ethical perspective.

- To distinguish the issue of punishment under the Eighth Amendment, and how capital punishment and life in prison can be evaluated using ethical principles.

His lack of education is more than compensated for by his keenly developed moral bankruptcy.

—Woody Allen (b. 1935)

THE ETHICS OF PUNISHMENT

In South Carolina, a young mother, Susan Smith, killed her two children by leaving them in a car she rolled into a lake. Smith could have been convicted of involuntary manslaughter or murder and received a death sentence, or she could have been found guilty but mentally ill. At trial, the defense pointed out that she came from a troubled background. Her parents had divorced and her father had committed suicide when she was 6. She had been molested by her stepfather at age 15 and later, even after she was married. Her mother covered up the molestation. After her divorce, her new boyfriend rejected Smith because she had two children. She had a long history of depression. The defense also noted that she had confessed to her crime and showed deep remorse.[1]

Which of these factors should be considered in deciding on a sentence? And how should an appropriate sentence be determined? In the actual case, Smith was convicted of murder and sentenced to 30 years in prison. It is easy to see that other sentencing choices were available to the judge, and that other sentences could have been imposed and defended rationally. This case illustrates why it is important to understand the underlying rationale or philosophy of sentencing.

When an offender violates the law, society attempts to accomplish some combination of retribution, incapacitation, deterrence, or rehabilitation.

- **Retribution** is punishment and is applied simply in proportion to the seriousness of the offense. The "eye for an eye" system of justice described in the Old Testament is an early form of retribution.[2] According to this concept, the more serious the crime, the more serious the punishment should be.
- **Incapacitation** aims to prevent further criminal behavior by physically restraining the offender from engaging in future misconduct. The primary method of incapacitation in the United States is incarceration, although other methods also are used, such as suspending a driver's license or license to practice law in cases of crimes committed by drivers or lawyers.
- **Deterrence** aims to prevent crime through the example of offenders being punished. General deterrence is directed at preventing crime among the general population, whereas special (or "specific") deterrence is aimed at preventing future crimes by the offender.
- **Rehabilitation** or "reformation" sees criminal behavior as a consequence of social or psychological shortcomings. The purpose of the sentence is to correct or treat these shortcomings in order to prevent future crimes.

A utilitarian rationale would clearly support sentences justified by deterrence, incapacitation, and rehabilitation if it was determined that they would benefit society in ways that would override (produce more total happiness) the harm to the offender. Formalism would support retribution only because it justifies punishment solely for the offender's past conduct. Each of the other justifications aims to prevent *future* crimes, using punishment as a means to another end. Formalism believes using current offenders in this way is unethical. Virtue ethics supports punishment that is designed to achieve civil peace and does not deprive one of liberty unjustly (seeking real goods via moral virtues). Rehabilitation that seeks to instill moral virtue in offenders would be especially appealing for virtue ethics. Retribution and incapacitation would be less appealing because they do nothing to improve the offender's ability to act morally. Which of these rationales (i.e., retribution, incapacitation, deterrence, and rehabilitation) do you think was used by the judge in the case of Susan Smith?

In a 2003 case, *Overton v. Buzzetta*, the U.S. Supreme Court held that regulations limiting visitors to prisoners did not violate the Eighth Amendment because "the regulations bear a rational relation to legitimate penological interests" relating to internal prison security. Restrictions on visits by minor children, adult children, and former prisoners, as well as elimination of most visits to inmates who commit two substance abuse violations, were, therefore, upheld because they had a "valid, rational connection" to a legitimate governmental interest in operating the prison securely.[3] If you were a prison warden, or policy maker, how would you balance the competing interests of operating a secure prison (ensuring retribution and incapacitation) with your interest in inmates maintaining close ties with their families and the community (which experience shows reduce the likelihood of recidivism—improving the likelihood of rehabilitation and deterrence)? Which ethical principles would you rely on in resolving this dilemma?

In moral terms, the ethics of punishment lie primarily in whether justice is done. As Aristotle said, justice consists of giving a person no more or less than he or she is due. It is difficult to determine the justice of punishment in the abstract because each offender and offense involves different motivations and circumstances. Determining the appropriate severity of punishment is a difficult task. In the case of Susan Smith, could a judge reasonably have found that she was emotionally unstable and sentence her to a prison term as punishment and then required her to undergo rehabilitation to correct her mental condition? Is it likely that deterrence or incapacitation is a significant issue in her case? Formalism would argue for punishment based solely on the severity of the offense (retribution), but if she was mentally unstable or otherwise impaired, she would not meet the "reasonable person" standard and not be blameworthy. Virtue ethics would seek justice (a moral virtue) giving her no more or less than she is due, so her background and circumstances would be relevant, especially if there was likelihood that she could become, or be restored to, a morally virtuous person. Utilitarianism would weigh the total good produced by a severe retributive sentence, a less severe punishment, or a punishment focused more on her rehabilitation. All relevant considerations, especially general deterrence and the likelihood of reoffending, would be important to weigh.

THE PROBLEMS OF SENTENCING

The lack of empirical evidence to support the four basic purposes of sentencing has contributed to concern about **disparity in sentences.** Disparity occurs when offenders with similar histories commit similar crimes but receive widely different sentences. Disparity must be expected, of course, when there is little agreement regarding what a sentence should accomplish. A result of disparity has been a trend toward mandatory and fixed sentences. This move toward uniformity in sentencing can be attributed to the widespread adoption of retribution and incapacitation as guiding sentencing philosophies in most jurisdictions.

Sentencing guidelines attempt to reduce disparity in sentencing by recommending a "guideline sentence" based on the seriousness of the crime and the offender's prior record. The guidelines are developed by examining averages of past sentences imposed on various combinations of offenders and offenses. Guideline sentences achieve the goals of proportionality and uniformity without mandating specific sentences for certain crimes or offenders. The U.S. Supreme Court ruled in 2005 that federal sentencing guidelines are not binding on judges but only advisory.[4] Judges usually deviate from the guideline sentence, however, only if they provide written reasons for doing so. For example, if a sentence of 5–7 years is typical for past robbery offenders, judges may sentence outside this range only if they state their reasons for doing so. These reasons might include a particularly serious prior record or severe injury to a victim.

Sentencing guidelines make possible more accurate predictions of prison populations, and prison populations can be controlled by modifying the guidelines.[5] It can be argued, however, that the size of prison populations should not be a factor in sentencing guidelines because it is unrelated to a particular crime in question. Prison populations are a utilitarian concern, having nothing to do with what the offender *deserves*, which is a fundamental consideration of both formalism and virtue ethics. Nevertheless, the public's fear of crime and willingness to support longer prison sentences has resulted in high prison expenses and new construction when, at the same time, there is pressure to reduce government spending (utilitarian concerns). Sentencing guidelines may help to limit the use of incarceration so that available prison capacity is restricted to serious offenders and habitual offenders, rather than being used for nonserious offenses (concerns central to formalism and virtue ethics).[6]

ETHICS CHECKUP
Punishment by Electric Shock

It has been argued that an alternative punishment is needed that is "properly painful," proportional to the offense, humane, and less expensive than incarceration. Such a punishment would be used to sentence those offenders who fall between minor criminals and those who are violent. "Corporal punishment which applies a nonlasting intense pain, such as electric shock, can do the job. It can be over in seconds, not years" [like prison], and it would not have "the severe long term effects of prison." It punishes the offender, and only the offender, for the offense. "Prison in contrast punishes innocent people, such as the offender's family by depriving it of support."[7]

Applying ethical principles, what is the moral permissibility of punishment by electric shock?

TABLE 8.1 Ethical Issues in Corrections

Ethical Issues in Corrections	Types of Unethical Conduct
Preferential or selective treatment	• Undeserved favors (smuggling, transfers) • Selective punishment or harsh treatment (unwarranted use of force, verbal abuse)
Misuse of authority	• Exploitation of offenders under supervision (sex, extortion) • Concealment of rule violations (failure to act upon known violations among offenders or between offenders, visitors, or supervisors)

Consider the case of Bernard Madoff who at age 71 was sentenced to 150 years in prison for fraud—a Ponzi scheme where he had individuals and institutions allow him to invest their money for a high interest return, while Madoff simply kept the money for himself, keeping the scheme alive only by continually adding more new investors. His scam went on for many years, resulting in losses estimated at $13 billion. The judge defended the very long prison sentence on grounds of the scheme's many victims, its size, and also deterrence, arguing "the symbolism is important here because the strongest possible message must be sent to those who would engage in similar conduct . . . that they will be punished to the fullest extent of the law." On the other hand, Madoff's defense attorney called the long prison sentence "absurd" because "there's nothing in the sentencing guidelines that talks about making symbols of people."[8] This disagreement over both the nature and purpose of the sentence reflects differences in ethical reasoning (summarized in Table 8.1). Whereas formalism looks at past conduct and punishes solely on the seriousness of the crime committed, utilitarianism looks to the future in punishing for purposes of deterrence. Virtue ethics justifies punishment only when specific real goods (such as civil peace) are achieve in a way consistent with the moral virtues.

CORRECTIONAL ETHICS

Once convicted and sentenced, there are a range of ethical issues that arise regarding the state's obligation to supervise the offender until his or her release from custody or supervision. These issues center on the proper treatment of the offender and the ethical obligations of those entrusted with their supervision.

Preferential or selective treatment of offenders and misuse of one's official position are the two largest categories of ethical difficulty. Preferential or selective treatment of offenders includes provision of undeserved favors or selective punishment or harsh treatment. Undeserved favors most often include smuggling of contraband, such as cigarettes, cash, or drugs in exchange for money or favors the offender can provide. Selective punishments and harsh treatments involve the unwarranted use of physical force or verbal abuse to control an offender, assert one's authority, or obtain an advantage to be used against the offender.

Misuse of authority include exploitation of offenders under supervision or concealment of rules violations. Exploitation of offenders most often involves sex or extortion. The sex can be for purposes of control or gratification, and the extortion involves threat of physical or reputational harm in the future in exchange for money. Another kind of misuse of authority is concealment of known rule violations between offenders or between offenders and visitors or other supervisors. Known sexual relationships, extortion, or abuses that are not reported are examples. These types of unethical conduct in corrections are summarized in Table 8.1.

It is clear that each type of ethical misconduct in corrections can occur in prisons or jails or to probationers or paroles. Those in prison or jail have their liberty revoked, so they are more subject to abuse given their captivity, but those on probation or parole have more access to others in the community, making them greater targets for extortion. The correctional misconduct described here cannot be justified under any ethical perspective, and laws and court decisions have been developed over the years to circumscribe the legal rights of offenders. Nevertheless, interactions between corrections personnel and offenders are of low visibility, less visible than police–public interactions. As a result, there must be an even greater reliance on ethical conduct, because there are fewer empowered witnesses to these interactions, making discovery less likely.

The American Correctional Association has a code of ethics (see Appendix D). It consists of seventeen principles, which, if followed by all correctional personnel, would result in universal ethical conduct on the job. In fact, every legal or ethical violation that occurs in corrections violates one or more of these principles, because they address the ethical issues described in Table 8.1. Whether the issue is unwarranted use of force, prison rape, extortion of inmates, or concealment of rule violations, the conduct is unethical under all three ethical perspectives. Virtue ethics requires the pursuit of real goods via the moral virtues, formalism requires pursuit of conduct consistent with the categorical and practice imperatives, and utilitarianism requires conduct that results in the greatest total happiness objectively considered. It is difficult to imagine a circumstance in which correctional misconduct can be justified in ethical terms. Nevertheless, there are unusual pressures in corrections that can contribute to a climate that fosters unethical conduct. These influences can include unqualified supervisory personnel, persistent deviant subcultures of staff or offenders, and failure of authorities to act on past reports or complaints.[9] A system of accountability that is not working properly directly promotes unethical conduct through its failure to hold individuals responsible for their actions as either offenders or staff.

With regard to offender treatment, there is some evidence that programs that endeavor to change the moral thinking of offenders has some impact on their subsequent conduct and reduces recidivism (compared to other offenders).[10] These cognitive-behavioral programs employ techniques such as Moral Reconation Therapy or attempt to move clients from selfish, hedonistic conduct to higher levels of thinking involving concern for others and longer-term outcomes. There is some evidence, therefore, that improvements in ethical

thinking by offenders can lead to lower recidivism. This is likely due to increased appreciation for the wrongfulness of illegal conduct and the impact of that conduct on others, which
ethical thinking promotes.

CORPORAL PUNISHMENT

An Ohio teenager, Michael Fay, committed acts of vandalism while visiting Singapore. Along
with some friends, he spray painted and threw eggs and bricks at eighteen cars over a 10-day
period. Singapore police also found stolen flags and signs in Fay's Singapore apartment. Fay was
sentenced to 4 months in prison, a $2,320 fine, and six lashes with a wet rattan cane. This kind of
caning, administered by an expert in martial arts, breaks the skin and leaves permanent scars on
the buttocks.[11] The sentence caused an uproar in the United States, with some people defending
it and others vehemently opposing it.

Corporal punishment is physical punishment short of the death penalty. It has often been
associated with torture and mutilation, and most forms of corporal punishment are illegal in the
United States under the Eighth Amendment's prohibition against cruel and unusual punishment.
During the 1990s, however, legislation was introduced in Texas that would result in a finger
being amputated for each conviction of a drug dealer.[12] This bill was an effort to imitate the
penalty for theft in some Islamic countries, which is amputation of the offender's right hand.[13]
Although such a penalty would seem to constitute a violation of the Eighth Amendment, it is up
to the courts to decide whether it is within the "limits of civilized standards" or "totally without
penological justification."[14] Do statements such as these make implied assumptions about ethical
standards?

The U.S. State Department protested Michael Fay's punishment in Singapore, claiming
that it was too severe. President Clinton called the punishment extreme and asked that it be
reconsidered. This reaction is interesting in view of the long history of whipping as a form of
punishment in the United States and elsewhere. Whipping was used as a form of punishment as
far back as ancient Egypt, where Hebrew slaves were whipped by their Egyptian masters if they
failed to produce enough bricks.[15] The Romans, and later the English, used whipping to punish
slaves and vagrants. During the early 1800s, England prohibited the whipping of women, but it
was not until 1948 that whipping was abolished altogether as a form of punishment.[16] Whipping
was employed more often in the American colonies than it was in England. Lying, swearing,
failure to attend church services, stealing, selling rum to Indians, adultery (for women), and
drunkenness were among the offenses for which people could be whipped. After the American
Revolution, incarceration came into use as an alternative to whipping. By 1900, all states except
Maryland and Delaware had abolished whipping. The last known "floggings" occurred around
1950 in those two states, and the Delaware law was not repealed until 1972.[17]

Despite the U.S. protests of the caning in Singapore, the penalty is still used in many
countries. A bill to permit whipping of drug dealers was introduced in the Delaware legislature in 1990 but was not passed. Similar legislation was introduced in California and St.
Louis to punish vandals.[18] Amnesty International has reported that whipping is legal in at
least thirteen countries, including countries in the Middle East, Africa, the Caribbean, and the
Far East.[19]

Singapore responded to criticism of its use of corporal punishment by stating that "it is
because of our tough laws against anti-social crime . . . that we do not have a situation like, say
New York, where even police cars are not spared by vandals."[20] This leads to the question of

whether whipping is effective as a deterrent to crime. An evaluation of the impact of whipping on subsequent criminal behavior of offenders in the United States found that 62 percent of offenders who were whipped were later convicted of another offense. Further, 65 percent of those who were whipped twice were convicted a third time.[21] Despite its failure as a deterrent, whipping and other forms of corporal punishment, such as paddling of schoolchildren, continue to attract attention from the public and some policy makers.[22] There are two reasons for this: Corporal punishment more directly imitates the pain suffered by the victim, and it is of short duration and, therefore, much less expensive to administer than traditional incarceration. The line must be carefully drawn between sanctions that attempt to be more authentic in relation to the crime committed and those that are simply cruel or vindictive.

Try to evaluate whipping or caning of offenders on ethical grounds. Singapore's claim of low crime suggests that caning might be an effective deterrent. Which ethical perspective would see this as an important consideration? Why did Emmanuel Kant believe deterrence of others in the future was a violation of the practical imperative? Is it a good universal rule that those who commit certain crimes be caned? Finally, are there any grounds on which virtue ethics might find caning of an offender ethical?

INNOVATIVE PENALTIES

Darlene Johnson, a mother of four children and pregnant with a fifth, was convicted of three counts of child abuse. The judge sentenced her to a year in jail, to be followed by implantation of a birth control device that would prevent her from conceiving any more children. According to the judge, "It is not safe for her to have children."[23] Is such a sentence cruel and unusual, or is it appropriate and just?

The contraceptive Norplant was approved by the U.S. Food and Drug Administration in 1990 for public use. **Norplant** prevents conception when six small rods containing hormones are placed under the skin in a woman's arm. The rods can be implanted for up to 5 years.[24] The question for criminal justice is whether such a device can or should be used for sentencing in cases involving mistreatment of children. Norplant may prevent abuse of new victims, but it does not address the current or future harm done to present victims. Those who advocate use of Norplant believe it forces the offender to suffer the consequences of misconduct in the parental role and prevents the offender from continuing in that role in the future. Once again, however, *existing* victims are not protected, only *future* victims.

Norplant was made available in school clinics in Baltimore in response to the city's high teenage pregnancy rate. A similar program was initiated in Washington, D.C., where teenage mothers accounted for 18 percent of all births.[25] This use of Norplant outside the criminal justice system points to growing acceptance of this form of contraception, although the coercion inherent in criminal sentencing poses important legal and social issues. Is forced birth control a weak technological attempt to solve a problem that is educational, social, and cultural in nature? Does the use of Norplant discriminate against women inasmuch as it holds them entirely responsible for parenting and abuse, even though males also play significant roles in this process? Is it used in discriminatory fashion against minorities and the poor? Can the use of Norplant be extended beyond the length of a normal jail or probation sentence? These questions have yet to be addressed by the criminal justice system as it looks for sentences that more directly mirror the nature of the harm inflicted by offenders.

What is the moral permissibility of using Norplant applying the three major ethical perspectives? Does it contribute more to the greater total happiness than other penalties? Is it a good universal rule for use in cases of maltreatment of children? Does it do justice without being excessive? These are the questions that ethics would ask, and thoughtful answers to them show

TABLE 8.2 Major Ethical Perspectives and Punishment

Ethical Perspective	Founder	How Should a Person Act?	Limitations	Why Punish Wrongdoers?
Virtue	Aristotle	Moral virtue is the habit of right desire—wanting what is really good for you and nothing else. We are obliged to seek real goods common to all humans guided by the moral virtues.	Focuses on being a good person versus good acts. Moral behavior depends more on one's motivation than on the act committed.	Purpose of society is to provide civil peace and protect liberty from those who would infringe on it by rendering justice. This must be carried out in accord with the moral virtues.
Formalism	Immanuel Kant	Moral worth comes from doing one's duty. Act in a way so that your conduct can become a universal rule. People are never to be treated as a means to another end.	If something is wrong, it is wrong all the time—there are no exceptions. Morality is limited to duty—the baseline, not the highest aspiration of morality.	Because wrongdoers deserve punishment (are blameworthy), punishment should be proportionate based solely on the seriousness of the conduct.
Utilitarianism	John Stuart Mill	Act in a way that results in the greatest good for the greatest number.	Morality is determined by the consequences of an action, leading to problems of measurement and speculation regarding its future impact.	Punishment should deter others, thereby obtaining a greater good. Punishment is aimed at its future impact.

how ethical thinking can inform and enlighten criminal justice decisions, especially as innovative penalties are increasingly sought for offenders.

Table 8.2 illustrates the differences among the three major ethical perspectives and their implications for criminal punishment. Note that formalism looks *backward*, basing punishment solely on the seriousness of the crime committed, whereas utilitarianism looks *forward*, with punishment aimed at its deterrent impact in the future. According to virtue ethics, punishment is justifiable only when it promotes the real good of civil peace and the protection of liberty of others in a manner consistent with the moral virtues.

CAPITAL PUNISHMENT

The **Eighth Amendment** to the U.S. Constitution deals largely with the final stages of the criminal justice process. It is also one of the shortest amendments. It reads as follows: "Excessive bail shall not be required, nor excessive fines imposed, nor cruel and unusual punishment inflicted."

The portion of the Eighth Amendment that has been most rigorously scrutinized is the prohibition of *cruel and unusual punishment*. A punishment is considered cruel and unusual if it violates "evolving standards of decency that mark the progress of a maturing society."[26] Thus, torture is cruel and unusual punishment under the Eighth Amendment. In extreme cases of solitary confinement, corporal punishment, mechanical restraints, and poor medical and sanitary conditions for prisoners, these practices sometimes have been held to be cruel and unusual.[27] No penalty has received more attention than capital punishment—that is, the death penalty.

The penalty of death for the commission of a crime is controversial, yet it is permitted in most states. Proponents argue that death serves as just retribution for murder, prevents future murders, and costs less than life imprisonment. Opponents argue the opposite: It does not serve as just retribution, does not deter murders, and costs more than life in prison. These are empirical arguments that can be resolved with the use of objective evidence. To what extent has the death penalty been used as retribution in the past? What impact does it have on homicide rates? How expensive is an execution compared to life imprisonment?[28] The important moral question is whether capital punishment is morally permissible *as a form of punishment*.

According to utilitarianism, the empirical issues previously noted would be significant because they would help determine the total good (in balancing pain versus pleasure) produced by capital punishment. If greater total happiness was increased through the use of capital punishment, then it would be a good policy according to utilitarianism. Its economic cost and whether it deters future crimes would weigh heavily in this decision. Formalism would determine the moral permissibility of capital punishment on entirely different grounds, depending on whether it would make a good universal rule to employ in all cases of murder. The ethics of the penalty would never include deterrence because that aims to prevent the future crimes of others—using the current offender as a means to another end (violating the practical imperative). A third view would examine the imposition of capital punishment using virtue ethics. Does capital punishment seek a real good via the moral virtues? If it was determined that capital punishment contributes to the civil peace (a real good) and that its imposition is just (i.e., gives an offender what she or he is due, not more, not less), then it would be morally permissible. The contemporary issue of errors in a number of capital cases is serious for virtue ethics because it creates doubt about whether justice (a moral virtue) is served by capital punishment, especially considering that there is no way to correct a mistake.[29] An unjust capital sentence cannot be undone once an execution occurs.

LIFE IMPRISONMENT MORE SEVERE THAN DEATH?

An interesting question has been raised in contemporary society that was raised 250 years ago: Is life imprisonment a more severe punishment than the death penalty? During the 1960s, a majority of Americans opposed the death penalty, but today public opinion polls show widespread support for capital punishment. This support is manifested in the death penalty laws of thirty-seven states and the federal government. The current support continues despite concerns about the deterrent effect of capital punishment and despite the fact that most other nations have abolished it. Even South Africa abolished capital punishment in 1995 after it had been in effect for 350 years. This leaves the United States among the few countries in the world that still carries out death sentences.[30]

In death penalty cases, a jury often may choose between the death penalty and life imprisonment. Supporters of capital punishment argue that life imprisonment is a less severe penalty than the death penalty. An argument can be made, however, that life imprisonment is actually a *more* severe sentence than the death penalty. This argument was made most persuasively by Cesare Beccaria in his 1764 book, *An Essay on Crimes and Punishments.* Beccaria argued, "It is not the terrible yet momentary spectacle of the death of a wretch, but the long and painful example of a man deprived of liberty . . . which is the strongest curb against crimes." He believed that the impression left by an execution is mitigated by a tendency to forget the event because of its brevity. In addition, some offenders may desire death because they are vain or fanatic or because they simply wish to escape their misery. Beccaria goes on to argue that life imprisonment is a better deterrent to crime than the death penalty. An execution provides only a single deterrent example, whereas "the penalty of a lifetime of servitude for a single crime supplies frequent and lasting examples" to others. "Adding up all the moments of unhappiness and servitude," Beccaria concludes, life imprisonment "may well be even more cruel; but [it is] drawn out over an entire lifetime, while the pain of death exerts its whole force in a moment."[31]

Beccaria also states that the death penalty is not useful "because of the example of barbarity it gives men." He notes, "It seems to me absurd that the laws, which are an expression of the public will, which detest and punish homicide, should themselves commit it, and that to deter citizens from murder, they order a public one."

Former New York state governor Mario Cuomo opposed capital punishment on grounds similar to those set forth by Beccaria. His opposition to the death penalty was seen by many as a major cause of his failure to win reelection. A year before the election, Cuomo refused to send an inmate serving a life sentence from New York state to Oklahoma, where the inmate faced the death penalty, despite the inmate's stated wish to die. After the election, the new governor sent the inmate to Oklahoma to be executed. Ironically, prior to execution the inmate wrote a statement that said, "Let there be no mistake, Mario Cuomo is wright [sic]. . . . All jurors should remember this. Attica and Oklahoma State Penitentiary are living hells." Cuomo later remarked about the inmate, "He admitted that being allowed to die was an act of clemency for a double murderer, relieving him of the relentless confinement he dreaded more than death."[32]

These are fascinating arguments to assess in moral terms. Given the comments of Beccaria and Cuomo, can you determine their ethical perspectives?

Controversy regarding capital punishment in recent years focused on whether executions of juveniles violate the Eighth Amendment of the U.S. Constitution. From an ethical perspective, the interesting aspect of the appeal to the U.S. Supreme Court was the court's increasing willingness to cite international law and foreign judgments to support its decisions. For example, a friend-of-the-court brief was written on behalf of forty-eight countries that urged the Supreme Court justices to declare the death penalty for juveniles unconstitutional, a position that the Court ultimately adopted.[33] Critics argue that this trend is a bad idea because judges might use international decisions to support their preferences rather than following the original intent of the Constitution's founders. Supporters of this trend see it as a safeguard from narrow parochial views, reflecting recognition of international legal norms and shared values across the world not contemplated by the writers of the U.S. Constitution more than 200 years ago. In ethical terms, the trend toward citing international laws and decisions reflects growing international consensus on issues of crime and justice and the decline of moral relativism, leading nations in the contemporary world to judge one another's laws and policies in moral terms. For example, the international Convention on the Rights of the Child entered into force in 1990, and it has since been ratified by 192 nations, including all UN members plus one nonmember country.[34] No other international agreement relating to justice has such universal support. This suggests international movement toward common legal and ethical standards in the justice process.

ETHICS IN BOOKS

Ethics is everywhere, even in the books we read, which sometimes are written without ethics specifically in mind. Here is a summary of such a book, followed by questions that ask you to reflect on the ethical connections.

THE PRINCE

by Niccolo Machiavelli
(written in 1512)
(Bantam, 1984)

Niccolo Machiavelli was born in 1469 and spent his entire life in Florence, Italy. He worked for the ruling Medici family, which maintained power during most of his life, and he was in a position to observe and interact with major political and military leaders of Europe of that period.

The Prince offers advice on how a prince should obtain and stay in power. His approach is pragmatic to the extreme, emphasizing power, advantage, and success over truth and virtue—coining the phrase "politics is the art of the possible." Whereas Aristotle (and Plato before him) makes a connection between being good and being successful, Machiavelli sees them as contradictory. He has none of the idealism of the earlier writers, arguing that only practical goals are achievable, and ideals should be lowered so they can be attained. Machiavelli observes that "unarmed prophets have failed, armed prophets have succeeded," making the point that those with high moral principles often become martyrs. Thus, according to Machiavelli, the goal to be achieved is not virtue, but success.

Assumptions that underlie *The Prince* are that the greatest good is success, and that honest men do not survive: "a prudent ruler cannot and should not honor his word when it places him at a disadvantage." He also states that for a leader "it would be best to be both loved and feared. But because the two rarely come together, anyone compelled to choose will find greater security in being feared than in being loved." Machiavelli argues further that without penalties the law has no value because there is no strong moral force in individuals that exists outside the law. His views of success without moral constraint separate him from most writers in the fields of ethics and politics.

Machiavelli's views are challenging and some find them offensive, but no one has been more influential, yet more despised, than Machiavelli. His book forces us to examine our assumptions about human nature and to defend our expectations of an often disappointing political system. Although written 20 years earlier, *The Prince* was published in 1532, 5 years after Machiavelli died.

QUESTIONS

1. What would Aristotle and Kant say of Machiavelli's views? What specifically would they object to?
2. Are there areas in which John Stuart Mill would agree on some of Machiavelli's positions? Can you offer a controversial example of the exercise of political power that both Mill and Machiavelli would accept?

ETHICS IN THE MOVIES

Movies seek to entertain and inform the audience about a story, incident, or person. Many good movies also hit upon important ethical themes in making significant decisions that affect the lives of others. Read the movie summary here (and watch the movie if you haven't already), and answer the questions to make the ethical connections.

DEAD MAN WALKING

Tim Robbins, Director
(1996)

The movie opens with Sister Helen Prejean (Susan Sarandon), a nun from Louisiana, who receives a letter from an inmate on Death Row asking for a visit. Prejean works in an inner-city neighborhood and decides to visit the inmate. She is warned by the prison chaplain about being manipulated, and the inmate Matthew Poncelet (Sean Penn) wants her to help him with his appeal. At one point Poncelet says that he and Prejean have nothing in common, but Prejean says, "We both live with the poor," something that apparently never occurred to the inmate before. Prejean agrees to help him with his last-minute appeal before his pending execution.

Dead Man Walking is based on the nonfiction book by Sister Helen Prejean. The movie is notable for its objectivity about capital punishment. There is no intention to change the viewer's mind about capital punishment. Instead, it forces you to reflect on the facts, emotions, and beliefs of the offender, the victims, and all those involved in cases like this. The inmate is on Death Row for a rape and murder of a couple on a lover's lane. The film is absorbing as Prejean meets the parents of the murdered girl, the father of the dead boy, and the inmate's family; she even faces the anger of her own mother, who resents her befriending a murderer. These scenes are emotional and sometimes troubling, but they are thoughtful, looking to provide insight rather than shock or sensationalism.

As a nun, Sister Prejean believes in the Christian principle that all sins can be forgiven because God's love is available to everyone, but she does not push Poncelet, hoping only that he will die understanding the impact of his crimes and his life. The movie's theme might be "finding meaning"—how people strive to move on after tragedy strikes (as a victim or parent) and how to find meaning when your life has been devoid of meaning (Poncelet). Susan Sarandon won the Academy Award for Best Actress for her performance, and both Sean Penn (Best Actor) and Tim Robbins (Best Director) received Oscar nominations.

QUESTIONS

1. Is it morally permissible to execute a murderer if he truly is remorseful and apologizes for his actions?
2. The imposition of capital punishment has been marred by errors in convictions, racial discrimination, and other problems in its administration over the years. Do you believe these problems will ever be eliminated? If they were eliminated, would it be permissible to use capital punishment more frequently as a penalty for major crimes?

Discussion Question

Find an example of an innovative kind of sentence imposed in a criminal case. Apply the three major ethical perspectives to evaluate its moral permissibility.

Critical Thinking Exercises

All ethical decisions affect others (by definition) and, as Aristotle points out, ethical decision making is achieved consistently only through practice. Given the outline of virtue ethics, formalism, and utilitarianism, evaluate the moral permissibility of the conduct in question in each scenario.

Important note on method: *Critical thinking requires the ability to evaluate viewpoints, facts, and behaviors objectively to assess information or methods of argumentation to establish the true worth or merit of an act or course of conduct. Please evaluate these scenarios, first analyzing pros and cons of alternate views,* before *you come to a* conclusion. Do not *draw a conclusion first, and then try to find facts to support it—this frequently leads to narrow (and incorrect) thinking.*

To properly evaluate the moral permissibility of a course of action using critical thinking skills:

1. *Begin with an open mind (no preconceptions!),*
2. *Isolate and evaluate the relevant facts on both sides,*
3. *Identify the precise moral question to be answered, and*
4. *Apply ethical principles to the moral question based on an objective evaluation of the facts, only then drawing a conclusion.*

8.1 Ethics of Sniping and Negotiating

With disturbing regularity we hear of a person, usually a man, who takes his family hostage and provokes a standoff with the police. Often the man has a gun and fires shots out the window in the direction of the police. In some cases, members of the family are killed, bystanders wounded, and police officers shot. These hostage-takers usually have significant family problems, employment problems, substance abuse problems, and sometimes are mentally unstable. When surrounded by police, they have little to negotiate for other than to surrender because their loved ones are being held hostage with them.

You are a hostage negotiator for the police department in the middle of such a situation in which you are talking by telephone with a man who is holding his own family hostage, is making unreasonable demands, and is shooting out the window. One bystander has already been hit by

gunfire. After many hours of unsuccessful attempts to get the man to surrender, you are asked by your supervisor to try to lure the man near a window at the rear of the house because a police sharpshooter has a clear shot to that position. The intention is to kill the hostage-taker.

- Evaluate the moral permissibility of luring the hostage-taker into a position to be shot.

8.2 Ethics and Mandatory Minimums

A 27-year-old African American accepted $500 from a neighbor for sending in the mail what he knew was a package of drugs, although he did not know the kind of drugs or their value. He did it because he faced mounting debts. He has a college education, a job, and no prior criminal record. He pleaded guilty to the federal crime, which requires a mandatory minimum sentence for anyone convicted of trafficking more than 50 grams of crack cocaine.

You are the federal judge assigned this case. The defendant faces a mandatory minimum sentence of 10 years in federal prison with no possibility of parole. A mandatory minimum requires anyone convicted of the crime to receive the minimum sentence prescribed by law, regardless of any others factors that may be present in the case.[35]

Mandatory minimum sentences increased dramatically in the 1980s as a result of the so-called war on drugs during the Reagan administration. The issue posed by mandatory minimums is that any features of the defendant's character, history, or circumstances that might call for a lesser punishment must be ignored. The sentence can be increased, however, if the defendant has a criminal record, sells drugs to children, or sells very large amounts of drugs.

You are having trouble with this case because it appears that the mandatory minimum sentence law treats all drug law violations of this type as if they were the same; however, offenders and circumstances dramatically differ in terms of seriousness and dangerousness, and you do not believe this offender is dangerous or deserving of 10 years in prison.

- Evaluate the moral permissibility of your decision to impose the mandatory minimum sentence in this case.

8.3 Lawyer-Assisted Suicide

Although the death penalty has been abolished in most countries around the world, thirty-seven states in the United States allow capital punishment for the conviction of certain crimes. These usually involve cases of homicide or treason. There are a record number of prisoners on death row in the United States, and successful appeals to reduce death sentences or review the facts of cases are rare. Courts and legislators have also restricted the possible grounds and opportunities for appeal in recent years.[36]

This situation has led some death row inmates to give up hope and not pursue the appeals allotted to them by law. Even though there are hundreds of documented cases of death sentences of innocent persons, the lack of hope for offenders on death row is pervasive.[37] The U.S. Supreme Court held in 1997 that terminally ill patients have no constitutional right to assisted suicide, but death row inmates appear to have the legal right to expedite their own executions by foregoing appeals.[38]

What should the offender's lawyer do if his or her client does not wish to appeal? Should that choice be respected? If it is, can this be considered lawyer-assisted suicide?

The choice by a death row inmate to expedite the execution process may be a rational one. Life on death row is both undesirable and uncertain.[39] Expediting the state's execution is much more certain and perhaps unavoidable, given trends in the outcomes of death penalty appeals. As one attorney has characterized the situation, "In the real world this death row client has only two options: the state can kill him now, or it can kill him later. He chooses now."[40]

Should a lawyer pursue appeals, despite the wishes of his or her client? If so, can this be considered state-assisted suicide? If the offender's attorney does not challenge the case facts or the penalty, it could make future executions easier by lowering further the legal and procedural barriers to executions. Should the attorney represent the client's wishes, even if those wishes lead to certain death?

- Evaluate the moral permissibility of the lawyer's possible actions under these circumstances.
- What would you do as an *attorney* in this situation? What would you do as an *offender* in this situation?

8.4 Predisposed to Re-offend?

The New York State legislature passed a law that permits the state to lock up individuals for crimes they might commit, rather than for crimes they have already committed. The law requires mental health professionals to screen all prison inmates doing time for sex offenses and determine if they are disposed to committing more sex crimes upon release. Those found likely to re-offend would be placed on trial, and if a jury agrees they are dangerous, they would be confined or placed under very strict supervision in the community.[41]

This law is a departure from traditional criminal procedure, which requires a crime to be committed before a person can be held legally responsible and punished. It also assumes as fact the controversial proposition that mental health professionals can accurately predict future dangerousness of offenders. Nevertheless, the law responds to public fears regarding potential repeat crimes by sex offenders.

- Is it morally permissible to punish offenders for future crimes that they are found to be at high risk of committing?

8.5 An Affair, a Trial, and an Execution

With less than a week to go before the scheduled execution of a man who contended his murder trial was tainted by a love affair between the judge and the prosecutor, a state judge ordered a hearing into the accusation. It was argued that if the love affair occurred, the condemned man did not receive a fair trial. Several prominent former judges and prosecutors urged the governor to delay the execution to allow more time for a hearing to determine if the affair took place. "It is an irrevocable wrong to send a man to his death without ever hearing this critical evidence," the group said in a letter to the Governor.

In a separate letter to local prosecutors, the Texas Attorney General said the state would ask the district court to "thoroughly review the defendant's claims before the execution proceeds" in order to "protect the integrity of the Texas legal system."

The convicted murderer, Charles Hood, age 39, was to be executed for the murder and robbery of a couple he lived with in Plano, just north of Dallas. Fingerprints linked Mr. Hood to the murders, and he was arrested the next day in Indiana driving a car belonging to the murdered man, who had been Mr. Hood's supervisor at a strip club where they both worked. The supervisor's girlfriend, Tracie Lynn Wallace, a former dancer at the club, was also killed in this incident.

Having exhausted all other appeals, Mr. Hood's lawyers have tried to prove in recent months that Mr. Hood's trial was tainted because the judge, Verla Sue Holland, and the Collin County district attorney at the time, Thomas S. O'Connell Jr., were having an affair.

Lawyers for Mr. Hood contend that the affair was long rumored in Collin County's legal circles, but no one with evidence about it had been willing to testify under oath. Mr. Hood's lawyers got a sworn affidavit from a former assistant district attorney, who said the romantic relationship "was common knowledge in the district attorney's office, and the Collin County bar, in general," at the time of the trial.[42] With this testimony in hand, Mr. Hood's lawyers asked the Texas Court of Criminal Appeals, the state's highest court, to stay the execution.

- Evaluate the moral permissibility of a judge and prosecutor having a romantic affair while working the same case.
- Assess any potential remedies for the offender(s) in the case(s).

Key Concepts

Retribution *105*	Rehabilitation *105*	Corporal punishment *109*
Incapacitation *105*	Disparity in sentences *106*	Norplant *110*
Deterrence *105*	Sentencing guidelines *106*	Eighth Amendment *111*

Notes

1. Susan Estrich, "A Just Sentence for Susan Smith," *USA Today* (August 3, 1995), p. 11.
2. Exodus 21:12–25; Leviticus 24:17–21; Numbers 35:30–1; Deuteronomy 19:11–12.
3. *Overton v. Buzzetta*, 123 S.Ct. 2162 (2003). See also *Turner v. Safley*, 107 S.Ct. 2254 (1987).
4. *United States v. Booker*, 125 S.Ct. 738 (2005).
5. Don M. Gottfredson, *Effects of Judges' Sentencing Decisions on Criminal Careers* (Washington, DC: National Institute of Justice, 1999); Jeffrey Y. Ulmer and John H. Kramer, "The Use and Transformation of Formal Decision-Making Criteria: Sentencing Guidelines, Organizational Contexts, and Case Processing Strategies," *Social Problems*, vol. 45 (May 1998), p. 248.
6. Dale Parent, Terence Dunworth, Douglas McDonald, and William Rhodes, *The Impact of Sentencing Guidelines* (Washington, DC: National Institute of Justice, 1996), p. 5.
7. Kevin McCoy, "Appeal of Madoff's 150-year Sentence Wouldn't Matter," *USA Today* (July 2, 2009).
8. Scott D. Camp, Gerlad G. Gaes, Neil P. Langan, and William G. Saylor, "The Influence of Prisons on Inmate Misconduct: A Multilevel Investigation," *Justice Quarterly*, vol. 20 (September 2003), pp. 501–533; Maureen Buell and Susan W. McCampbell, "Preventing Staff Misconduct in the Community Corrections Setting," *Corrections Today*, vol. 65 (February 2003), p. 90.
9. Gregory L. Little, Kenneth D. Robinson, Katherine D. Burnette, and E. Stephen Swan, "Twenty-Year Recidivism Results for MRT-Treat Offenders," *Cognitive Behavioral Treatment Review*, vol.

19 (2010), pp. 1–9; Sally F. Stevenson, Guy Hall, and J.M. Innes, "Rationalizing Criminal Behaviour: The Influence of Criminal Sentiments on Sociomoral Development in Violent Offenders and Nonoffenders," *International Journal of Offender Therapy & Comparative Criminology*, vol. 48 (April 2004), pp.161–174.
10. Graeme Newman, *Just and Painful: A Case for the Corporal Punishment of Criminals*, 2nd ed. (Albany, NY: Harrow & Heston, 1983), p. 6.
11. Andrea Stone, "Whipping Penalty Judged Too Harsh—by Some," *USA Today* (March 10, 1994), p. 3.
12. Tom Squitieri, "Proposals Seek More Drastic Punishments," *USA Today* (February 14, 1990), p. 3.
13. Sam S. Souryal and Dennis W. Potts, "The Penalty of Hand Amputation for Theft in Islamic Justice," *Journal of Criminal Justice*, vol. 22 (1994), pp. 249–265.
14. *Trop v. Dulles*, 356 U.S. 86 (1958); *Rhodes v. Chapman*, 452 U.S. 337 (1981).
15. W. M. Cooper, A History of the Rod in All Countries (London, UK: John Camden Hotten, 1870).
16. L. A. Parry, *The History of Torture in England* (Montclair, NJ: Patterson Smith, 1934); Graham Newman, *The Punishment Response* (New York, NY: J. B. Lippincott, 1978).
17. S. Rubin, *The Law of Criminal Correction* (St. Paul, MN: West Publishing, 1973).
18. Paul Leavitt, "Calls for Caning Keep on Coming," *USA Today* (May 25, 1994), p. 3.
19. Amnesty International, *1995 Report* (New York, NY: Amnesty International, 1995).
20. Cited in Stone, "Whipping Penalty Judged Too Harsh—by Some." p. 3.

21. R. G. Caldwell, *Criminology*, 2nd ed. (New York, NY: Ronald Press, 1965).

22. Tamara Henry, "Groups Seek to Lay Down Law on Corporal Discipline," *USA Today* (March 8, 1994), p. 6D; Graham Newman, *The Punishment Response* (New York, NY: J. B. Lippincott, 1978).

23. Paul Leavitt, "Birth Control Sentence," *USA Today* (January 7, 1991), p. 3.

24. Kim Painter, "Norplant Gets a Shot in the Arm," *USA Today* (August 22, 1995), p. 4D.

25. Paul Leavitt, "Baltimore Schools Offer Teens Norplant," *USA Today* (December 4, 1992), p. 3.

26. *Thompson v. Oklahoma*, 108 S.Ct. 2687 (1988).

27. See *French v. Owens*, 777 F.2d 1250 (7th Cir. 1985).

28. See Jay S. Albanese, *Criminal Justice*, 3rd ed. (Boston, MA: Allyn & Bacon, 2005); Hugo Adam Bedau and Paul Cassell, Eds., *Debating the Death Penalty* (New York, NY: Oxford University Press, 2003).

29. Barry Scheck, Peter Neufeld, and Jim Dwyer, *Actual Innocence* (New York, NY: Signet, 2001); Stanley Cohen, *The Wrong Men* (New York, NY: Carroll & Graf, 2003).

30. Charles Lane, "Why Japan Still Has the Death Penalty," *The Washington Post* (January 16, 2005), p. B1.

31. Cesare Beccaria, *Essay on Crimes and Punishments* (1764) (Indianapolis, IN: Bobbs-Merrill, 1984), ch. 16.

32. Doug Ferguson, "Grasso, Just before Dying, Says Cuomo Is Right: Life in Prison Would Be Worse," *The Buffalo News* (March 21, 1995), p. 14.

33. Warren Richey, "Global Legal Trends Make Waves at High Court," *The Christian Science Monitor* (October 25, 2004), p. 1; *Roper v. Simmons*, 543 U.S. 551 (2005).

34. UN Convention on the Rights of the Child. (1990). http://www.unicef.org/crc/ (accessed August 1, 2004).

35. David Dolinko, "Ethical Problems of Mandatory Minimum Sentences," *Tikkun* (March–April 1998), p. 3.

36. Stephen B. Bright and Patrick Keenan, "Judges and the Politics of Death," *Boston University Law Review*, vol. 75 (May 1995), pp. 759–765; Vivian Berger, "Herrera v. Collins: The Gateway of Innocence for Death-Sentenced Offenders Leads Nowhere," *William & Marry Law Review*, vol. 35 (Spring 1994), p. 943.

37. Micahel Radelet, Hugo Adam Bedau, and Constance E. Putnam, *In Spite of Innocence: Erroneous Convictions in Capital Cases* (Boston, MA: Northeastern University Press, 1992); John McCormick, "The Wrongly Condemned," *Newsweek* (November 9, 1998), p. 64; Stanley Cohen, *The Wrong Men: America's Epidemic of Wrongful Death Row Convictions* (New York, NY: Carroll & Graff, 2003).

38. *Vacco v. Quill*, 117 S.Ct. 36 (1997).

39. Richard M. Rossi, *Waiting to Die: Life on Death Row* (New York, NY: Vision Books, 2004); Jan Arriens, *Welcome to Hell: Letters and Writings from Death Row* (Boston, MA: Northeastern University Press, 1997).

40. Michael Mello, "Representing Death Row: An Argument for Attorney-Assisted Suicide," *Criminal Law Bulletin*, vol. 34 (January–February 1998), pp. 48–64; Michael Mello, *Deathwork: Defending the Condemned* (Minneapolis, MN: University of Minnesota Press, 2002).

41. "Punishment without Crime," *Newsday* (New York) (March 2, 2007); see also Bill Mears, "Can Sex Offenders be Held After Serving Criminal Sentences?" *CNN* (January 12, 2010).

42. James C. McKinley, Jr. "As Texas Execution Nears, Hearing Is Set on Claim Judge and Prosecutor Had Affair," *The New York Times* (September 5, 2008), p. 15.

CHAPTER 9

Liability
What Should Be the Consequence of Unethical Conduct?

Learning Objectives:

- To understand the nature of civil remedies for ethical misconduct, such as compensation and blacklisting.

- To recognize the double standards often placed on public officials regarding liability for conduct that is accepted when acting as private citizens.

- To evaluate the ethical dilemmas posed by sex offender notifications laws.

- To distinguish "right versus right" ethical dilemmas.

- To assess the liabilities faced in unethical individual, corporate, and government misconduct.

Everyone's for ethics until it begins to exact a cost.

—Michael Josephson (1998)

In 2004, President Bush nominated Bernard Kerik, former commissioner of the New York City Police Department, to head the Department of Homeland Security (which oversees immigration and border security among other agencies). It was soon revealed, however, that a nanny that Kerik had employed was in the country as an illegal immigrant and that he had failed to pay taxes on her behalf.

It also was reported that Kerik had an ongoing extramarital affair with the editor of his autobiography and had engaged in questionable business dealings as a private citizen.[1]

Kerik's case bears a striking resemblance to another that occurred during the 1990s, when President Clinton nominated Zoe Baird for the position of U.S. attorney general. It came to light that she had hired a nanny in her home but failed to pay Social Security taxes for her employee as required by law. Interestingly, a publication called for Baird to withdraw her name (which Baird ultimately did), and an editor of the publication later confided that she also had a nanny for whom she was not paying Social Security taxes, "but her situation was different" because she was not trying to become U.S. attorney general.[2] This tortured reasoning illustrates the **double standard** often placed on public officials. Conduct we often accept from private citizens somehow becomes objectionable when it is done by public officials. It is true that public officials represent others and, therefore, should be worthy of the public trust, but the same can be said of corporate officials who are entrusted with shareholder assets, private attorneys entrusted with their clients' funds, the automobile mechanic entrusted with your car, and so on for teachers, cooks, construction workers, and virtually all other professions. Ethics by definition involves conduct that affects others, so the public official versus private citizen distinction is misleading. Instead, it is crucial to recognize that all unethical conduct is serious because it affects others whose interests are equally valued as fellow human beings regardless of the social status of the wrongdoer or the victim.

CIVIL REMEDIES FOR ETHICAL MISCONDUCT

The remedies for ethical misconduct can lie outside the criminal law. Civil penalties, which seek compensation rather than punishment, often are used to "correct" wrongful actions. Civil penalties are used because the **burden of proof for liability** is lower than that for criminal cases (preponderance of evidence versus beyond a reasonable doubt). Also, wronged parties are often more interested in compensation for their losses than in seeing the offender punished.

Macy's department store paid $600,000 to settle a civil complaint by the New York state attorney general who found that Latino and African American customers suspected of shoplifting were arrested, handcuffed, and detained three to five times more often than white customers—accounting for police arrests of different racial and ethnic groups for theft in the areas surrounding Macy's stores. Macy's had a formal company policy banning racial and ethnic profiling, but it was ignored by employees.[3] Although the behavior in question was not criminal, Macy's was civilly liable, and the victims were compensated for their maltreatment. An ethical analysis suggests that the profiling and abuse of targeted groups was probably justified on grounds of utility (deterrence) because neither formalism nor virtue ethics could defend such tactics. Of course, the utilitarian consideration fails to account for the fact that over the long term such a policy would produce complaints, might result in legal liability, and probably would affect both Macy's reputation and its competitive business. Clearly, the greatest total happiness was not produced by Macy's actions, illustrating that faulty anticipation of the consequences of a course of conduct can result in unethical conduct and unhappiness for all involved.

Repeat offenders sometimes draw special attention because civil compensation may not have a strong deterrent effect for future violations. For example, New York City engaged in a concerted effort to rid itself of "mob-connected" contractors who were doing business with the city. One of the recommended solutions to the problem was "blacklisting" businesses or individuals who defrauded the city in the past or who executed past contracts in a way that constituted gross negligence.[4] **Blacklisting** is future punishment (by exclusion from participation) for a pattern of past violations. Is this ethical? Should a person or business suffer in the future for past misconduct?

The nature and extent of "punishment" and "compensation" outside the criminal justice system continues to be debated. For example, once an offender has served a prison sentence for a crime, on release should he or she continue to be excluded from certain professions or from voting?

This issue of continuing civil penalties after a criminal sentence has been served has been hotly debated in the case of registering former sex offenders. Public concern reached a crescendo during the 1990s, when a 7-year-old New Jersey girl, Megan Kanka, was raped and murdered by a twice-convicted sex offender who was living across the street. Within 6 months of the incident, New Jersey passed a **sex offender notification law,** requiring ex–sex offenders to register with police and for communities to be warned when such an offender was living nearby. The law also required offenders to notify police of their location every 90 days with penalties of 7 months in jail and fines if they did not comply. Despite legal challenges, most states followed New Jersey's lead.

Once an offender has served his or her sentence, it has been argued, the punishment has ended. Sex offender notification laws allow a criminal sentence to continue as long as the offender lives, thereby continuing to "punish" the ex-offender through civil restrictions. Court challenges have gone all the way to the U.S. Supreme Court, which held that it is constitutional to notify a community when a former sex offender lives in its midst or moves into the area.[5] The Supreme Court also ruled that judges must hold hearings to determine whether an individual sex offender is subject to the notification law and the extent of the warning to be given to the community, but the impact of this provision is unclear, given that California released a CD-ROM with the locations of 64,000 registered sex offenders, and about half the states now have publicly accessible Internet sites that contain information on individual sex offenders.[6]

The availability of this information to the public has resulted in instances of vigilante behavior. Four days after one offender's name was listed, a paroled child molester's car was fire-bombed; the crime was allegedly carried out by his neighbors.[7] A New Jersey man was attacked and beaten by two men who mistakenly believed that he was a child molester.[8] Five bullets were shot through the front window of the house of a former sex offender after police had circulated fliers in the area identifying him by name, address, and photograph.[9] Notification of the community regarding the release of sex offenders implies that the state has some belief that the ex-offenders may still be dangerous, so it is not surprising that it has produced panic in a number of cases. Even though a small proportion of all offenders are sex offenders, these cases are highly publicized, and public concern is quite high.[10] Nevertheless, few incarcerated sex offenders receive treatment, and the treatment they do receive appears to be ineffective in many cases.[11]

Is it morally permissible to disseminate the location of former sex offenders to the public? From the perspective of virtue ethics, what is the real good being sought? Is liberty or civil peace being served? In addition, are the moral virtues of prudence and justice served by community notification? Formalism requires adherence to both the categorical and practical imperatives. Is community notification a good universal rule, and does it involve using a person for another end? Conclusions are not obvious. The total happiness sought by utilitarianism requires an objective weighing of the potential "costs" (e.g., impeding offender reform, incorrect addresses, possible vigilante behavior by the public) versus the "benefits" (e.g., public knowledge of the location of former sex offenders). The case of sex offender notification makes it clear that a policy found to be constitutional does not automatically mean the policy is also ethical. Determining moral permissibility is distinct from determining legal permissibility.

INDIVIDUAL MISCONDUCT

Given that different ethical perspectives can sometimes produce different results, it is sometimes asked, "Isn't there a general rule to follow in *all* cases to determine whether my conduct is ethical?" For a **test to know whether your conduct is ethical,** ask the questions, "Would I want the public to know about this?" and "Would I want this to appear in the newspaper?" Conduct you would not want publicly known is rarely ethical conduct.

In a similar way, Rushworth Kidder, founder of the Institute for Global Ethics, observes that right versus wrong scenarios are usually easy to decide in ethical terms. Stealing versus paying for merchandise is not a difficult ethical question. It is **"right versus right" ethical dilemmas** that are more difficult. For example, should a first offender be given a warning or arrested? Should a prosecutor file marijuana possession charges against a college student or let the university handle it as an on-campus disciplinary matter? Should you tell your supervisor about a colleague who is drinking on the job? In each of these cases, compelling arguments can be made on both sides. Kidder identifies four types of issues found in "right versus right" ethical dilemmas[12]:

- *Justice versus mercy.* Fairness and equity in applying the law sometimes conflict with compassion, empathy, and love.
- *Short term versus long term.* Immediate needs or desires conflict with future goals or prospects.
- *Individual versus community.* Conflict occurs in evaluating the positions of self versus others or a smaller group versus the larger group.
- *Truth versus loyalty.* Honesty or integrity conflicts with commitment, responsibility, or keeping a promise.

Kidder recommends that an ethical dilemma be assessed to determine which of these four conflicts is at issue. Most ethical dilemmas involve one of these conflicts, but some involve more than one. Once the nature of the conflict is identified, and information is gathered about the evidence on both sides, then ethical principles can be applied to assess the moral permissibility of the conduct in question.

For example, the Pennsylvania Supreme Court banned prosecutors from urging jurors to "send a message" with their verdicts. In this case, prosecutors used a strong rhetorical flourish in speaking to the jury of a murder case, saying, "When you think of the death penalty, there are messages to be sent. There is a message on the street saying, 'Look at that, he got death; you see that, Honey, that's why you live by the rules, so you don't end up like that.' "[13] The court held that such send-a-message exhortations are "particularly prejudicial and should be avoided." So although prosecutors are expected to make their cases earnestly and with vigor, the court says that statements that go beyond the facts of the case at hand are "deliberate attempts to destroy the objectivity and impartiality" of the jury, whose decision should be based on reflective judgment rather than emotion.[14] Using the four-part typology of ethical dilemmas, send-a-message verdicts are of the "individual versus community" type, where the argument to the jury relies on general emotional appeal to *community* safety versus the *individual* facts of the case and the defendant at hand. This helps to frame the ethical question: "Is it morally permissible to ask juries to send a message to others in their sentencing deliberations rather than to consider only the facts of the case and the sentence they believe the offender deserves?" Although valid arguments can be made on both sides of this issue (making it a "right versus right" dilemma), application of utility, formalism, and virtue ethics make it clear that the aims of justice, the categorical imperative, and total happiness are more likely to be achieved by focusing solely on the case at hand.

A particularly difficult ethical dilemma exists in the case of **assisted suicide.** In the 1990s, Dr. Jack Kevorkian claimed to have provided deadly drugs to 130 terminally ill patients. His work has been alternately called "assisted suicide" or "murder." Many people believe that provision of these drugs allows for "death with dignity." Others believe Kevorkian is "playing God" and has no right to provide people with the means to hasten their deaths. The application of the criminal law to this kind of behavior is not uniform because not all states include these acts in their definition of homicide. The ethics of assisted suicide are still being debated in evaluating a patient's right to determine his or her own destiny and the physician's role in that choice. After a highly publicized, televised assisted suicide in 1999, Jack Kevorkian was convicted of second-degree murder and sentenced to 10–25 years in prison in Michigan.[15] Application of the law is complicated in these cases because the physician plays a passive role (does not administer the drug) and because the patient gives his or her consent or self-administers a lethal dose. Nevertheless, consent is not a valid defense to the crimes of assault or homicide because the law generally does not permit people to victimize themselves. As a result, the debate has focused on the role of the physician. The state of Oregon passed a law that permitted physicians to prescribe lethal medicines to terminally ill patients near the ends of their lives. After the first year, only fifteen people ended their lives with lethal medication, although six others obtained the medications but died of their diseases.[16] The impact of a law is only one consideration in determining its desirability, of course, as the morality of the action also must be deemed acceptable.

In the case of assisted suicide, there are three types of ethical dilemmas: justice versus mercy (imposing liability on physicians versus mercy deaths of terminally ill patients), short term versus long term (allowing for short-term relief from pain when death is never certain), and individual versus community (permitting individuals to make decisions to end their lives prematurely when such "consent" is not a defense to other consensual offenses and it might promote euthanasia). This issue is evaluated further in Chapter 10 in the landmark case of *Vacco v. Quill.*

ETHICS CHECKUP
Employee E-Mail Surveillance

In one of the largest sexual harassment settlements in U.S. history, a company agreed to pay more than $2 million to settle a lawsuit brought by four women employees who complained of being targets of online sexual harassment. The women found pornographic messages on a computer system and an anonymous sadistic pornographic image through company e-mail. In response to the women's complaints, the company began monitoring the e-mail of all employees so that anyone engaging in misconduct in the future would be discovered. Surveillance of employees' Internet and e-mail use can affect employee trust and morale, but employers can reduce the risk of being sued by informing employees that they cannot expect privacy in either their Internet or e-mail use. Businesses are trying to formulate policies that seek to establish a fair balance between security and trust. Such policies will "actually protect users in their organizations from discrimination, harassment, and embarrassment," said one expert, adding that companies that implement these policies are "looking at the greater good."[17]

Using ethical principles, attempt to justify employer monitoring of employee e-mail and Internet use. What is your conclusion?

CORPORATE MISCONDUCT

A growing trend in U.S. law is to bring charges against those deemed responsible for the death of others, although those potentially responsible were not present at the scene of the crime. For example, a carnival ride owner was charged with manslaughter when a 15-year-old girl was thrown from a ride into a wall and killed. The lap bar on her seat was not secure. It was the first time a carnival ride owner was held criminally responsible for causing a death as a result of a malfunctioning ride.[18] In years past, cases like this were resolved through civil suits in which the responsible party would pay damages (in the form of money) to the victim or the victim's family. Criminal charges are now being added as further punishment to the parties found responsible. The ethics of such actions are questionable because the more that liability is removed from the individuals involved in the conduct, the less responsible the principal actors become, thereby reducing individual responsibility (e.g., shifting responsibility from the rider to the ride operator, to the amusement park management, to the state regulatory inspector, to the ride manufacturer). The infamous McDonald's coffee spilling case of the 1990s is illustrative: A woman won a $2.9 million jury award after she accidentally spilled McDonald's coffee on herself while riding in a car and was burned.[19] The judgment was later significantly reduced in amount, but it has become a symbol for blaming others (especially large corporations or others with deep pockets) for individual accidents or errors. Although it is clear that both ethical and legal responsibility belong to the persons or entities whose actions were most responsible for the outcome, the troubling trend is to look first not to those involved in the incident but instead to those with the greatest financial resources.

Corporations have faced significant ethical issues as a result of both their own conduct and the conduct of others. For example, Royal Caribbean Cruises, the second-largest passenger cruise line in the world, had promoted itself as an environmentally responsible company. It pled guilty to twenty-one felony charges for dumping waste oil and hazardous chemicals at sea and then lying about it to the U.S. Coast Guard. Royal Caribbean admitted it routinely dumped oil from its ships a year earlier, but continued the conduct while under court supervision. The investigation found that some of the company's ships had no oil-contaminated wastewater, when these ships produce 100,000 gallons of wastewater annually. Hazardous chemicals from photo processing equipment, dry cleaning shops, and printing presses also were dumped at sea, in ports, and in environmentally sensitive areas. The company was fined a record $18 million in addition to $9 million fines it was assessed a year earlier. Federal investigators said Royal Caribbean crew members wore buttons declaring "Save the Waves" at the same time the company was engaged in illegal dumping.[20]

Corporate codes of ethics have been criticized for being too general and focusing on clearly wrongful conduct, rather than "right versus right" conflicts, where two competing, but legitimate, interests collide.[21] A classic case occurred during the 1980s when someone poisoned Tylenol capsules and replaced them on store shelves in the Chicago area. Six people died from these random poisonings. The chair of Johnson & Johnson (the makers of Tylenol) had to make a decision to balance the company's interests (they warned consumers about checking for compromised seals and packaging) versus the public safety threat of an unknown number of contaminated containers, and the impact of a recall of all Tylenol on store shelves. The company ultimately made the decision to pull all containers of Tylenol from store shelves, valued at $100 million.[22] In many ways, this was a defining moment for the company, costing it millions in the short run but gaining public confidence and respect in the company's products and image. On the other end of the spectrum, the owner of a peanut company was under investigation after some peanuts tested positive for salmonella, yet the owner apparently ordered the product be shipped anyway. The result was a salmonella outbreak resulting in

600 illnesses, eight deaths, more than 1,800 products pulled from store shelves, and one of the largest recalls in history. Company e-mails showed that the owner was worried about lost sales.[23] Therefore, it is clear that ethics always requires a decision, and it is crucial to know to make ethical decisions when needed.

Lockheed Martin Corporation has an ethics program that has been identified as a model.[24] It contains several significant elements:

1. Mandatory ethics awareness training is required of all 130,000 employees each year. This 1-hour training involves scenarios from actual cases.
2. Ethics tools for leaders are provided through a self-directed course required of all management personnel. It includes topics such as creating an ethical environment, responding to ethics complaints, and barriers to communication.
3. The organizational ethics assessment program is designed to evaluate the ethical environment in the company and existing ethical "disconnects."
4. One-minute video messages on ethics issues are delivered periodically via e-mail to all employees to enhance ethical awareness.
5. A clear, formal reporting process for fraudulent or ethically questionable behavior has been established, and each major unit within the company has a full-time ethics officer.

These five major components of the corporate ethics policy are designed to create a continuously reinforcing ethical environment that reflects well on the corporation's reputation, on its employees, and in the marketplace—while also reducing exposure to liability.

A leading expert on character education has made nine general recommendations for organizations to help promote a climate that fosters ethical conduct.[25] Even though all ethical decisions are ultimately individual ones, organizations can let individuals know how much they value those decisions.

1. Develop a code of ethics, regardless of the size of your company or agency.
2. Create ownership in the code of ethics by asking all levels of employees to participate in creating the code.
3. Keep the code of ethics alive by making it part of the language and culture of the company or agency.
4. Make values and ethics an integral part of your interview, orientation, and review procedures.
5. Ensure that ethical leadership starts at the top. Ethics must be a central belief and practice of management.
6. Institute ongoing training in ethics and values.
7. Institutionalize the notion that ethical dilemma can be reduced through communication, awareness, discussions, training, and practice.
8. Support character education in the schools.
9. Recognize and reward ethical behavior. Ethical practices do have an impact on the bottom-line performance of the organization.

These recommendations emphasize the importance of organizations to take responsibility for creating both rules and a climate that values and enforces ethical conduct. For example, the Swiss Bank UBS was publicly embarrassed by charges that it helped wealthy clients evade taxes. The bank was fined $780 million. It has since adopted a new policy, which requires all employees to sign an ethics code to comply with all the laws, rules, and regulations of the countries in which the bank operates and not provide assistance to clients aimed at breaching their financial obligations. All employees must also pass a test demonstrating knowledge of the detailed ethics code.[26] When these rules, climate, values, and enforcement are not made explicit, ethical conduct often lapses.

Corporate ethical conduct is also being encouraged through deterrence efforts, such as requiring a company to publish an apology in local newspapers as a part of settlement agreements. In Massachusetts, for example, a local ferry operator was forced to placed an ad in the *Boston Herald* newspaper, which stated, "[O]ur company has discharged human waste directly into coastal Massachusetts waters," and that it paid a heavy fine.[27] The objective is that such public "shaming" will deter both this company and others from violating the law, although the long-term impact of these kinds of sentences on future corporate conduct is unclear.

GOVERNMENT MISCONDUCT

"Corruption in large-scale public projects is a daunting obstacle to sustainable development and results in a major loss of public funds needed for education, health care, and poverty alleviation, both in developed and developing countries," according to the chair of **Transparency International (TI).** TI is a nongovernmental organization dedicated to anticorruption activities. It publishes an annual "Corruption Perceptions Index," which reports on the extent of corruption in countries by combining a number of surveys and interviews of businesspersons, public officials, and citizens around the world. A perfect score for noncorruption is ten, and according to the 2004 Index, 106 of the 146 countries included scored less than a five. A summary of the scores is presented in Table 9.1.

Sixty countries (more than 40 percent of the total) scored less than three out of ten, suggesting rampant corruption. Corruption is seen as most rampant in Bangladesh, Haiti, Nigeria, Chad, Myanmar, Azerbaijan, and Paraguay, which each has a score of less than two. Countries with low levels of corruption tend to be wealthier industrialized countries distinguished by significant efforts to avoid conflicts of interest among public officials and open media access to public finances.[28]

Corruption lies at the core of virtually all major governmental problems, and ethical misconduct underlies corruption. Measures to enact and enforce antibribery laws, competitive bidding processes, oversight, and transparency of government agencies are all important measures, but lying underneath them is the need for public officials and a public that demands conduct in the public interest versus self-interest. Overcoming self-interest that lacks just consideration of others is the fundamental domain of ethics.

One common ethical mistake related to corruption involves treating loyalty as a virtue. Misplaced loyalty inhibits reporting of unethical conduct and whistle-blowing on observed governmental misconduct. **Loyalty** is often a good attribute, but it is **not a virtue** in itself. When it is treated as a virtue, loyalty can be misguided, leading to protection of illicit conduct of all kinds in the name of "loyalty." At the U.S. Naval Academy, part of the honor educational program entails a visit to the Holocaust Museum in Washington, D.C. Its purpose is to show the sailors the extreme consequences of misplaced loyalty, blind obedience, and lack of compassion.[29]

Instances and patterns of governmental misconduct can be addressed systematically by the agency to change the existing culture to one that recruits, values, and rewards ethical conduct. Consider the case of the police department in Chandler, Arizona, which evaluated its operations and training to address the issues of police professionalism and ethical conduct. According to the

TABLE 9.1 Countries Ranked by Perceived Corruption

Least Corrupt

1. Finland	9.7
2. New Zealand	9.6
3. Denmark	9.5
4. Iceland	9.5
5. Singapore	9.3
6. Sweden	9.2
7. Switzerland	9.1
8. Norway	8.9
9. Australia	8.8
10. Netherlands	8.7

Most Corrupt

133. Angola	2.0
Congo, Democratic Republic	2.0
Cote d'Ivoire	2.0
Georgia	2.0
Indonesia	2.0
Tajikistan	2.0
Turkmenistan	2.0
140. Azerbaijan	1.9
Paraguay	1.9
142. Chad	1.7
Myanmar	1.7
144. Nigeria	1.6
145. Bangladesh	1.5
Haiti	1.5

Source: Transparency International's (TI) Corruption Perceptions Index 2004. TI notes "many countries, including some which could be among the most corrupt, are missing because there simply is not enough survey data available." (www.transparency.org)

assistant city attorney, "The department is trying to develop the highest standard, train its officers and civilian staff according to that standard, and develop the administrative mechanisms to hold every member of the department accountable to it."[30] The five main elements of this program involve increasing ethical conduct by:

1. changing hiring standards,
2. commanding responsibility,
3. developing training programs with ethical components that set the standards,
4. conducting evaluations stressing ethical standards, and
5. providing awards and promotions reinforcing the standards.

A new written-entry test was developed, one-third of which stresses ethics. Ethics is also included as part of the oral interview. The department found that sergeants and lieutenants were not spending enough time in the field, largely because of unfinished paper work. A new goal was established for all sergeants to spend 85 percent of their time in the field and all lieutenants to spend 75 percent of their time in the field with the advent of a wireless report-writing system. The objective is to improve direct supervision and command, thereby reducing exposure to liability for unethical conduct. The department has incorporated ethics components into all its training programs, emphasizing the morally right things to do instead of the legally right things. Legally appropriate conduct changes regularly with new laws, regulations, and court decisions, whereas morally permissible conduct remains constant. Emphasis on the moral, rather than the legal, is expected to further reduce exposure to liability. The employee evaluation form was revised to include a category that specifically addresses ethical conduct. The overall ethical standard is set forth in a department code of ethics, which applies to all employees, as well as an Oath of Honor, which every officer takes on being commissioned. Finally, the department recognizes that people need positive reinforcement for their good actions, so the department reorganized its awards program to recognize those employees "who behave ethically and those who foster the ethical core in the department."[31]

ETHICS IN BOOKS

Ethics is everywhere, even in the books we read, which sometimes are written without ethics specifically in mind. Here is a summary of a book that looks at actions taken in the interest of others, followed by questions that ask you to reflect on the ethical connections.

DO UNTO OTHERS: EXTRAORDINARY ACTS OF ORDINARY PEOPLE

Samuel P. Oliner
(Westview Press, 2004)

Samuel Oliner is a sociologist, and holocaust survivor, who has written extensively on altruism and why people help others when they can just as easily not do so. His book was inspired by the heroism he saw after the terrorist attacks of September 11, 2001, leading him to a wider inquiry of altruism during the Holocaust, and by both ordinary and notable people throughout history, from moral leaders to military heroes to philanthropists to the heroes of 9/11. The stories he recounts are inspiring and lead him to ask the question, "Why did these people do it, and why is altruistic behavior so common?"

Altruism is derived from the Latin *alter*, which means "other." Altruistic behavior is conduct in the interest or for the good of others; the opposite of self-centered desire.

Helping others in time of emergency (e.g., the Holocaust and 9/11) is dangerous, helping others who are seriously ill can be risky, and taking time to help others in general interferes with a person's individual pursuits. Given these limitations, it is surprising that altruism is so common. Oliner reviewed more than forty empirical studies with a total of more than 6,000 respondents on the question of why they volunteered to help others. The most frequently mentioned motivating factors were empathy and compassion, followed by social responsibility, a sense of moral obligation, and spiritual and religious reasons. He also interviewed a large number of hospice and nonhospice volunteers about their motivations and found similar results. He found that "altruistic tendencies are learned early in life, so it is never too early to learn the joys of giving or too early to learn that it's wrong to hurt, it's wrong to oppress, it's wrong to neglect and exclude." The stories his book recounts "demonstrate that goodness is possible and that it doesn't take any superhuman effort to inculcate in people the desirability of the moral road."

Oliner concludes with a suggestion to decrease the number of bystanders by celebrating, publicizing, and appreciating the millions of people who are already helping and can serve as role models. He adds that "when people are aroused and are given a good reason for helping, they exhibit courage, helping behavior, devote more time to others, and often leave a moral legacy for future generations."

QUESTIONS

1. Given the three major ethical perspectives of utilitarianism, formalism, and virtue, do they see altruistic behavior as being morally required of a person?
2. Do you believe that celebrating and publicizing altruistic acts would increase the frequency of this kind of behavior?

ETHICS IN THE MOVIES

Movies seek to entertain and inform the audience about a story, incident, or person. Many good movies also hit upon important ethical themes in making significant decisions that affect the lives of others. Read the movie summary here (and watch the movie if you haven't already), and answer the questions to make the ethical connections.

SHATTERED GLASS

Billy Ray, Director
(2003)

Shattered Glass tells the story of Stephen Glass, who began as a writer for the magazine *The New Republic* when he was only 23 years old. Glass wrote a number of very dramatic stories, which supposedly reported on actual events. One story he wrote was called "Hack Heaven," about a 15-year-old computer hacker, hired to work for a large company as a consultant after he broke into its computer system and had exposed its weaknesses. Like his other stories, the account was vivid and read as if Glass was present as the story unfolded.

Soon after this article was published, a *Forbes* magazine Internet reporter checked the facts in the story carefully and presented evidence that the story was fabricated, and the company described in Glass's story did not exist. An investigation confirmed this allegation and discovered that Glass created false Web and e-mail accounts for the company to deceive his own editors about the truthfulness of the story.

He was fired from *The New Republic* for journalistic fraud, and the magazine subsequently determined that at least twenty-seven of forty-one stories written by Stephen Glass for the magazine contained false content. In the movie version of this scandal, Stephen Glass (Hayden Christensen) tells the story of what occurred, and the behavior of a very likable person who apparently was a pathological liar is illustrated.

In 2003, the real Stephen Glass appeared on television's *60 Minutes* to promote his "biographical novel" titled *The Fabulist*. Glass said on this program, "I wanted them to think I was a good journalist, a good person. I wanted them to love the story so they would love me." He said that small fabrications and false quotes were used at first to make a story better, and that practice mushroomed until some stories were entirely false. He "wanted every story to be a homerun." The *60 Minutes* interview is included as a special feature added to the DVD edition of *Shattered Glass*.

QUESTIONS

1. This case was an embarrassment for *The New Republic*, which apologized to its readers, but the fabricated stories were not considered crimes. What specifically makes his actions unethical from the perspectives of virtue, formalism, and utilitarianism?

2. An issue was raised whether he should be suspended for a few months or fired outright as an employee of the magazine. Are there arguments based in ethics that would lead you to recommend suspension versus firing?

Discussion Question

What is questionable about the ethics of shifting liability to corporations and others not involved in the conduct in question (e.g., the McDonald's case, the carnival ride owner)?

Critical Thinking Exercises

All ethical decisions affect others (by definition) and, as Aristotle points out, ethical decision making is achieved consistently only through practice. Given the outline of virtue ethics, formalism, and utilitarianism, evaluate the moral permissibility of the conduct in question in each scenario.

Important note on method: *Critical thinking requires the ability to evaluate viewpoints, facts, and behaviors objectively to assess information or methods of argumentation to establish the true worth or merit of an act or course of conduct. Please evaluate these scenarios, first analyzing pros and cons of alternate views,* before *you come to a conclusion. Do not draw a conclusion first, and then try to find facts to support it—this frequently leads to narrow (and incorrect) thinking.*

To properly evaluate the moral permissibility of a course of action using critical thinking skills

1. *Begin with an open mind (no preconceptions!),*
2. *Isolate and evaluate the relevant facts on both sides,*
3. *Identify the precise moral question to be answered, and*
4. *Apply ethical principles to the moral question based on an objective evaluation of the facts, only then drawing a conclusion.*

9.1 The Scarlet Driver's License

A Delaware law features a new version of the scarlet letter. Anyone convicted of a sex crime (including sexual abuse of a child) is immediately issued a new driver's license with a "Y" stamped on the front. The meaning of the code is explained on the back of the license.

If the ex-offender moves to another state and turns in the Delaware license, that state would be alerted as to the offender's past conviction. This new law was added to the existing Megan's law, now passed in virtually every state, that requires convicted sex offenders to register with local police and child welfare agencies so that neighbors can be notified even after the offender's sentence has been completed.

The sponsor of the new law said, "This additional information will give police the ability to thwart some sex crimes before they occur." Simply checking a person's identification will alert police to a past conviction for a sex crime.

Opponents argue that such a label will interface with an ex-offender's ability to get a job, cash a check, rent an apartment, or do anything that requires picture identification. This will impede efforts of former sex offenders to live law-abiding lives. It also unfairly discriminates against sex offenders versus other kinds of ex-offenders.[32]

- Assess the moral permissibility of a scarlet letter such as that used in Delaware.

9.2 Paying for Legislative Results?

Many commercial interests hire lobbyists in Washington, D.C., to promote their interests to members of Congress as it considers new legislation, regulations, taxes, and other changes. Media companies are no exception with interests that include cable company regulations and fees, Internet provider access and regulations, broadcast of programs with adult content, film ratings and restrictions, as well as newspapers and magazines.

Concern has been expressed about lobbying and political contributions from the media industry because it helps shape public (and political) opinion through newspapers, radio, television, and film. During the late 1990s, for example, Congressman Thomas Bliley (R–VA) chaired the House of Representatives Commerce Committee, which regulates communications. He received more than $81,000 in contributions from media companies. Senator Ernest Hollings (D–SC) was ranking Democrat on the Senate Commerce Committee and received more than $250,000 in contributions from media organizations. Many other senators and congressional representatives also received contributions. The leading contributors were General Electric's political action committee, the National Cable Television Association, the National Association of Broadcasters, and Time Warner, each of which contributed between $468,000 and $1 million to federal legislators during this period.

Under law, individuals can contribute up to $2,000 to any political candidate, and political action committees can contribute up to $10,000 in each federal election cycle, but there are no limits on contributions to political parties (which may then use the money any way they want—including for the support of individual candidates).[33]

Media companies lobby for protection in the same way that other industries do. Media companies have sought to protect profitable tobacco ads in newspapers and magazines, to avoid Internet taxes, to gain government allocation of free broadcast spectrum space, to curb cable regulation and taxes, and to avoid giving free airtime to political candidates. The conduct of both the media companies and legislators in giving and receiving contributions has been questioned, given the appearance of advancing private gain over public interest.

- Evaluate the moral permissibility of these payments to legislators.

9.3 Would You Do It for $1 Million?

A survey of 2,000 people by Roper/Starch Worldwide found that art may be imitating life. Following a scenario from the movie *Indecent Proposal* (1993), the survey found that 10 percent of respondents would accept an offer of $1 million from a stranger who wanted to sleep with his or her spouse, and 16 percent would seriously consider it.

- What is the strongest argument *in favor* of the moral permissibility of accepting the money?
- What is the strongest argument *against* the moral permissibility of accepting the money?

- What is the correct moral course of action in this case, given your assessment of the preceding arguments?

9.4 Bananas and Terrorism

Banana company Chiquita Brands International was charged with allegedly paying Colombian terrorists to protect its banana-growing operations. Prosecutors said the company agreed to pay about $1.7 million between 1997 and 2004 to the United Self-Defense Forces of Colombia (known as AUC for its Spanish initials). The AUC has been responsible for some of the worst massacres in Colombia's civil conflict and also for a sizable percentage of the country's cocaine exports. The U.S. government designated the AUC a terrorist group in 2001. In addition to paying the AUC, prosecutors said Chiquita made payments to the National Liberation Army (ELN) and the leftist Revolutionary Armed Forces of Colombia (FARC), as control of the company's banana-growing geographic area shifted.

Chiquita has said it was forced to make the payments and was acting only to ensure the safety of its workers. From the company's viewpoint, leftist rebels and far-right paramilitaries have fought viciously over Colombia's banana-growing region producing many civilian casualties. Most companies in the region, including Chiquita, made extensive security arrangements for the purpose of protecting employees.

But federal prosecutors noted that while Chiquita made $825,000 in illegal payments, the Colombian banana operation earned $49 million and was the company's most profitable unit. "Funding a terrorist organization can never be treated as a cost of doing business," U.S. Attorney Jeffrey Taylor said.[34] Chiquita sold Banadex, its Colombian subsidiary, in 2004 for $44 million.

- Assume you were CEO of Chiquita from 1997 to 2004 and faced the same situation in Colombia. Assess the moral permissibility of your decisions.

9.5 Psychologist Ethics and Interrogations

Psychologists have played a central role in the military and C.I.A. interrogation of people suspected of being enemy combatants. But the profession, long divided over this role, is considering whether to make any involvement in military interrogations a violation of its code of ethics.

At the American Psychological Association's annual meeting, prominent members denounced such work as unethical by definition, while other key figures—civilian and military—insist that restricting psychologists' roles would only make interrogations more likely to harm detainees. Like other professional organizations, the association has little direct authority to restrict their members' ability to practice. But state licensing boards can suspend or revoke a psychologist's license, and experts note that these boards often take violations of the association's ethics code into consideration.

For the first time, lawyers for a detainee at the United States Navy base at Guantanamo Bay, Cuba, singled out a psychologist as a critical player in documents alleging abusive treatment. At the center of the debate are the military's behavioral science consultation teams, made up of psychologists and others who assist in interrogations. Little is known about these units, including the number of psychologists who take part. Defenders of that role insist that the teams are crucial in keeping interrogations safe, effective, and legal. Critics say their primary purpose is to help break detainees, using methods that might violate international law.

The psychological association's most recent ethics amendments strongly condemn coercive techniques adopted during the Bush administration's antiterrorism campaign. But its guidelines covering practice conclude that "it is consistent with the A.P.A. ethics code for psychologists to serve in consultative roles to interrogation and information-gathering processes for national-security-related purposes," as long as they do not participate in any of 19 coercive procedures, including waterboarding, the use of hoods, or any physical assault.

How these guidelines shape behavior during interrogations is not well understood. Documents from Guantanamo made public suggest that at least some of the coercive methods the military has used were derived from a program based on Chinese techniques used in the 1950s that produced false confessions from American prisoners. These techniques included "prolonged constraint," "exposure," and "sleep deprivation," known informally as the frequent flier program.

According to the standard operating procedure for Camp Delta, at Guantanamo, the "behavior management plan" for new detainees "concentrates on isolating the detainee and fostering dependence of the detainee on his interrogator." Some psychologists, though appalled by these techniques, emphasize that there is a danger in opting out as well. "There's no doubt that the psychologist's presence can be abused," said Robert Resnick, who is in private practice in Santa Monica, California, "but if there's no presence at all, then there's no accountability, and you walk away feeling noble and righteous, but you haven't done a damned thing."[35]

Interrogators, too, are split on the question of whether psychologists provide valuable assistance. Some say that their advice can be helpful; others point out that there is no evidence that it improves the quality of the information obtained.

- Evaluate the moral permissibility of making psychologist participation in military interrogations a violation of their professional ethical code.

Key Concepts

Notes

1. Elisabeth Bumiller and Eric Lipton, "Kerik's Position Was Untenable, Bush Aide Says," *The New York Times* (December 12, 2004), p. 1; William Rashbaum and Kevin Flynn, "Beyond the Disclosure of Kerik's Nanny, More Questions Were Lurking," *The New York Times* (December 13, 2004), p. 25.
2. Cited in Stephen L. Carter, "In Defense of Privacy," in M. Josephson and W. Hanson, Eds., *The Power of Character* (San Francisco, CA: Jossey-Bass, 1998), p. 213.
3. Andrea Elliott, "Macy's Settles Complaint of Racial Profiling for $600,000," *The New York Times* (January 14, 2005), p. D1.
4. James B. Jacobs and Frank Anechiarico, "Blacklisting Public Contractors as an Anti-Corruption and Racketeering Strategy," *Criminal Justice Ethics*, vol. 11 (Summer/Fall 1992), pp. 64–76.
5. Steve Marshall, "Megan's Law Upheld," *USA Today* (July 26, 1995), p. 2; "New Jersey's Megan's Law on

Sex Offenders Left Intact by Nation's Highest Court," *The Buffalo News* (February 23, 1998), p. 4.

6. Devon B. Adam, *Summary of State Sex Offender Registry Dissemination Procedures* (Washington, DC: Bureau of Justice Statistics, 1999).

7. Arlyn Tobias Gajilan and Beth Glenn, "Sex-Crime Database," *Newsweek* (August 11, 1997), p. 12.

8. Paul Leavitt, "Sexual Predators," *USA Today* (August 28, 1993), p. 3.

9. Robert Hanley, "Shots Fired at House of Rapist," *The New York Times* (June 17, 1998), p. B1.

10. Peter Finn, *Sex Offender Community Notification* (Washington, DC: National Institute of Justice, 1997).

11. D. M. Polizzi, D. L. MacKenzie, and L. J. Hickman, "What Works in Adult Sex Offender Treatment? A Review of Prison- and Non-Prison-Based Treatment Programs," *International Journal of Offender Therapy and Comparative Criminology*, vol. 43 (September 1999), p. 357.

12. Rushworth M. Kidder, *How Good People Make Tough Choices* (New York, NY: Simon & Schuster, 1996).

13. Mark Scolforo, "Pennsylvania High Court Bans 'Message' Verdicts," *Philadelphia Inquirer* (October 23, 2004), p. 1.

14. Scolforo, "Pennsylvania High Court Bans 'Message' Verdicts."

15. Joseph P. Shapiro, "Dr. Death's Last Dance," *U.S. News & World Report* (April 26, 1999), p. 44.

16. Joseph P. Shapiro, "Casting a Cold Eye on 'Death with Dignity,' " *U.S. News & World Report* (March 11, 1999), p. 56.

17. Rebecca T. Michael, "Online Hate Increasing," *United Press International* (May 18, 2004).

18. "Carnival Ride Owner Guilty in Teen's Death," *apbnews.com* (accessed November 21, 2001).

19. Matt Fleischer-Black, "One Lump or Two? The Infamous Coffee-Burn Case Is about to Get a Tenth-Anniversary Rerun," *The American Lawyer*, vol. 26 (June 2004).

20. Reuters, "Royal Caribbean to Plead Guilty on Dumping Charges," *The New York Times* (July 21, 1999), p. 1.

21. Joseph L. Badaracco, Jr., *Defining Moments: When Managers Must Choose between Right and Right* (Boston, MA: Harvard Business School Press, 1997), pp. 28–30.

22. Badaracco, *Defining Moments: When Managers Must Choose between Right and Right,* pp. 85–86.

23. Julie Schmit, "Broken System Hid Peanut Plant's Risks: Case Reveals Every Link in Food Safety Chain Failed," *USA Today* (April 27, 2009), p. 1B; Ricardo Alonso-Zaldivar and Brett J. Blackledge, "Peanut Company Owner Urged Shipping Tainted Products," *Associated Press* (February 11, 2009).

24. "Profile of a 'Walk-the-Talk' Corporate Ethics Program," *White-Collar Crime Fighter*, vol. 7 (January 2005), pp. 1–3.

25. B. David Brooks, "The Bottom Line on Character," in M. Josephson and W. Hanson, Eds., *The Power of Character* (San Francisco, CA: Jossey-Bass, 1998), pp. 168–169.

26. Carl Hausman, "Scandal-Stung Swiss Bank UBS to Require All Employees to Sign Ethic Code," www.globalethics.org (January 19, 2010).

27. Tovia Smith, "Companies 'Names and Shamed' for Bad Behavior," *National Public Radio.* www.npr.org (March 7, 2010); see also Janet Romaker, "Fashion Police: Judge Tailors Punishment that Fits Criminals to a T," *The Toledo Blade* (September 7, 2009).

28. Transparency International, Global Corruption Report, www.tranparency.org (2004) (accessed March 1, 2005).

29. Charles R. Larson, "Training Leaders," in M. Josephson and W. Hanson, Eds., *The Power of Character* (San Francisco, CA: Jossey-Bass, 1998), p. 176.

30. Michale McNeff, "One Agency's Effort to Reduce Liability Risk through Emphasis on Ethics." www.theiacp.org/documents/index.cfm?fuseaction=document&document_type_id=1&document_id=13 (accessed October 24, 2004).

31. McNeff, "One Agency's Effort to Reduce Liability Risk through Emphasis on Ethics."

32. Kelly McMurry, "Delaware Label Drivers' Licenses of Sex Offenders," *Trial*, vol. 34 (July 1998), p. 116; Stephen P. Garvey, "Can Shaming Punishments Educate?" *University of Chicago Law Review*, vol. 65 (Summer 1998), pp. 733–794; James Q. Whitman, "What Is Wrong with Inflicting Shame Sanctions?" *Yale Law Journal*, vol. 107 (January 1998), pp. 1055–1092.

33. Sheila Kaplan, "Payments to the Powerful," *Columbia Journalism Review* (September–October 1998), p. 118.

34. Matt Apuzzo, "Chiquita Pleads Guilty in Terrorism Probe," *The Associated Press* (March 19, 2007).

35. Benedict Carey, "Psychologists Clash on Aiding Interrogations," *The New York Times* (August 16, 2008), p. 1.

CHAPTER 10

The Future
Will We Be More or Less Ethical?

Learning Objectives:

- To recognize the importance of the "24-hour test."

- To evaluate the ethical dilemma in the case of the Unabomber.

- To appreciate the reason behind the establishment of the CDC panel of ethicists.

- To understand the ethical distinctions between killing and letting die in a medical context.

- To recognize the ethical importance of the story of Alfred Nobel.

Maybe this world is another planet's bell.

—Aldous Huxley (1894–1953)

The daily course of unhappy human events can sometimes make us cynical about the prospects for ethical behavior. Is there any hope in the future for more ethical conduct, more of the time, and by more people?

Can you go for 24 hours without saying anything unkind to anyone or *about* anyone? This would seem to be a simple task, but it is amazing how many people have trouble accomplishing it. People routinely curse out other drivers or make disparaging comments about coworkers, bosses, friends, or even family members. Just as a person who can't go for a day without drinking or smoking has alcohol or nicotine addiction problems, a person who cannot go a day without speaking ill of others has a character problem. The **24-hour test** is a good way to begin a baseline ethical test for yourself.

RECOGNIZING ETHICAL DECISIONS WHEN THEY ARISE

Most decisions involve ethics, although some do not. This book is designed to raise awareness of the pervasiveness of ethics in everyday life. Ethics is not at war with common sense, but it guides our decisions in unclear situations.

In the future, ethical dilemmas will become increasingly complex as individuals become more interdependent as a result of more expedient communications, such as cell phones, e-mail, and the many new cable and satellite television and radio channels. Given these trends, the actions of an individual will become more widely known, and have a greater impact on others, than ever before. Ethical dilemmas become more complicated as the interests of more individuals are involved.

Consider the case of the **Unabomber,** who killed three people and injured thirty during a 17-year period using mailed packages that contained explosives. The Unabomber wrote letters to the *New York Times*, *Washington Post*, and *Penthouse Magazine* threatening to kill again if his 35,000-word manifesto (on the evils of industrialization) was not published by one of the two newspapers within the next 90 days.

The editors at both the *Times* and the *Post* believed there was no journalistic reason to publish the manifesto, but there was a clear public safety concern. The editors at the newspapers talked to the public officials involved, and, at the urging of the U.S. attorney general, the two papers decided to print the manifesto as an eight-page insert. The editors at the newspapers were concerned that other newspapers and television stations would be the victims of future threats such as this, and they asked the FBI to weigh the pros and cons of publication. An FBI spokesman said, "This [the Unabomber] has been going on for 17 years, and until we get this guy and are in a position to ask all the questions, there is no way to predict what he may do."

Some in the journalism community saw publication of the manifesto as an "outrageous decision." They believed the Unabomber was a terrorist and that two of the nation's leading newspapers had succumbed to the demands of a terrorist, which both is a bad idea and sets a dangerous precedent. Also, it is likely the Unabomber was not a rational individual, so there was no clear evidence he would not keep killing.[1]

Analyzing this situation in ethical terms shows the difficulty of the dilemma. Using a utilitarian rationale, the decision should weigh on the balance struck between the possibilities for positive or negative consequences. If there was a reasonable probability that lives would be saved, then succumbing to the demands of a terrorist would be acceptable. In Kantian terms, however, the question would be whether publication of the manifesto would be a good universal rule, regardless of the consequences. According to virtue ethics, publication would be pursuing a real good (civil peace), but was it in accord with the moral virtues (was it courageous to publish or was it cowardly or rash; was it prudent or was it excessive)? Careful ethical reasoning could lead to different results depending on the perspective taken.

As it turned out, a completely unanticipated result occurred in this case when the Unabomber's brother saw the published manifesto in the newspaper and recognized some of the writing and phrasing as resembling his brother's. He notified the authorities of his suspicions, leading to the apprehension of the Unabomber. This surprising result serves as a reminder of Kant's warning that the future is so uncertain that it is not wise to make ethical decisions based on predictions of future outcomes.

IS THE BAR RISING?

The ethical bar will rise in the future because decisions will impact more people. The reasons for this difficulty are advances in technology, increasing life span, and globalization, which allow decisions in one part of the world to affect others thousands of miles away. Therefore, consideration of ethical decisions will have greater consequences than ever before.

Ethics are becoming more relevant than ever in everyday life. In 2004, the **Centers for Disease Control and Prevention (CDC)** created a **panel of ethicists** for the first time in its history to help it deal with the life-and-death questions of who should receive flu vaccine after a major shortage of the vaccine occurred.[2] The panel was established in recognition of the fact that ethics provides a reasoned and objective basis on which to make important decisions. The decision regarding who should receive priority for vaccination when flu vaccine is scarce is a difficult one because babies, young children, the elderly, health care professionals, the seriously ill, emergency workers, and other groups are all at high risk. The formation of the panel illustrates the direct relevance of ethics in everyday life.

The City of Alexandria, Virginia, had worked for several years to establish a program to provide housing for homeless people who suffered from mental illness. Facing major budget cuts, however, the City realized it could balance the budget if it delayed the start of the housing program. The City had trouble in deciding which programs to cut, and turned to an ethicist for an opinion, so the discussion would not deteriorate into a politicized debate.[3] Here again, the importance of ethical thinking is directly relevant to making decisions that affect an entire jurisdiction.

A related major issue is increasing life span and the issue of "quality of life." Consider the following case, which is based on actual diagnosis and treatment decisions that found their way to the criminal justice system. Timothy Quill, a physician, wrote an article in the *New England Journal of Medicine* in 1991 in which he recounted the difficult decisions he made in working with a terminally ill leukemia patient who chose to commit suicide with medication he prescribed. In the article Quill recounted that he was well aware of the patient's intention in taking the painkiller medication he prescribed and the emotional and physical struggle that the patient experienced in dealing with the disease, its effects, and the decision to end her life prematurely.[4] Dr. Quill's case was brought before a grand jury in New York State where he practiced medicine, but the grand jury refused to indict him for homicide. In New York, as in most states, it is a crime to aid another in committing or attempting suicide, but patients may refuse even lifesaving medical treatment.

In a subsequent case that went to the U.S. Supreme Court, Quill and other physicians claimed that terminally ill patients who are suffering great pain and desire a doctor's help in ending their own lives are deterred from doing so by New York's assisted-suicide ban, while at the same time the standards of medical practice permit physicians to prescribe lethal medication for mentally competent terminally ill patients. The physicians (together with three terminally ill patients) claimed in court that this was unfair and unconstitutional because the law accords different treatment to those competent, terminally ill persons who wish to hasten their deaths by self-administering prescribed drugs than it does to those who wish to do so by directing the removal of life-support systems. The U.S. Supreme Court held, however, that state law prohibition on assisting suicide does not violate the Equal Protection Clause of the U.S. Constitution.[5] Therefore, physician-assisted suicide of this nature is still prohibited.

There is heated debate about the desirability of these laws and even whether such personal decisions should be subject to law at all. On the one hand, it is argued that the **distinction between killing and letting die** is of no moral significance.[6] It is said the law's allowance for one kind of assistance (withholding treatment) and criminalization of the other (prescribing lethal doses of drugs to be self-administered) is not morally justified, resulting in needless suffering of patients and their families. On the other hand, it is contested that whether active or passive, participation of physicians in ending life is immoral and should not be permitted under law or under medical ethics.[7] A utilitarian argument has been made to justify "voluntary euthanasia."[8]

How would you assess the moral permissibility of these two types of end-of-life assistance by physicians? To what extent should the desires of the patient be controlling? Ethical reasoning in cases such as these is difficult without knowledge of the facts of the individual cases being decided. Perhaps this is what makes creating generalized legislation or developing guidelines difficult. Nevertheless, these cases illustrate the far-reaching ethical implications of conduct in a world where medicine and technology have the ability to both extend and end life in new ways.

In a recent twist on this dilemma, several states have passed laws that permit a pharmacist to refuse to fill a prescription on moral grounds. The laws are directed primarily at contraceptives, but they also may include drugs that could be used for assisted suicide. One woman who was denied a prescription said of the pharmacists, "Their job is not to regulate what people take or do. It's just to fill the prescription that was ordered by my physician."[9] The American Pharmacists Association already has a policy that allows druggists to refuse to fill prescriptions if they object on moral grounds, but they must make arrangements for the patient to obtain the prescription somewhere else. In several instances, however, this has not occurred. In Wisconsin, a pharmacist would not return a prescription to a woman seeking birth control pills, and he would not transfer it to another druggist because of his religious views. Is this morally permissible? From the viewpoint of the pharmacists, how would you evaluate their decisions from the perspectives of virtue, formalism, and utility?

FINDING DEFINING MOMENTS IN LIFE

Harold Kushner, author of *When Everything You Ever Wanted Isn't Enough: The Search for a Life That Matters*, believes that we all have a yearning to make some kind of difference through our conduct. "Our souls are hungry for meaning, for the sense that we have figured out how to live so that our lives matter, so that the world will be at least a little bit different for our having passed through it."[10] Yet at the same time, we continue to see instances of people who attempt to exploit the system for selfish ends. For example, a Tennessee woman sued McDonald's, claiming she was badly burned on the chin by a hot pickle after biting into a McDonald's hamburger.[11]

Simple methods are sometimes used to remember the meaning of ethics in everyday decisions. An example is expressed as follows:

E Everywhere

T all the *Time*

H be *Honest*

I act with *Integrity*

C have *Compassion*

S —for what is at *Stake* is your reputation, your self-esteem, and your inner peace.

This is one way to remember our ethical mandate as human beings.[12] Moral conviction is not a matter of personal taste; it is a matter of judgment and actions according to objective principles.

ETHICS CHECKUP
A Bathrobe Bonus

A letter to advice columnist Ann Landers illustrates that ethical questions are persistent. A retired man, living on a fixed income, enjoyed going to auctions and garage sales to purchase household items inexpensively. On one occasion he purchased items from a dealer who had bought an entire houseful of furniture and clothing from a man whose wife had died. The widower wanted to sell all the house's contents and move away. Included in the purchase from the dealer was a bathrobe. Back home, the retired man went through the goods he bought and was stunned to find large wads of bills in the pocket of the bathrobe. He wrote to Ann Landers for advice; his wife thinks he is morally obligated to return the money because it wasn't an intended part of the purchase. He believes he should keep the money because he bought the bathrobe from a dealer and doesn't believe the dealer would return the money to the owner.[13]

Applying ethical principles, which course of action is morally correct for the retired man?

BEING ETHICAL WHEN NO ONE IS LOOKING

Stephen Covey has described character as consisting of integrity, maturity, and abundance mentality. Integrity is making and keeping promises (to yourself and to others). Maturity is the ability to balance courage and kindness. Abundance mentality involves realizing that the ability to accomplish great things is limitless; excellence and virtue are achievable by everyone, and everyone should be encouraged toward them. As Covey explains, "most people are deeply scripted in the **scarcity mentality.** They see life as a finite pie: If another person gets a big piece of the pie, it means less for them and for everyone else. They have a zero-sum attitude toward life."[14] This causes them to have a difficult time in sharing recognition or to be genuinely happy for those who perform well. Without integrity, maturity, and abundance mentality, it is difficult to follow the moral virtues and be of good character.

It has been argued that criminal justice professionals should ask the following questions when faced with a decision or dilemma: What does the law require? What does departmental policy require? What do personal ethics require?[15] Perhaps these questions are in the wrong order, however, because ethics precede policy, which precedes law. In other words, ethics provides the principles on which *all* decisions should be framed. Department policies and laws address specific situations, but they cannot anticipate all the possibilities. Therefore, a grounding in ethics helps the professional frame all situations, regardless of whether they are anticipated, in moral terms ensuring a rational and principled response, rather than a decision based on mere emotion or self-interest.

Think for a moment about what will be said about you when you die. Write what you might wish to appear on your tombstone. How would your inscription be different if you were utilitarian, Kantian, or Aristotelian? Such an exercise helps you clarify and prioritize central ethical principles in your life.

Consider **the story of Alfred Nobel,** a chemist best known for inventing dynamite. His brother died while Alfred was still alive, and the newspaper inadvertently printed Alfred's obituary instead of his brother's. He read an obituary that saluted him as the inventor of dynamite (perhaps the most destructive explosive of his time) and described how he made a lot of money in the process. He was horrified by his own obituary and resolved to establish a different legacy. So he gave away his wealth and established the Nobel Prize for achievement in various fields.

What will be said about you in *your* obituary? As it was once said, if you want to know how to live your life, think about what you'd like people to say about you after you die—then live backward.

ETHICS IN BOOKS

Ethics is everywhere, even in the books we read, which sometimes are written without ethics specifically in mind. Here is a summary of a book that looks at actions that affect others, followed by questions that ask you to reflect on the ethical connections.

THE LUCIFER EFFECT: UNDERSTANDING HOW GOOD PEOPLE TURN EVIL

Philip Zimbardo
(Random House, 2007)

Philip Zimbardo is a psychologist and professor emeritus at Stanford University. He is best known as the creator of the Stanford Prison Experiment in 1971, which used a simulated prison involving student volunteers who were randomly chosen to be "guards," while others became "inmates." Within a week, however, the experiment had to be abandoned, as the student volunteers who were guards became cruel and sadistic, and those playing inmates became seriously depressed and emotionally distraught.

This book contains a complete and detailed description of the Stanford Prison Experiment, and the author compares it with what occurred in the Abu Ghraib prison scandal in Iraq in 2004, where U.S. soldiers treated Iraqi inmates in brutal fashion. Zimbardo was called as an expert witness for one the Abu Ghraib trials. He believes that the "experimental dehumanization" of the Stanford Experiment is instructive in understanding the abusive conduct of guards at Abu Ghraib.

Zimbardo finds that the abusing persons in these situations were not "bad apples," but instead were products of a "bad barrel"—the social setting they were placed in contaminated the individual. He concludes that we must give "greater consideration and more weight to situational and systemic processes than we typically do when we are trying to account for aberrant behaviors and seeming personality changes. Human behavior is always subject to situational forces." The author finds fault with the military and political leadership who were "complicit in creating the conditions that in turn made possible such wide-ranging wanton abuse and torture" in U.S. military prisons. Ironically, the United States decided to shut down the prison at Abu Ghraib, for the same reasons the Stanford Prison Experiment was ended three decades earlier.

Zimbardo does not excuse individual misconduct however: "the view I have provided does not negate the responsibility of these MPs (in Abu Ghraib Prison), nor their guilt; explanation and understanding do not excuse such misdeeds. Rather, understanding how the events happened and appreciating what were the situational forces operating on the soldiers can lead to proactive ways to modify the circumstances that elicit such unacceptable behavior. Punishing is not enough. 'Bad systems' create 'bad situations' create 'bad apples' create 'bad behaviors,' even in good people."

Zimbardo ends the book with a chapter on heroism, involving a number of case studies. He observes that thousands of ordinary people make the decision to act heroically in the face of "situational and systemic forces that propel some of us toward social pathology." Although he does not offer an answer to this dilemma, he does recognize the fundamental issue: "the decisive question for each of us is whether to act in helping others, to prevent harm to others, or not to act at all. We should be preparing many laurel wreaths for all those who will discover their reservoir of hidden strengths and virtues enabling them to come forward to act against injustice and cruelty and to stand up for their principled values."

QUESTIONS

1. If the decision to engage in deviant or criminal conduct is strongly influenced by situational factors, how should we balance our crime prevention efforts between attention to ethical (personal) versus situational (social) factors?

2. What would the major ethical perspectives (of Aristotle, Kant, and Mill) say about the difficulty of ethical conduct in the face of situational pressure to be unethical?

ETHICS IN THE MOVIES

Movies seek to entertain and inform the audience about a story, incident, or person. Many good movies also hit upon important ethical themes in making significant decisions that affect the lives of others. Read the movie summary here (and watch the movie if you haven't already), and answer the questions to make the ethical connections.

GATTACA

Andrew Niccol, Director
(1997)

Gattaca is a science fiction thriller about the near future when we reach the point where we can correct our defects through cloning and DNA manipulation, and the decisions that such a situation would force upon us. Vincent (Ethan Hawke) works as a maintenance man at the space center. Genetic tests show he has bad eyesight, heart problems, and should die by age 30. Vincent does not accept this fate and dreams of becoming a crew member on a planned expedition to the moons of Saturn.

Vincent makes a deal with Jerome (Jude Law), an illegal DNA broker, who possesses the correct genes but was paralyzed in an accident. Using Jerome's blood, urine sample, and identity, Vincent "becomes" Jerome and thereby becomes a finalist for the space mission. There is great tension in Vincent as he protects his new identity as Jerome.

Tension is also caused by the murder of the director of the space center, who questioned the wisdom of the mission to Saturn. The detective (Alan Arkin) may stumble on Vincent's fraud, and his interest in Irene (Uma Thurman) who works at the space center is also threatening because it is common in this future world of DNA for a woman to have a man's saliva swabbed from her mouth after kissing him to determine his genetic prospects. In this future society, genetic discrimination is prohibited by law, but in practice a person's genotype is easily profiled, so the "Valids" qualify for the best jobs, while the "In-Valids" are relegated to menial jobs because they have genetic defects of some kind.

QUESTIONS

1. Cloned sheep and tomatoes have already been developed with ideal traits for food production. If it became scientifically possible, would it be morally permissible for a parent to order a "perfect" baby (genetically)?

2. In today's society, a person can be prevented from pursuing certain careers if they have physical defects. What are some examples? How is this justified in moral terms?

Discussion Question

If your obituary was to be summarized in two sentences, what would it reveal about you?

Critical Thinking Exercises

All ethical decisions affect others (by definition) and, as Aristotle points out, ethical decision making is achieved consistently only through practice. Given the outline of virtue ethics, formalism, and utilitarianism, evaluate the moral permissibility of the conduct in question in each scenario.

Important note on method: *Critical thinking requires the ability to evaluate viewpoints, facts, and behaviors objectively to assess information or methods of argumentation to establish the true worth or merit of an act or course of conduct. Please evaluate these scenarios, first analyzing pros and cons of alternate views,* before *you come to a conclusion. Do not draw a conclusion first, and then try to find facts to support it—this frequently leads to narrow (and incorrect) thinking.*

To properly evaluate the moral permissibility of a course of action using critical thinking skills:

1. *Begin with an open mind (no preconceptions!),*
2. *Isolate and evaluate the relevant facts on both sides,*
3. *Identify the precise moral question to be answered, and*
4. *Apply ethical principles to the moral question based on an objective evaluation of the facts, only then drawing a conclusion.*

10.1 Both Sides of Genetic Testing

Gary works for the Burlington Northern Sante Fe Railroad as a tracklayer. It is a physically demanding job requiring extensive use of both hand tools and heavy machinery. Sometimes, workers such as Gary develop a condition called carpal tunnel syndrome, which is a musculoskeletal disorder caused by repetitive and strenuous hand motions that result in nerve damage, causing weakness or disability in the use of the hands or wrists.

After he had returned to work from time off for carpel tunnel–related surgery to reduce pressure on the median nerve in his arm, Gary received a letter from his employer directing him to get his blood tested. His wife called the employer and discovered that the purpose of the blood work was genetic testing. Gary refused to submit to the blood test, and the first federal suit against a private company resulted, charging that such secret genetic testing violated the Americans with Disabilities Act and other laws barring DNA testing of employees.

Some industry and insurance officials claim that such genetic testing could reveal genetic defects that predispose a person to the syndrome. Thus, preventive treatment or job accommodations can be made, lowering company insurance premiums. However, there have been cases where workers were denied disability insurance or health care coverage based on the results of positive blood tests, which were interpreted as a "preexisting condition." Similarly, there are fears that hiring or promotions may be blocked based on the results of a genetic test. Some scientists are skeptical of genetic testing because so little is known about the role of genes in most diseases, most tests are inconclusive, and the comparative impact of environmental factors on disease is still hotly debated.[16]

- Is it morally permissible for Gary's employer to require a blood test for genetic testing?
- Understanding the company's purposes in requesting a blood test, is it morally permissible for Gary to refuse to submit to the test?

10.2 Transplant or Prosecute?

Michael Costin was knocked unconscious during a fight at a hockey rink and died. He had indicated that he wanted his heart donated as an organ transplant on his death, but the district attorney (DA) blocked the donation.

Costin's death at the hockey rink resulted in a criminal prosecution of the other "hockey-dad" who assaulted him. On Costin's death, the charge against the defendant became manslaughter. The DA blocked the heart donation because she didn't want the defendant to claim at trial that Costin died of a preexisting heart condition rather than from the fight.

The result of this decision was that it may have cost a heart patient the opportunity for a life-saving transplant. Doctors claimed that preserving (and not transplanting) Costin's heart offered little medical evidence because it was healthy—the heart would have been rejected if it was defective in any way. Several doctors believed it was clear that Costin died from head trauma and that his heart was fine. One physician declared, "It's very, very likely that, because of this decision, someone with heart disease died."

However, a professor argued, "there is also the interest in making sure we have all the evidence necessary so that justice is served." The DA said that according to an EMT at the fight scene, "it was a possible heart attack [and] we didn't want to give the defense an issue at trial to allow them to say, 'We really don't know the cause of death' " to raise doubt in the minds of jurors.[17]

- Assess the moral permissibility of the DA's decision.
- Should the wishes of the family play a role in assessing the morality of this decision?

10.3 A Marriage Proposal

Oklahoma has the second-highest divorce rate among U.S. states. This led the governor to initiate a program to reduce divorces there. He requested that churches mandate premarital counseling. In addition, Oklahoma funded "relationship-skills" education for welfare recipients, promarriage rallies led by hired "marriage ambassadors," and prenuptial counseling classes for couples who could not afford private counseling.

President George W. Bush liked the Oklahoma programs and presented a plan to spend $300 million to promote marriage. According to Bush, "Strong marriages and stable families are incredibly good for children, and stable families should be the central goal of American welfare policy." His proposal called for premarital education, relationship counseling, and publicity to convince high-risk groups that "marriage is cool."

Critics call the Oklahoma and Bush plans a "conservative version of big-government social engineering." They also raise questions about the proper role of government in the private lives of its citizens. At the same time, however, states spend millions of dollars on services such as child support enforcement, child abuse response, and divorced persons driven to welfare because of financial problems. It is argued that some government-funded promarriage programs ultimately could reduce the human and social costs brought about by failed marriages.[18]

- Assess the moral permissibility of a mandatory promarriage program.

10.4 Good Warrant, Wrong House

Los Angeles County Sheriffs obtained a search warrant for the home of four black suspects in an identify-theft fraud scheme. When police went to the home, a white teenage boy answered the door and was ordered to lie facedown on the floor, while police went into the bedroom and ordered the two naked white people in it to stand naked next to the bed, while police searched the home.[19]

It turned out that the black suspects had moved 3 months earlier. The couple sued the police, contending the search was an unreasonable invasion of privacy, as the color of their skin should have immediately tipped police that they were not the suspects and that the premise for the search (the warrant) was flawed.

- The U.S. Supreme Court ruled against the couple holding that valid search warrants will sometimes result in innocent people being searched, "and people like [the couple] unfortunately bear the cost." Assess the moral permissibility of this finding.
- If police discovered unrelated incriminating evidence during their search of the couple's house (e.g., drugs), would it be morally permissible to use it against them in court?

10.5 Monitoring Workers on Social Networks

As more employees start to use Twitter and Facebook, executives are becoming increasingly concerned with the message their digitally savvy workers are conveying to the public. A new survey underscores the growing role of social networks and the dilemma they present for corporations that spend huge amounts on their image. The survey found that 60 percent of the executives interviewed believe they have a right to know how employees portray themselves and their organizations. Employees, on the other hand, bristle at the thought that employers would monitor their online activity. Overall, about 53 percent say their social networking activities should not be any concern of their employer, although about 74 percent recognize that social networks make it easier to damage a company's reputation.

Few companies have given employees guidelines about how to use social networks. "We found a high percentage of employers who are thinking about what they should do but not a high percentage of employers who have concluded what those procedures and policies should be," says Deloitte chairman Sharon Allen.

Some news organizations have issued guidelines, but there's little agreement about what those rules should be. Last week, my colleague Diane Brady wrote about *The Wall Street Journal*'s ground rules for how employees should use social networking sites such as Twitter. *Editor & Publisher* noted that the *WSJ* guidelines included the warning that "business and pleasure should not be mixed on services like Twitter." *Editor & Publisher* followed up with a report on how different newspapers have issued a variety of guidelines and quoted this policy from the *Los Angeles Times,* "Assume that your professional life and your personal life merge online regardless of your care in separating them.

Don't write or post anything that would embarrass the LAT or compromise your ability to do your job."

Having my colleagues follow me on Twitter and Facebook probably makes me more cautious. But, I'm not yet ready to abandon my personal life when I tweet. My personal life is what it is, and if people know I'm a geek who saw *Star Trek* or *The Notebook* on opening day, it doesn't compromise my ability as a worker.[20]

• Evaluate the moral permissibility of employers having a say in what workers share on social networking sites.

Key Concepts

24-hour test *136*
Unabomber *136*
Centers for Disease Control and Prevention
 (CDC) panel of ethicists *137*

Distinction between killing and letting
 die *137*
Scarcity mentality *139*
The story of Alfred Nobel *39*

Notes

1. Alexandra Marks, "Ethics of Publishing Terrorist Tracts," *Christian Science Monitor* (September 20, 1995), p. 1.
2. Gardiner Harris, "U.S. Creates Ethics Panel on Priority for Flu Shots," *The New York Times* (October 28, 2004), p. 1.
3. Laura Olson, "In Alexandria, Va., Weighing Ethics in Decisions about Budget Cuts," *The Chicago Tribune*, (January 1, 2009).
4. Timothy E. Quill, "Death and Dignity: A Case of Individualized Decision Making," *New England Journal of Medicine*, vol. 324 (March 7, 1991), pp. 691–694.
5. *Vacco v. Quill*, 117 S.Ct. 2293 (1997).
6. James Rachels, "Active and Passive Euthansia," *The Elements of Moral Philosophy* (New York, NY: McGraw-Hill, 1986), pp. 90–103.
7. Daniel Callahan, "Killing and Allowing to Die," *Hastings Center Report*, vol. 19 (January/ February 1989), pp. 5–6.
8. Peter Singer, "Justifying Voluntary Euthansia," *Practical Ethics* (New York, NY: Cambridge University Press, 1993), pp. 176–200.
9. Charisse Jones, "Druggists Refuse to Give Out Pill," *USA Today* (November 9, 2004), p. 3.
10. Harold Kushner, *When Everything You Ever Wanted Isn't Enough: The Search for a Life That Matters* (New York, NY: Fireside, 2002).
11. John Leo, "Victims of the Year," *U.S. News & World Report* (December 4, 2000), p. 24.
12. Wayne Dosick, "Love Your Neighbor," in M. Josephson and W. Hanson, Eds., *The Power of Character* (San Francisco, CA: Jossey-Bass, 1998), p. 293.
13. "Ann Landers: Stuck with a Bathrobe," *The Buffalo News* (December 30, 1992), p. B10.
14. Stephen R. Covey, "Growing Great Children," in M. Josephson and W. Hanson, Eds., *The Power of Character* (San Francisco, CA: Jossey-Bass, 1998), p. 104.
15. Jocelyn Pollock and Ronald Becker, "Ethical Dilemmas in Police Work," in M. Braswell, B. McCarthy, and B. McCarthy, Eds., *Justice, Crime and Ethics* (Cincinnati, OH: Anderson Publishing, 2002), p. 101.
16. Dana Hawkins, "The Dark Side of Genetic Testing," *U.S. News & World Report* (February 19, 2001), p. 30; Dana Hawkins, "Guard Your Genetic Data from Those Prying Eyes," *U.S. News & World Report* (March 5, 2001), pp. 59–60.
17. Sean P. Murphy, "Heart Transplant Was Blocked by DA in Junta Case," *The Boston Globe* (January 25, 2002), p. 3.
18. Michael Schaffer, "Marriage Proposal: Should the Government Spend Your Tax Dollars to Encourage Holy Cows," *U.S. News & World Report* (March 11, 2002), p. 26.
19. *Los Angeles County v. Rettele*, no. 06–605 (decided May 21, 2007).
20. Rachael King, "Companies Want to Monitor Workers on Social Networks," *Business Week* (May 17, 2009); John Schwartz, "For Judges on Facebook, Friendship has Limits," *The New York Times* (December 11, 2009).

APPENDIX A

International Association of Chiefs of Police (IACP) Law Enforcement Code of Ethics

As a law enforcement officer, my fundamental duty is to serve the community; to safeguard lives and property; to protect the innocent against deception, the weak against oppression or intimidation, the peaceful against violence or disorder; and to respect the constitutional rights of all to liberty, equality and justice.

I will keep my private life unsullied as an example to all and will behave in a manner that does not bring discredit to me or to my agency. I will maintain courageous calm in the face of danger, scorn or ridicule; develop self-restraint; and be constantly mindful of the welfare of others. Honest in thought and deed both in my personal and official life, I will be exemplary in obeying the law and the regulations of my department. Whatever I see or hear of a confidential nature or that is confided to me in my official capacity will be kept ever secret unless revelation is necessary in the performance of my duty.

I will never act officiously or permit personal feelings, prejudices, political beliefs, aspirations, animosities or friendships to influence my decisions. With no compromise for crime and with relentless prosecution of criminals, I will enforce the law courteously and appropriately without fear or favor, malice or ill will, never employing unnecessary force or violence and never accepting gratuities.

I recognize the badge of my office as a symbol of public faith, and I accept it as a public trust to be held so long as I am true to the ethics of police service. I will never engage in acts of corruption or bribery, nor will I condone such acts by other police officers. I will cooperate with all legally authorized agencies and their representatives in the pursuit of justice.

I know that I alone am responsible for my own standard of professional performance and will take every reasonable opportunity to enhance and improve my level of knowledge and competence.

I will constantly strive to achieve these objectives and ideals, dedicating myself before God to my chosen profession . . . law enforcement.

Note: Revised in 1991

Source: www.lib.jjay.cuny.edu/cje/html/codes/codes-usa-organizational/lece-r.html

APPENDIX B

Federal Bureau of Investigation (FBI) Core Values

The strategic plan for accomplishing the FBI's mission must begin by identifying the core values which need to be preserved and defended by the FBI in performing its statutory missions. Those values are: rigorous obedience to the Constitution of the United States; respect for the dignity of all those we protect; compassion; fairness; and uncompromising personal and institutional integrity. These values do not exhaust the many goals which we wish to achieve, but they capsulize them as well as can be done in a few words. Our values must be fully understood, practiced, shared, vigorously defended and preserved.

Observance of these core values is our guarantee of excellence and propriety in performing the FBI's national security and criminal investigative functions. Rigorous obedience to constitutional principles ensures that individually and institutionally we always remember that constitutional guarantees are more important than the outcome of any single interview, search for evidence, or investigation. Respect for the dignity of all whom we protect reminds us to wield law enforcement powers with restraint and to recognize the natural human tendency to be corrupted by power and to become callous in its exercise. Fairness and compassion ensure that we treat everyone with the highest regard for constitution, civil and human rights. Personal and institutional integrity reinforce each other and are owed to the Nation in exchange for the sacred trust and great authority conferred upon us.

We who enforce the law must not merely obey it. We have an obligation to set a moral example which those whom we protect can follow. Because the FBI's success in accomplishing its mission is directly related to the support and cooperation of those whom we protect, these core values are the fiber which holds together the vitality of our institution.

Source: www.lib.jjay.cuny.edu/cje/html/codes/codes-usa-organizational/fbicode.html

APPENDIX C

Judicial Conference of the United States Code of Conduct

The code of conduct of the Judicial Conference of the United States applies to all federal judges but is only advisory and nonbinding on Supreme Court justices. The rules explicitly permit judges to accept and participate in awards programs and to receive certain benefit from legal publishers. Listed here are the official canons, followed by excerpts of commentary provided by the Judicial Conference.

Canon 1: A judge should uphold the integrity and independence of the judiciary. ("Public confidence in the impartiality of the judiciary is maintained by the adherence of each judge to this responsibility.")

Canon 2: A judge should avoid impropriety and the appearance of impropriety in all activities. ("A judge must expect to be the subject of constant public scrutiny. A judge must therefore accept restrictions that might be viewed as burdensome by the ordinary citizen and should do so freely and willingly.")

Canon 3: A judge should perform the duties of the office impartially and diligently. ("A judge shall disqualify himself or herself in a proceeding in which the judge's impartiality might reasonably be questioned, including but not limited to instances in which the judge has a personal bias or prejudice concerning a party . . .")

Canon 4: A judge may engage in extrajudicial activities to improve the law, the legal system and the administration of justice. ("A judge, subject to the proper performance of judicial duties, may engage in . . . law-related activities, if in doing so the judge does not cast reasonable doubt on the capacity to decide impartially any issue that may come before the judge.")

Canon 5: A judge should regulate extrajudicial activities to minimize the risk of conflict with judicial duties. ("Complete separation of a judge from extrajudicial activities is neither possible nor wise; a judge should not be isolated from the society in which the judge lives. The changing nature of some organizations and of their relationship to the law makes it necessary for a judge regularly to reexamine the activities of each organization with which the judge is affiliated to determine if it is proper for the judge to continue the judge's relationship with it. For example, in many jurisdictions charitable hospitals are now more frequently in court than in the past.")

Canon 6: A judge should regularly file reports of compensation received for law-related and extrajudicial activities. ("A judge may receive compensation and reimbursement of expenses for the law-related and extra-judicial activities permitted by this Code, if the source of such payments does not give the appearance of influencing the judge in the judge's judicial duties or otherwise give the appearance of impropriety . . .")

Source: www.newshare.com/west/guidelines.html

APPENDIX D

American Correctional Association Code of Ethics

PREAMBLE

The American Correctional Association expects of its members unfailing honesty, respect for the dignity and individuality of human beings and a commitment to professional and compassionate service. To this end, we subscribe to the following principles.

Members shall respect and protect the civil and legal rights of all individuals.

Members shall treat every professional situation with concern for the welfare of the individuals involved and with no intent to personal gain.

Members shall maintain relationships with colleagues to promote mutual respect within the profession and improve the quality of service.

Members shall make public criticism of their colleagues or their agencies only when warranted, verifiable, and constructive.

Members shall respect the importance of all disciplines within the criminal justice system and work to improve cooperation with each segment.

Members shall honor the public's right to information and share information with the public to the extent permitted by law subject to individual's right to privacy.

Members shall respect and protect the right of the public to be safeguarded from criminal activity.

Members shall refrain from using their positions to secure personal privileges or advantages.

Members shall refrain from allowing personal interest to impair objectivity in the performance of duty while acting in an official capacity.

Members shall refrain from entering into any formal or informal activity or agreement which presents a conflict of interest or is inconsistent with the conscientious performance of duties.

Members shall refrain from accepting any gifts, service, or favor that is or appears to be improper or implies an obligation inconsistent with the free and objective exercise of professional duties.

Members shall clearly differentiate between personal views/statements and views/statements/positions made on behalf of the agency or Association.

Members shall report to appropriate authorities any corrupt or unethical behaviors in which there is sufficient evidence to justify review.

Members shall refrain from discriminating against any individual because of race, gender, creed, national origin, religious affiliation, age, disability, or any other type of prohibited discrimination.

Members shall preserve the integrity of private information; they shall refrain from seeking information on individuals beyond that which is necessary to implement responsibilities and perform their duties; members shall refrain from revealing nonpublic information unless expressly authorized to do so.

Members shall make all appointments, promotions, and dismissals in accordance with established civil service rules, applicable contract agreements, and individual merit, rather than furtherance of personal interests.

Members shall respect, promote, and contribute to a work place that is safe, healthy, and free of harassment in any form.

Note: Adopted August 1975 at the 105th Congress of Correction, revised August 1990 at the 120th Congress of Correction, revised August 1994 at the 124th Congress of Correction

Source: www.bmi.net/wca/ethics_code.html

APPENDIX E

United Nations Code of Conduct for Law Enforcement Officials

ARTICLE 1

Law enforcement officials shall at all times fulfil the duty imposed upon them by law, by serving the community and by protecting all persons against illegal acts, consistent with the high degree of responsibility required by their profession.

Commentary:

a. The term "law enforcement officials", includes all officers of the law, whether appointed or elected, who exercise police powers, especially the powers of arrest or detention.

b. In countries where police powers are exercised by military authorities, whether uniformed or not, or by State security forces, the definition of law enforcement officials shall be regarded as including officers of such services.

c. Service to the community is intended to include particularly the rendition of services of assistance to those members of the community who by reason of personal, economic, social or other emergencies are in need of immediate aid.

d. This provision is intended to cover not only all violent, predatory and harmful acts, but extends to the full range of prohibitions under penal statutes. It extends to conduct by persons not capable of incurring criminal liability.

ARTICLE 2

In the performance of their duty, law enforcement officials shall respect and protect human dignity and maintain and uphold the human rights of all persons.

Commentary:

a. The human rights in question are identified and protected by national and international law. Among the relevant international instruments are the Universal Declaration of Human Rights, the International Covenant on Civil and Political Rights, the Declaration on the Protection of All Persons from Being Subjected to Torture and Other Cruel, Inhuman or Degrading Treatment or Punishment, the United Nations Declaration on the Elimination of All Forms of Racial Discrimination, the International Convention on the Elimination of All Forms of Racial Discrimination, the International Convention on the Suppression and Punishment of the Crime of Apartheid, the Convention on the Prevention and Punishment of the Crime of Genocide, the Standard Minimum Rules for the Treatment of Prisoners and the Vienna Convention on Consular Relations.

b. National commentaries to this provision should indicate regional or national provisions identifying and protecting these rights.

ARTICLE 3

Law enforcement officials may use force only when strictly necessary and to the extent required for the performance of their duty.

Commentary:

a. This provision emphasizes that the use of force by law enforcement officials should be exceptional; while it implies that law enforcement officials may be authorized to use force as is reasonably necessary under the circumstances for the prevention of crime or in effecting or assisting in the lawful arrest of offenders or suspected offenders, no force going beyond that may be used.

b. National law ordinarily restricts the use of force by law enforcement officials in accordance with a principle of proportionality. It is to be understood that such national principles of proportionality are to be respected in the interpretation of this provision. In no case should this provision be interpreted to authorize the use of force which is dispropor-tionate to the legitimate objective to be achieved.

c. The use of firearms is considered an extreme measure. Every effort should be made to exclude the use of firearms, especially against children. In general, firearms should not be used except when a suspected offender offers armed resistance or otherwise jeopardizes the lives of others and less extreme measures are not sufficient to restrain or apprehend the suspected offender. In every instance in which a firearm is discharged, a report should be made promptly to the competent authorities.

ARTICLE 4

Matters of a confidential nature in the possession of law enforcement officials shall be kept confidential, unless the performance of duty or the needs of justice strictly require otherwise.

Commentary:

By the nature of their duties, law enforcement officials obtain information which may relate to private lives or be potentially harmful to the interests, and especially the reputation, of others. Great care should be exercised in safeguarding and using such information, which should be disclosed only in the performance of duty or to serve the needs of justice. Any disclosure of such information for other purposes is wholly improper.

ARTICLE 5

No law enforcement official may inflict, instigate or tolerate any act of torture or other cruel, inhuman or degrading treatment or punishment, nor may any law enforcement official invoke superior orders or exceptional circumstances such as a state of war or a threat of war, a threat to national security, internal political instability or any other public emergency as a justification of torture or other cruel, inhuman or degrading treatment or punishment.

Commentary:

a. This prohibition derives from the Declaration on the Protection of All Persons from Being Subjected to Torture and Other Cruel, Inhuman or Degrading Treatment or Punishment, adopted by the General Assembly, according to which: "[Such an act is] an offence to human dignity and shall be condemned as a denial of the purposes of the Charter of the United Nations and as a violation of the human rights and fundamental freedoms proclaimed in the Universal Declaration of Human Rights [and other international human rights instruments]."

b. The Declaration defines torture as follows:

> "... torture means any act by which severe pain or suffering, whether physical or mental, is intentionally inflicted by or at the instigation of a public official on a person for such purposes as obtaining from him or a third person information or confession, punishing him for an act he has committed or is suspected of having committed, or intimidating him or other persons. It does not include pain or suffering arising only from, inherent in or incidental to, lawful sanctions to the extent consistent with the Standard Minimum Rules for the Treatment of Prisoners."

c. The term "cruel, inhuman or degrading treatment or punishment" has not been defined by the General Assembly but should be interpreted so as to extend the widest possible protection against abuses, whether physical or mental.

ARTICLE 6

Law enforcement officials shall ensure the full protection of the health of persons in their custody and, in particular, shall take immediate action to secure medical attention whenever required.

Commentary:

a. "Medical attention", which refers to services rendered by any medical personnel, including certified medical practitioners and paramedics, shall be secured when needed or requested.

b. While the medical personnel are likely to be attached to the law enforcement operation, law enforcement officials must take into account the judgement of such personnel when they recommend providing the person in custody with appropriate treatment through, or in consultation with, medical personnel from outside the law enforcement operation.

c. It is understood that law enforcement officials shall also secure medical attention for victims of violations of law or of accidents occurring in the course of violations of law.

ARTICLE 7

Law enforcement officials shall not commit any act of corruption. They shall also rigorously oppose and combat all such acts.

Commentary:

a. Any act of corruption, in the same way as any other abuse of authority, is incompatible with the profession of law enforcement officials. The law must be enforced fully with respect to any law enforcement official who commits an act of corruption, as Governments cannot expect to enforce the law among their citizens if they cannot, or will not, enforce the law against their own agents and within their agencies.

b. While the definition of corruption must be subject to national law, it should be understood to encompass the commission or omission of an act in the performance of or in connection with one's duties, in response to gifts, promises or incentives demanded or accepted, or the wrongful receipt of these once the act has been committed or omitted.

c. The expression "act of corruption" referred to above should be understood to encompass attempted corruption.

ARTICLE 8

Law enforcement officials shall respect the law and the present Code. They shall also, to the best of their capability, prevent and rigorously oppose any violations of them.

Law enforcement officials who have reason to believe that a violation of the present Code has occurred or is about to occur shall report the matter to their superior authorities and, where necessary, to other appropriate authorities or organs vested with reviewing or remedial power.

Commentary:

a. This Code shall be observed whenever it has been incorporated into national legislation or practice. If legislation or practice contains stricter provisions than those of the present Code, those stricter provisions shall be observed.

b. The article seeks to preserve the balance between the need for internal discipline of the agency on which public safety is largely dependent, on the one hand, and the need for dealing with violations of basic human rights, on the other. Law enforcement officials shall report violations within the chain of command and take other lawful action outside the chain of command only when no other remedies are available or effective. It is understood that law enforcement officials shall not suffer administrative or other penalties because they have reported that a violation of this Code has occurred or is about to occur.

c. The term "appropriate authorities or organs vested with reviewing or remedial power" refers to any authority or organ existing under national law, whether internal to the law enforcement agency or independent thereof, with statutory, customary or other power to review grievances and complaints arising out of violations within the purview of this Code.

d. In some countries, the mass media may be regarded as performing complaint review functions similar to those described in subparagraph (c) above. Law enforcement officials may, therefore, be justified if, as a last resort and in accordance with the laws and customs of their own countries and with the provisions of article 4 of the present Code, they bring violations to the attention of public opinion through the mass media.

e. Law enforcement officials who comply with the provisions of this Code deserve the respect, the full support and the co-operation of the community and of the law enforcement agency in which they serve, as well as the law enforcement profession.

Note: Adopted by General Assembly resolution 34/169, December 17, 1979

Source: http://www2.ohchr.org/english/law/codeofconduct.htm

INDEX

Note: The letter followed by 't' refer to tables presented in the text